THE NEW COMPLETE
GUITARIST

THE NEW
COMPLETE
GUITARIST

RICHARD CHAPMAN

LONDON, NEW YORK, MUNICH, MELBOURNE, DELHI

REVISED EDITION
Project editor Anna Fischel
Art editor Edward Kinsey
Senior editor Neil Lockley
Senior art editor Kevin Ryan
DTP designer Rajen Shah
Production controller Sarah Sherlock

Managing editor Adèle Hayward
Managing art editor Karen Self
Category publisher Stephanie Jackson

This book is dedicated to Carol

ORIGINAL EDITION
Editors Laurence Henderson and Katie John
Project editor Terry Burrows
Managing editor Sean Moore
Designers Heather McCarry, Gurinder Purewall, and Dawn Terrey
Deputy art director Tina Vaughan
Deputy editorial director Jane Laing

Special Contributors:
Rack-mounted systems Jim Barber
Care and maintenance Bill Puplett
Sound and amplification John Seabury

Original edition produced and art directed in Great Britain
by Nigel Osborne, 115J Cleveland Street, London W1

Revised edition first published in 2003
by Dorling Kindersley Ltd. 80 Strand, London WC2R 0RL
A Penguin Company

First published in 1993 by Dorling Kindersley Limited,
9 Henrietta Street, London WC2E 8PS

First published in paperback 1994

A CIP catalogue record for this book is
available from the British Library

ISBN 1405301899

Reproduced in Singapore by Colourscan
Printed in China by L.Rex Printing Company

See our complete catalogue at
www.dk.com

CONTENTS

INTRODUCTION

The guitar has established itself as the world's most popular musical instrument. It is adaptable, portable, and attractive and its myriad forms and versatility have led to a vast range of fascinating music. The captivating sounds of the guitar can be heard in every corner of the world. Its unparalleled diversity ranges from indigenous folk music with simple home-made instruments through to sophisticated compositions and improvisation using electric guitars linked up to computers.

Books of guitar music were popular as long ago as 1552

The guitar has ancient and mysterious origins. Stone-cut reliefs from central Turkey show guitars in the Hittite civilization from over 3,000 years ago. The emergence and widespread adoption of the instrument in Europe during the Middle Ages produced some of the first written references to the guitar and the earliest music we can hear and understand today. By the 16th century the guitar was firmly established in many European countries and had even reached the Americas. Primarily a small-bodied instrument with four or five strings predominantly arranged in pairs, it was played at all levels of society for songs and dances. Instrumental compositions were circulated and the guitar started to evolve into its present form.

The earliest surviving guitars come from the end of the 16th century and the 17th century. They are fragile and often highly decorated. The guitar took an important step towards its modern-day form during the late 18th century, when instruments in Italy appeared with six single strings tuned EADGBE. During the mid-19th century the Spanish maker Antonio de Torres built a large-bodied instrument, which is the template for modern classical and flamenco guitars. America became the centre for guitar innovation in the late 19th century and 20th century, with a whole range of dramatic and revolutionary designs. These have established virtually all modern guitar designs with steel strings, ranging from flat-top steel-string acoustics to archtops, resonators, and amplified electric guitars. The guitar continues constantly to evolve with acoustic and electronic innovations.

GUITAR MUSIC

Today every type of music can be heard on the guitar. One of the strengths of the instrument is that it is not dominated by any one style or approach. Each genre has different facets and various areas of musical activity. Styles include classical, flamenco, blues, country, jazz, rock, pop, folk, and a whole range of music from around the world such as Brazilian and African. There are also many indefinable hybrid crossovers. This explosion of styles took place during the 20th century. Before that, there was classical music, popular songs and dances, flamenco, and various folk styles including early blues and gypsy music. Music has evolved both where the guitar is integral, as in, for instance, flamenco and modern rock and pop, and within sophisticated areas such as jazz, led and developed by saxophone and piano.

It is helpful and inspiring to listen and be aware of different types of guitar music. There are many outstanding individuals from the past whose music can be appreciated on recordings. These range from the gypsy jazz genius Django Reinhardt through to the rock visionary Jimi Hendrix.

Five-course guitar dated around 1590

PLAYING THE GUITAR

At first it is best to concentrate on and stay within a chosen area of music. With certain popular styles, such as rock and pop, it is possible to work and develop within a simple framework. To be creative and learn to improvise in a fully developed way, it is important to understand and play jazz. Different areas use widely divergent techniques and material, yet there are interesting possibilities for cross-fertilization when it comes to writing or improvising. Consider carefully the long term before choosing one style. Take classical music, for example. To play classical music, it is essential to use a proper nylon-string guitar and develop an excellent right-hand technique. Overall sound, the variety of tone, and harmonic control are at the highest level with this approach. Classical study is based on accurately learning pieces from an extensive historical repertoire and interpreting them in a musically sensitive way with a highly polished technical execution. Yet such practice will not prepare the guitarist for playing in other styles. To step outside classical music and develop creative and improvisational skills and techniques, it is necessary to study theory, composition, and jazz.

The electric guitar was at the heart of the 1960s music boom

Every style and approach has different goals and values as well as strengths and weaknesses. Rock guitar can be incredibly limited but, with knowledge and inspiration, it is possible to absorb, adapt, and recreate ideas and techniques from anywhere. Blues is based on a small traditional vocabulary of chords and phrases, yet it can be profound and expressive. Jazz is an umbrella term for a wide range of different music from styles based on past eras to contemporary approaches. It is unlimited in its creative possibilities. The jazz area continues to produce much of the most advanced music as well as pointing to the future.

CHOOSING A GUITAR

Guitars can be divided into acoustic and electric. There are two general types of acoustic guitar: those with nylon strings and those with steel strings. Guitars with nylon strings are the only type for classical and flamenco music. They are also used in South American music, crossover styles, and certain other areas. Steel-string guitars are played in most popular styles. They are particularly widely used by singers to support the voice.

Most players start on an acoustic guitar of some type. This is a sensible choice as it helps the guitarist to focus on playing with a real sense of touch and to develop a solid fingering technique. It also enables the guitarist to practise properly on the production of a good tone, and work at dynamics and nuance. From an acoustic it is relatively easy to move over to an electric guitar at an early stage. Many players start on cheap small-bodied nylon-string or steel-string guitars.

Electric guitars are the mainstay of rock and pop as well as jazz, country, and blues. If you are particularly keen on music with electric guitars and want to eventually play in a group, obtain an electric guitar as soon as possible and learn to use this effectively with an amplifier and effects. Although not essential to play an acoustic guitar as well, it is strongly recommended. Regular acoustic practice, as well as electric, helps to develop strength, touch, and sensitivity for sound production and playing technique.

John D'Angelico archtop guitar

For those who are very young, it is best to start on a small instrument or one that is easy to play with a low string action. Avoid really poor instruments or those with flaws such as a bent neck. It is offputting to play on something that will never sound good!

On a personal note, I have written this book to provide a wide range of source material, ranging from all kinds of techniques to advanced theories. My aim is to enlighten and inspire guitarists at every level, from the beginner to the professional. I wish everyone the best of luck!

RICHARD CHAPMAN

Jimi Hendrix developed his own approach to playing, and produced some of the greatest guitar music

THE GUITAR

The contemporary guitar can be separated
into four main types: the nylon-strung classical,
the steel-string acoustic, the archtop, and the
solid-body electric. This section of the book
traces the history of the instrument to the
present day and details the principles on
which each type of guitar is constructed.

THE GUITAR TIMELINE

AN ILLUSTRATED HISTORY OF THE GUITAR

The evolution of tuning
The development of the modern tuning system can be traced in stages. One of the tunings from the 16th century is C-F-A-D. This is equivalent to the top four strings of the modern guitar tuned a tone lower. However, the absolute pitch for these notes is not equivalent to modern "concert pitch". The tuning of the four-course guitar was moved up by a tone, and, towards the end of the 16th century, five-course instruments were in use with an added lower string tuned to A. This produced A-D-G-B-E, one of a wide number of variant tunings of the period. The low E string was added during the 18th century.

An instrument bearing a close resemblance to the guitar existed before 1500; it emerged in Mediterranean Europe during the Renaissance. Representations from the 13th and 14th centuries show a distinctive *figure-of-eight* shaped instrument, which may have been played with a quill plectrum. Some sources from this period also refer to a Latin guitar, or *guittara latina*. The first books to feature music for the guitar date from the 16th century. They refer to a four-course guitar: three or four of the strings are doubled to form paired unison courses. The bottom course is sometimes tuned with an octave interval and the top string is often single. Guitars with five courses also existed in the 16th century. Early guitars were built with a solid headstock and friction pegs that were adjusted from the back. The fingerboard of such a guitar is level with the top of the instrument and has between eight and ten tied gut frets. The body is small by today's standards, with less curvature. The back is either vaulted or flat, and the soundhole has a decorative parchment, or wooden rose. The fragility of this type of guitar, changing fashions and tunings, and the use of metal strings has led to many instruments being lost, damaged or altered over the centuries.

Timeline
Over the next eight pages, the guitar is shown on a timeline from around the end of the 16th century to the present day. This is not wholly based on the most important makers or instruments. Twentieth-century classical instruments have been omitted, and manufactured models from various periods have been placed at their launch dates.

Strings The vihuela has twelve strings in six double courses.

This instrument was reproduced from a study of the early 16th-century Spanish vihuela in the Jacquemart-André Museum in Paris.

THE LUTE
With its pear-shaped body and curved back, the lute is a relative of the Arabic U*d*. An early type of lute, referred to as the *guitarra moresca*, appeared during the Renaissance. This was probably introduced to Europe from the Middle East. By the 16th century, the lute was nearly always a six-course instrument, played with the fingers. It was used widely throughout Europe as an instrument for accompaniment and composition.

The chitarrone has ten bass strings set off the fingerboard.

QVATRIESME LIVRE
CONTENANT PLVSIEVRS FANTASIES,
Chanſons, Gaillardes, Paduines, Branſles, reduict't en Tabulature de Guyterne,
&c aux ins de la Cistre, par Maiſtre Guillaume Morlaye,
&c autres bons autheurs.

A PARIS,
De l'imprimerie de Michel Fezandat, au mont ſainct Hylaire, à l'hoſtel d'Albret,
1552.
Auec priuilege du Roy, pour dix ans.

Early guitar music
This is a fourth book of guitar music produced in Paris by G. Morlaye in 1552. It contains different tunings, as well as popular songs and dances written in tablature for the four-course guitar.

THE VIHUELA
A considerable body of music was written for this popular instrument which, in the 16th and 17th centuries, was considered to be superior to the early guitar. It has a large, guitar-shaped body with a flat back. Like the early lute, the twelve strings in six double courses are tuned to G-C-F-A-D-G. The evolution of the guitar contributed to the demise of the vihuela in the 17th century. There are thought to be only two authentic surviving examples.

Chitarrone Like the vihuela on the right, this is a remake by London-based luthier Stephen Barber.

1614 Matteo Sellas (right)

Matteo Sellas worked in Venice in the first half of the 17th century. He was one of the first members of the Sellas family to become prominent as an outstanding maker of guitars and lutes. This guitar has a decorated spruce soundboard. The body is constructed with a vaulted back and an ornate rosette. The fingerboard has nine frets. Many outstanding luthiers were trained in the Sellas workshops; among them were Andreas Oth and the Englishman, Christopher Cocks.

Headstock with "scalloped" outline

1641 René Voboam (left)

This is a copy of the only surviving instrument that can be attributed to the 17th-century French guitar maker René Voboam, who was based in Paris. Voboam guitars by other members of the family were made later in the 17th century. This guitar has a foliate design on the fingerboard and a three-dimensional rose with a star design. The body uses ebony and bone inlays with a tortoiseshell veneer.

1760 Jean Salomon (right)

The French guitar maker Jean Salomon was based in Paris. This type of instrument was constructed towards the end of a conservative period during which the guitar was modified slightly in size and shape. During the second half of the 18th century, a low E sixth string was added by a number of makers. In Spain, fan bracing was introduced, and, around 1780 in most European countries outside Spain, the six double courses were gradually replaced by six single strings.

Bridge The type of unit used on early guitars is known as a "moustache" bridge.

1507	1521	1535	1549	1563	1577	1591	1605	1619	1633	1647	1661	1675	1689	1703	1717	1731	1745	1759	1773	1787	1801
1500	1514	1528	1542	1556	1570	1584	1598	1612	1626	1640	1654	1668	1682	1696	1710	1724	1738	1752	1766	1780	1794

16th-century guitar (right)

This guitar has been dated to a period between 1580 and 1600, making it one of a small number of surviving 16th-century guitars. It has been restored extensively. The guitar has five courses, a spruce top, and ten gut frets, which are tied around the neck. The decorated fingerboard and headstock has interwoven inlays. A variation on this type of inlay work was used on a small Portuguese guitar by Belchior Dias from 1581.

Headstock On early guitars, the headstock was often referred to as the "pegbox".

1627 Chittara Battente by Giorgio Sellas (left)

This instrument by Giorgio Sellas has wire strings, which produce greater volume. It was normally played with a quill plectrum and fitted with metal frets. This example has a highly ornate mother-of-pearl fingerboard and extensive ivory decorative inlays on the neck and body. It has a vaulted back made from ebony strips with foliate inlays.

Scale length The Stradivari guitar has a scale length of 74.3 cm (29 in). It was probably used for "continuo" playing.

The soundboard, bridge, and a part of the neck have been restored.

Five courses The strings run in five courses and are supported by a bridge and anchored to the base of the body.

1688 Stradivari (left)

This is one of two surviving guitars known to have been made by the famed Italian violin maker Antonio Stradivari of Cremona (1644-1737). This guitar has a very long scale length and eighteen frets. The body and neck are both made from maple, with an ebony fingerboard. The guitar has a spruce top with a coat of arms displayed on the upper fingerboard. The extended decorations on the bridge have been lost.

Spanish court guitar (right)
This guitar was probably made as a special commission for a member of the aristocracy in northern Spain in the first half of the 19th century. It has a rosewood body with a spruce soundboard, and a mahogany neck with a rosewood fingerboard. It features a high standard of craftsmanship with mother-of-pearl abalone and ivory decorations on the bridge, fingerboard, and around the soundhole. Floral inlays are set into black mastic around the edge of the instrument.

Headstock The slotted headstock and the use of six individual strings indicate that the design of this guitar was influenced by guitar-makers outside Spain.

1835 Lacote (right)
The Frenchman Rene-Francois Lacote (1785-1855) was one of the leading 19th-century guitar makers. He was born in Mirecourt and worked in Paris. This guitar has a spruce top, which carries the upper frets and extends along the neck to meet the ebony fingerboard on the 10th fret. This type of construction was used from the 16th to the early 19th century. The headstock has concealed machine heads.

Bridge Lacote used curved bridge-ends with pearl eyes.

1836 Panormo (right)
Louis Panormo came from a family of instrument makers. He was born in Paris in 1784 and was based in London during the first part of the 19th century before emigrating to New Zealand in 1854. His use of fan-strutting reveals the influence of Pagés and Martínez. His instruments were advertised and labelled as "guitars in the Spanish style". This example has a spruce top, a bridge without a separate saddle, and a finely carved headstock with large slots.

Machine heads Panormo guitars were often fitted with machine heads made in London by Baker.

Bridge The bridge has been extended and inlaid in an ornamental style.

| 1801 | 1802 | 1803 | 1804 | 1805 | 1807 1808 1809 1810 1811 | 1812 1813 1814 1815 1816 1817 1818 1819 1820 | 1821 | 1822 | 1823 | 1824 | 1825 | 1826 | 1827 | 1828 | 1829 | 1830 | 1831 | 1832 | 1833 | 1834 | 1835 | 1836 | 1837 | 1838 | 1839 | 1840 | 1841 | 184 |

1804 Pagés (left)
Based in Cadiz, José Pagés was one of the foremost Spanish luthiers working from the end of the 18th century to the beginning of the 19th century. The strings on this instrument run in six double courses tied to the bridge. The guitar has a spruce top with inlaid frets running up to the edge of the soundhole. José Pagés was one of a number of guitar makers in southern Spain who pioneered the use of a fan-bracing system beneath the soundboard.

Legnani-style guitar (right)
This model was made in Vienna around 1830. It features a sloping upper body and an asymmetric headstock. The machine head gears are concealed beneath a plate. The instrument has a mahogany neck, spruce top, and rosewood body. This type of design was constructed by the Austrian makers, Johann Staufer and Georg Ries, and influenced by Luigi Legnani, the Italian guitar virtuoso.

C. F. Martin
Born in Germany, C. F. Martin (1796-1873) worked as a foreman with the luthier Johann Staufer in Vienna. In 1833, he emigrated to America, settling in New York. He opened a shop making and selling musical instruments, and in 1839 he moved to Nazareth, Pennsylvania, to develop the company that has become one of the world's foremost guitar manufacturers.

Fingerboard The top end is cut just before the soundhole.

1838 Martin (right)
This instrument is the standard type of model built by C. F. Martin during his early period, clearly showing the influence of Johann Staufer and the Legnani model. It has an asymmetric headstock, an 18-fret fingerboard, a rosewood body, and a spruce top with a decorated purfling. The ebony bridge has an ivory saddle and the soundhole features a herringbone inlay.

Headstock All Torres guitars were built with a similar headstock shape.

1860 Torres (right)

The Torres guitar was constructed with a new type of large body whose outline and proportions had been redesigned. The string length of these guitars is usually 65 cm (25½ in) with seven fan-braces beneath a slightly domed spruce top to balance tonal response. This guitar has a cedar neck with an ebony fingerboard, and a cypress body with a four-piece back.

Sound Torres balanced the tonal response and increased the volume of the guitar.

1876 Torres (right)

This guitar has a cedar neck, a three-piece spruce top, and a cypress body with a two-piece back. It was originally built as an eleven-string instrument, with five additional bass strings. The design was modified in 1945 by Marcelo Barbero, who converted the headstock and tied bridge to carry six strings.

Body shape In comparison with the 1860 guitar this instrument has less rounded upper bouts.

Orville Gibson

The American Orville Gibson (1856-1918) is one of the key figures in the development of the guitar. He started as an instrument maker in the late 19th century, quickly establishing himself as an innovative manufacturer of fretted instruments. The Gibson company was founded in 1894. Gibson's designs were influenced by the methods of construction used for the violin family. This approach led him to develop the carved-body method for making guitars, in which the body of the instrument is given an arched back and top.

| 1843 | 1844 | 1845 | 1846 | 1847 | 1848 | 1849 | 1850 | 1851/1852/1853/1854 | 1855 | 1856 | 1857 | 1858 | 1859 | 1860 | 1861/1862 | 1863 | 1864 | 1865/1866/1867 | 1869 | 1870 | 1871 | 1872 | 1873 | 1874 | 1875 | 1876 | 1877 | 1878 | 1879 | 1880 | 1881/1883 | 1882 | 1884 | 1885 | 1886 | 1887 | 1888 | 1889/1890/1891/1892 | 1894 | 1895 | 1896 | 1897 | 1898 | 1899 | 1900 |

Antonio de Torres

Antonio de Torres was born in Almeria, Spain in 1817. He is the most important figure in the history of the modern classical guitar. After moving to Seville in the 1840s he set up a workshop and started making guitars. The models he created were used by many famous players, notably Arcas and Tarrega. His instruments were made during two separate periods: he worked in Seville from 1850 to 1869 before deciding to retire from guitar making, then resumed his craft in Almeria in 1880 and continued until his death in 1892.

Machine heads The majority of Martin guitars were fitted with German machine heads.

Martin Style 2 (left)

Martin developed an American acoustic guitar which combines a number of influences from European makers. This model has a rosewood body with the cross-braced top that Martin developed around 1850. The black-painted cedar neck has a cone-shaped heel and an 18-fret rosewood fingerboard. The ebony bridge has pyramid-shaped ends and a bone saddle, and the strings are held in place by pins.

Conversion This instrument originally had tuning pegs, but was converted to take machine heads in the early 20th century.

1894 Arias (right)

Vicente Arias (1845-1912) was based in Ciudad Real. He was one of a group of Spanish luthiers, which included Manuel Ramírez of Madrid, who started building instruments using the Torres design in the late 19th century. This example has a cedar neck, a rosewood body with an ebony fingerboard, and a spruce top with fan-bracing.

Martin O-45 (left)
Martin guitars with an "O-style" body and 34.5-cm (13½-in) lower bout were developed in the 19th century. The O-45 was produced from 1904 as a top of the range model with this body size. It has an ornamented headstock and fingerboard, soundhole inlays, and a decorated purfling, using abalone and mother-of-pearl. The body is made of rosewood with a spruce soundboard. The example shown is from 1929.

Gibson L-4 (left)
Gibson launched the L-4 in 1912 as their top-of-the-range, non-cutaway companion to the Style O. It has a 40.8-cm (16-in) lower bout, an archtop, oval soundhole, and a tapering "snakehead" headstock. During the early 1920s it was one of the first Gibsons to feature an internal truss rod. This example is from 1924.

National Style O (left)
In the mid-1920s, Resonator guitars were developed by the Dopyera brothers to enhance volume and sustain. They were made with wooden as well as metal bodies. Their internal construction with a circular metal resonator produced a new type of sound. This early 1930s' model has "f"-holes on the upper bouts, and is decorated with a sand-blasted Hawaiian landscape.

Maccaferri guitar (right)
The Italian guitarist and designer Mario Maccaferri developed a new type of instrument in the early 1930s, which was built in Paris by the Selmer Company. It has a zero fret, an unusual flat cutaway, a D-shaped soundhole, an extended register for the top string, and a metal tailpiece. The guitar has a flat spruce top and an internal sound box.

| 1901 | 1902 | 1903 | 1904 | 1905 | 1906 | 1907 | 1908 | 1909 | 1910 | 1911 | 1912 | 1914 1915 | 1916 | 1917 | 1918 1919 | 1921 | 1922 | 1923 | 1924 | 1925 | 1926 | 1927 | 1928 | 1929 | 1930 | 1931 | 1932 |

Gibson Style O (right)
This highly ornate guitar was introduced in 1908. It was one of the first commercially produced American guitars to feature a cutaway. The upper bout on the bass side has a scroll design similar to Gibson's mandolins. The archtop has an oval soundhole, a trapeze tailpiece, and a raised pickguard. Production was discontinued in 1923.

Soundhole Most early Gibson guitars have an oval-shaped soundhole.

Pickguard Gibson were one of the first companies to use a raised pickguard.

Metal tuning pegs

Martin OM-28 (right)
The "orchestral model" OM-28 was launched in 1929. To meet the demand for a Martin guitar with better access to the upper register, the neck joins the body at the 14th fret. It has a long scale-length and a redesigned standard Martin body. This model paved the way for the use of 14-fret necks on other Martin models. The OM series was discontinued in 1934 and replaced by the 000028, which had a shorter scale length.

Rickenbacker Electro Spanish (right)
Rickenbacker pioneered the use of electro-magnetic pickups in 1931 with their Frying Pan lap-steel instruments. A year later they launched one of the first commercially manufactured electric guitars. This archtop was fitted with a pickup using a horseshoe magnet. The success of the Electro Spanish guitar prompted other manufacturers to consider producing electric guitars.

Body Rickenbacker used the Harmony Guitar Company of Chicago to make wooden archtop bodies.

Gibson L-5 (right)
The L-5 was launched in 1922 as the company's most advanced model. It was developed by the visionary Gibson designer Lloyd Loar. It featured "f"-holes and an internal Virzi tone sound producer, which was a type of internal resonator.

Gibson ES-150 (left)
Gibson's first full-production "Electric Spanish" guitar – a modified version of their L-50 acoustic model – was launched in the mid-1930s. It featured a mahogany neck, a rosewood fingerboard, and a cross-braced, solid spruce top. The pickup, placed near the fingerboard, has a blade-shaped bar.

Solid-body pioneers
From the 1930s, a number of people started experimenting with electric guitars and a new type of body construction. Lloyd Loar, O. W. Appleton, and Les Paul were among the pioneers who used pickups and built unusual designs. This instrument was built by the guitarist Les Paul in the 1940s. It was constructed using a Gibson neck, and sections from an archtop acoustic body. The neck and fingerboard are attached to a solid piece of pine which is used to mount the pickups, bridge, and tailpiece. This adapted piece of cut timber was used regularly by Les Paul. The one-piece central section produces solid-body tonal characteristics and reduces feedback.

Gibson SJ-200 (left)
Gibson first made flat-top guitars in 1918. They developed a range during the 1920s. A "Jumbo" model was introduced in 1934, which paved the way for a redesigned "Super Jumbo" in 1937. This model has a spruce top, a rosewood body, a 20-fret ebony fingerboard with inlays and an ornate "moustache" bridge.

Bigsby Merle Travis (right)
The engineer and inventor Paul Bigsby produced one of the first solid-body electric guitars for country guitarist Merle Travis in the late 1940s. This hand-built guitar has a maple body with a "through-neck", and an unusual headstock derived from European designs. They had a considerable influence on other makers.

1933	1934	1935	1936	1937	1938	1939	1940	1941	1942	1943	1944	1945	1946	1947	1948	1949

Gibson Super-400 (left)
Launched in 1934, this archtop acoustic with a large 45.9-cm (18-in) maple body, and a 65-cm (25½-in) string-scale was designed to produce greater volume. The guitar features inlays and multiple binding on the headstock, fingerboard, and body rims. The top is made from carved spruce.

Bout Early models have a narrow upper bout.

Tailpiece The tailpiece transfers energy to the soundboard.

Gibson L5 Premier (left)
During the 1930s, demand grew for instruments with a cutaway to enable melodies and solos to be played in the higher register. In 1939, Gibson introduced a cutaway, for the first time since the early Style O, on their L-5 and Super-400 models . These were termed "Premier" models, and the cutaway was given a rounded Venetian shape. This example is from 1947.

Gibson ES-350 (right)
The first Gibson electric guitar with a cutaway, the Gibson ES-350 was initially launched with a single pickup. The top is made of laminated maple to produce a clear bright sound. This was considered to be effective with an amplified archtop for producing tone and response, and production was also cheaper.

Gibson ES-175 (right)
In 1949, Gibson produced their first modern instrument to feature the "Florentine" cutaway. The ES-175 has a rosewood fingerboard with double parallelogram inlays, a laminated maple top, and a single P90 pickup, with one tone and volume control. An extra pickup was added in the 1950s. The ES-175 remains in production today.

Leo Fender

Leo Fender (1909-1991) is a key figure in the history of the guitar. Born in California, he started building amplifiers and guitars in the 1940s, eventually leading, in 1950, to the launch of the Broadcaster solid-body electric guitar. This design revolutionized guitar making. Fender went on to develop the electric bass and a number of other classic guitars.

Gibson Les Paul (left)

In 1952, the Gibson company introduced their first solid-body guitar, the Les Paul. Elements of the Les Paul design were derived from the company's archtop electric guitars. The model shown features a mahogany body with a maple top finished in gold, and a 22-fret rosewood fingerboard with crown marker inlays. Two P90 pickups are controlled by a three-way selector switch.

Tailpiece Early Les Paul models were fitted with a trapeze tailpiece.

Gretsch 6120 (left)

The "Chet Atkins" hollow-body 6120 is an electric archtop featuring "f"-holes and a single cutaway. It has a 22-fret rosewood fingerboard and a laminated maple body with an amber finish. It is highly ornamented with "western" motifs. Two De Armond pickups have a selector switch and four controls, one of which is mounted on the cutaway bout. The strings run down to a Bigsby vibrato unit.

Gibson ES-335 (right)

The Gibson ES-335 thinline guitar was developed as a semi-acoustic instrument, combining solid-body features with a shallow arch-top design. The guitar has a 22-fret rosewood fingerboard with dot inlays. The symmetrical double cutaways improve access to the upper register.

1950	1951	1952	1953	1954	1955	1956	1957	1958	1959	1960	1961	1962

Fender Broadcaster (left)

The Broadcaster, soon renamed the Telecaster, was the first mass-produced, solid-body electric guitar. Its highly innovative design featured a maple 21-fret fingerboard with an asymmetric headstock. The neck is attached to the solid ash body with four screws and a metal neckplate. Two pickups are controlled by a three-way selector switch and one pair of tone and volume controls.

Pickups A single-pickup model – the esquire – was also produced.

Fender Stratocaster (left)

Following the success of the Telecaster, Fender launched a "futuristic" model with advanced features. This guitar has a 21-fret maple neck and a deep double cutaway for access to the upper register. The ash body has comfort contouring with a sunburst finish. Three pickups are controlled by a selector switch with one volume and two tone controls. An internal tremolo block is added as a standard feature.

Gibson Flying V (right)

This instrument, produced in very small numbers, was an imaginative departure in modern geometric styling. It has a pointed headstock with a 22-fret rosewood fingerboard, and a V-shaped, two-piece korina wood body with a clear finish. The two PAF humbucking pickups are controlled by a selector switch connected to two volume controls and one tone control.

Gibson SG (right)

The Gibson SG ("Solid Guitar") was introduced to replace the Les Paul in 1961. It was an attempt to produce a more playable guitar with a modern appearance. The 22-fret rosewood fingerboard is set clear of a mahogany body, which has a sharp double cutaway. Two PAF humbucking pickups are controlled by two pairs of tone and volume controls. The strings are attached to a large vibrato unit.

Vibrato On some later models, the vibrato unit was modified.

Rickenbacker 360/12 (left)
The 360/12 was the first popular 12-string electric guitar. Each pair of strings was reversed to give a distinctive sound quality. Derived from the company's Capri series, it has a thinline maple double-cutaway body finished in sunburst and a "cat's eye" "f"-hole. Two "toaster-top" pick-ups are controlled by a selector switch, two pairs of tone and volume controls, and a mixer control.

Yamaha SG2000s (left)
A third series of SG guitars was launched by Yamaha in 1973. Their design, derived from the Gibson Les Paul, featured a new symmetrical double cutaway. Their quality and styling helped to establish Japanese manufacturers with guitarists worldwide. This model has a 22-fret, ebony fingerboard with a laminated "through neck". The body has a black finish with white binding, two humbucking pickups, and gold-plated metal parts.

Jackson Soloist (left)
Grover Jackson produced the first of the "Superstrats" with pointed headstocks and modified body shapes in 1982. The Soloist features a 24-fret rosewood fingerboard, a "through-neck", three pickups, and, as a standard feature, a Floyd Rose tremolo unit.

Steinberger (left)
Steinberger guitars first appeared in 1982. Made with a very small body, they are among the most innovative and revolutionary guitars of the 1980s. They were produced without a headstock: the strings are adjusted for intonation by micro-tuners on the tremolo unit on the body of the guitar. The instrument is constructed from extremely strong fibre resin and graphite materials which produce a very clear and even tonal response. The model shown was introduced in 1989.

| 1964 | 1965 | 1966 | 1967 | 1969 | 1970 | 1972 | 1973 | 1974 | 1975 | 1976 | 1977 | 1978 | 1979 | 1980 | 1981 | 1983 | 1984 | 1986 | 1987 | 1988 | 1989 | 1990 | 1991 | 1993 | 1994 | 1996 | 1997 | 1998 | 1999 | 2000 | 2001 | 2002 | 2003 |

Ovation guitars (left)
In 1966, the Ovation company, started by aerospace industrialist Charles Kaman, developed a new type of guitar design with a fibreglass "Lyrachord" rounded-bowl back. The sitka spruce top has an unusual bracing system and a large soundhole. The company was one of the first to produce successful amplified acoustic guitars in the late 1960s: individual "piezo-electric" transducers were set under the bridge saddles.

Paul Reed Smith (left)
PRS guitars were first designed in the early 1980s before going into full production in 1985. This highly rated guitar has a mahogany body and neck with a 24-fret rosewood fingerboard, two humbucking pickups, a simplified control format with tone switches, and a tremolo unit and nut without locking strings.

Ibanez Jem (right)
The Ibanez Jem is a standard "superstrat" with a 24-fret fingerboard. The upper frets are scalloped to facilitate string bending. It has two humbucking pickups, a single-coil middle pickup, and a Floyd Rose tremolo unit. The guitar features a carrying handle cut through the upper section of the body.

Parker Fly (right)
Developed by maker Ken Parker and Larry Fishman, this radical design first appeared in 1993. Its light, contoured body has a hard "exoskeleton" outer shell of synthetic materials and a resonating internal centre made of wood. The guitar has excellent upper-register access. The two-octave fingerboard is synthetic and has 24 steel frets set directly into it. The guitar has standard pickups and a piezo pickup set into the bridge to add an acoustic element to the sound.

CLASSICAL GUITARS

THE DESIGN AND CONSTRUCTION OF THE CLASSICAL GUITAR

Innovation
Many established makers are refining and adjusting their work within the classical tradition. Australian Greg Smallman and German Matthias Dammann have revolutionized the guitar with new bracing systems and the incorporation of carbon fibre.

Today's classical guitar is based on the traditional design of the Spanish maker Antonio de Torres (1817-92). In the mid-19th century he developed a new large-body guitar with a pleasing outline and standardized rectangular bridge. His guitars took construction and sound a step forwards. The Torres guitar had extra volume and a good tone and was widely adopted by classical players. It replaced the small-body guitars of makers such as Panormo and Lacote.

Strings
Guitars were originally strung with gut treble and metal-wound silk bass strings. In the 1940s, nylon treble strings were introduced. Nylon strings are more consistent in quality, stronger, and may be used at high tension to produce a clear sound with good projection.

CHRISTOPHER DEAN CLASSICAL (BELOW)
One of the outstanding English guitar makers, Christopher Dean (b.1958) has been building guitars professionally for over 20 years. He is part of a tradition going back nearly half a century to the early work of David Rubio (1934-2000). Dean worked at one time with prominent maker Paul Fischer (b.1941), who in turn had worked with Rubio for a number of years. Dean continually strives to refine and enhance his sound. His guitars have a bright crisp string tone, and the body adds a pure resonance and depth. There is a good response in all registers. Dean's instruments are evolving within the tradition of European classical guitar building, influenced by Torres, Bouchet, Hauser, and the philosophy and approach behind English making. The guitars are used widely for performing and recording.

Materials Finished in 2003, the instrument is made principally of four woods: Indian rosewood for the body, bridge, and headstock facing, European spruce for the top, mahogany for the neck, and ebony for the fingerboard.

Bridge The rosewood bridge has a saddle set in a slot with a tie block for the strings. The internal bracing has five radiating fan struts and a cross bar under the saddle.

Fingerboard extension The one-fret extension of the fingerboard gives a high C note.

Flamenco feature The guitar has a *golpeador* plate to stop the top becoming damaged from the *golpe*, the technique where the fingers use the top for percussive, rhythmic tapping.

Headstock The solid headstock with friction pegs is a feature of early instruments.

Construction Flamenco guitars have a thinner top than classical instruments to make them more responsive.

FLAMENCO GUITARS

The flamenco guitar is a classical guitar in outline, shape, and proportions, but it has a number of important differences in construction that give it its own particular tonal qualities. It has lighter internal bracing than a classical guitar, a thinner top with a transparent *golpeador* tapping plate, and a light-coloured cypress-wood body with cedar neck. The string action is set lower. The overall effect is a warm, loose guitar with a pronounced string sound. Nevertheless, the

flamenco guitar player can produce a cutting attack from the instrument as well as a mellow, soulful quality.

The guitar featured here is the work of Domingo Esteso (1882-1937). His guitars are fragile, antique instruments, dating from the early 1900s, yet they are still valued for their remaining tonal qualities. There are many great makers in Spain today, among them the Hermanos Conde, successors to Esteso in Madrid, and Manuel Reyes in Cordoba.

Today, flamenco guitars have more in common with the modern classical guitar. Professional flamenco guitars have a slotted headstock with worm-and-gear tuners instead of pegs, which make the instrument difficult to tune. Many flamenco guitars are made with rosewood bodies, which give power and density to the sound. Many leading guitarists today, including the great Paco de Lucía, have to amplify their guitars on stage, particularly in a group.

Rosette One of the hallmarks of the maker is the rosette. It is handmade from a roll composed of hundreds of tiny strips of coloured wood, which are then cut across to form a pattern.

Neck The mahogany neck and 20-fret ebony fingerboard, with 5.2cm (2½in) nut width, joins the body at the 12th fret. There is an overall 65cm (25½in) string scale length.

Headstock The slotted head-stock has a rosewood facing and the maker's distinctive carved shape.

Low string action

Construction The guitar has standard construction, with a spruce top, rosewood body, mahogany neck, and ebony fingerboard.

Body and finish Beautifully proportioned with a 37cm (14½in) lower bout width, the top is carefully sanded for a superb tonal response. The instrument is finished with a light French polish made from shellac.

CUTAWAY GUITAR (RIGHT)

This innovative guitar, made for the author Richard Chapman by Russell Fong in London in 1993, was designed to meet the need for a more modern instrument. The upper bout body shape was altered to give easy access to a higher register, reaching notes that are just out of range on a standard design when using sophisticated fingering patterns and a stable thumb position. The neck joins the body one fret higher than normal, and a dropped shoulder on the treble side gives an extra two frets. The guitar has a rounded neck profile and the heel is cut in closer to the body than usual. Together, these structural changes let the player move three frets higher and play melodies, improvisation, and chords in a better register, similar to steel-string and electric guitars, while maintaining a beautiful full nylon-string sound.

STEEL-STRING ACOUSTICS

THE DEVELOPMENT OF THE STEEL-STRING ACOUSTIC GUITAR

Steel strings
By 1928 steel strings had gained wide acceptance and replaced gut as the standard fitting on virtually all Martin models. Gut is virtually unknown today. Nylon strings, associated with classical guitars, appeared in the 1940s.

Steel strings have existed for centuries but were used widely only from the late 1800s. Their incisive cutting edge created an entirely new guitar sound, and their tone has became an integral part of American blues, folk, and country music as well as acoustic rock and pop. Today, these styles are played with steel strings throughout the world. The American acoustic guitar is differentiated from the classical and archtop guitars as a steel-string "flat-top" acoustic.

Bracing
Unlike the classical guitar, the American flat-top acoustic has an internal X-bracing, developed by Martin as a simple, effective support. German-born C.F. Martin moved to the USA and founded his company, the premier American flat-top manufacturer, in 1833.

MARTIN 000-18 (BELOW)

With its mahogany body and functional design, the OOO-18 is one of the most popular mid-range Martin models. Its design changes describe the evolution of steel-string guitars. Small Style 18 guitars with a specific mix of woods and decoration were listed from 1857. In 1902 the demand for more volume led to the OOO body size with a 38cm (15in) lower bout width. The OOO-18 came out in 1911, with a rosewood body, cedar neck, and ebony fingerboard. It was offered primarily with steel strings from 1923. A solid headstock and 14-fret neck-to-body junction came in during 1934; a rosewood fingerboard from 1940. The modern OOO-18, with its metallic springy tone, has been popular with English folk guitarists such as Richard Thompson and Martin Carthy.

Saddle and bridge There is a compensating slanted saddle. The rosewood belly bridge has black pins with white eyes holding the strings.

Clear finish

Construction The spruce top is X-braced internally and has a round sound hole with three groups of black and white concentric ring inlays.

Body The OOO-18 was given a mahogany body and neck from 1917. The black binding came in during 1966. The lower bout width is 38cm (15in).

TWELVE-STRING ACOUSTICS

Guitars with doubled pairs of strings, termed courses, date from five centuries ago. After the ascendancy of six single strings, one of the few prominent guitars with 12 strings in the early 20th century was the interwar Stella instrument, used by many blues guitarists. Modern steel-string guitars with six pairs of strings became popular in the 1960s. The first 12-string guitar made by Martin in any numbers was the D12-20, which came out in 1964. The acoustic 12-string has a huge orchestral sound with a sensation of continual ringing. Folk virtuoso Leo Kottke and jazz and classical player Ralph Towner have used it to great effect.

MARTIN D12-28

The D12-28 was first produced in 1970. It has the Style 28 woods and decoration, and the D-shaped large body with square shoulders that was brought into full production by Martin in the 1930s. The guitar has the top two strings doubled at the same pitch. The four lower strings have an upper octave pair, which sits above the normal string and is struck first on a downstroke.

Large ebony pin bridge

Body The rosewood body has extra bracing to accommodate the increased string tension. The top is spruce.

Headstock with 12 tuners

Strings The overall string scale length is 63.5cm (25in).

Headstock The rosewood headstock facing has a gold Martin logo and tuners with metal buttons.

Sound There is a Fishman transducer pickup under the saddle and an internal microphone.

Neck The one-piece mahogany neck with a 20-fret unbound rosewood fingerboard with dot inlays joins the body at the 14th fret.

TAYLOR 714CE (RIGHT)

From 1931, Mario Maccaferri designed guitars with cutaways, played by Django Reinhardt. Gibson brought out a J160E acoustic with a fitted pickup in 1954, which the Beatles used. Yet acoustics with cutaways and fitted pickups did not become popular until the 1970s. The Taylor 714CE cedar-top electro-acoustic model from 1992 is high quality. The combination transducer and microphone gives attack and a full-bodied sound. It has a shimmering tone without strong bass, ideal for backing vocals and with other instruments. This guitar's Indian rosewood body has a sharp cutaway on the treble side, a two-piece back with centre stripe, and a Western Red cedar top with a round sound hole with concentric ring inlays of koa wood and abalone.

ACOUSTIC INNOVATION

THE DEVELOPMENT OF ARCHTOPS AND RESONATORS

Archtop makers
Gibson dominated the world of archtops. Rivals Epiphone brought out their own large Emperor in 1936, with its 47cm (18½in) wide body, to challenge the Gibson Super 400. Among individual makers, Jimmy D'Aquisto (1935–1995), who worked with D'Angelico, stands out.

The increasing popularity of the guitar in the USA and its use by performers in bars and clubs led to the development of new acoustic guitars with greater volume. The archtop guitar was developed by Orville Gibson in the late 19th century. Gibson made mandolins and used their construction as the basis for a new type of guitar. It paved the way for 20th-century developments, such as archtops with cutaways, the templates for the first electric guitars.

D'Angelico
New York archtop maker John D'Angelico (1905-64) started by copying the Gibson L-5 and, in the 1930s, incorporated art-deco styling. He focused on a large New Yorker and a smaller Excel model. D'Angelico greatly improved the tone of archtops.

Headstock
The bound "snake-head" headstock has the Gibson script logo and flowerpot motif, and tuners with ivory buttons mounted on plates.

GIBSON L-5 (LEFT)

When it first appeared in 1922, the Gibson L-5 Master Model was a milestone in the accelerating evolution of the guitar in America. Developed by Lloyd Loar with "f" holes and high-quality construction, it became the prototype for virtually all jazz guitars. With a new type of refined balanced sound, a smooth pure tone, and sustain, this model was adopted by jazz guitarists such as Eddie Lang and country star Maybelle Carter. Early L-5 models have birch bodies, replaced by maple from about 1924, and an internal Virzi-Tone sound chamber, later discontinued. The 1928 guitar featured has a 40.5cm (16in) wide maple body with an arched back and cream binding on the rims. The carved spruce arched top has narrow "f" holes with internal tone bars. There is a wooden height-adjustable bridge, trapeze tailpiece and raised pickguard. It has gold plated metal parts and a sunburst finish.

Construction A one-piece maple neck and 20-fret bound ebony fingerboard with dot inlays join the body at the 14th fret.

Headstock The bound headstock has a curved design inspired by the Radio City stage. It has the Monteleone logo, and Schaller gold-plated tuners with buttons cast as a stylized letter "M".

Neck The one-piece maple neck with internal truss rod and 24-fret bound ebony fingerboard has mother-of-pearl and turquoise inlays suggesting rays of light. It has an overall 65cm (25½in) string scale length.

MONTELEONE RADIO CITY (RIGHT)

John Monteleone (b.1947), based in Long Island, New York, is one of the world's outstanding guitar and mandolin makers. Each guitar is unique, with an exceptional sound and art deco aesthetics. One of a small range of handbuilt models, the Radio City featured is inspired by New York's art deco Radio City Music Hall. It has a 46cm (18in) wide bound curly maple body, 7.5cm (3in) deep at the rim, with a single cutaway and an arched back. The top is European spruce carved to form an arch, with bound "f" holes, internally supported by an asymmetric X-brace and tone bar system. There are ebony fittings, a height-adjustable bridge, a tailpiece with inlays, and a raised inlaid pickguard with a stepped edge that matches the upper fingerboard.

Body It has a maple body with a single rounded cutaway, a carved spruce arched top with "f" holes, adjustable ebony bridge, and a brass trapeze tailpiece.

Neck The guitar has a two-piece maple neck. The 20-fret bound ebony fingerboard with split block inlays has a 65cm (25½in) string scale length.

Headstock The bound headstock has the Gibson logo, split diamond inlays, and tuners with tulip shaped metal buttons.

Controls The guitar has two humbucking pickups with plastic surrounds, four rotary controls, and a three-way selector switch set on the lower bout.

GIBSON SUPER 400 CES (ABOVE)

Introduced in 1934 as a loud, high-quality model, the Gibson Super 400, with its 46cm (18in) wide body, was the company's largest archtop. The upper bout width was enlarged in 1936, and in 1939 a cutaway "Premier" model was added. The first electric Super 400 CES and L-5 CES models came out in 1951, with P-90 pickups and controls. Humbuckers were introduced in 1957. The Super 400 CES sounds deep and full bodied, ideal for jazz, country, and rock. George Benson, Scotty Moore, and Mark Knopfler have all used this guitar.

RESONATORS

In the late 1920s, a revolutionary instrument with internal resonating discs concealed below a top coverplate was designed by the Dopyera brothers' National company. They manufactured the "resonator" in response to the growing demand for a guitar that could be heard clearly in relation to other instruments in popular music ensembles. The energy from the string is transferred through the bridge to either one or more of the cone-shaped, aluminium discs. The discs vibrate to enhance the sound and percussively project it. Their all metal bodies further alter the effect, creating a bright, luminous sound with a cutting edge. Their punchy attack, and increased volume and projection, were ideal for a duo or group. The new sound was taken up by blues, Hawaiian, and jazz players.

Body The ornate body has art-deco styling and lily-of-the-valley engraving. Slide models were made with square necks as well.

Headstock The slotted headstock has a shield with the National logo.

NATIONAL STYLE 3 (ABOVE)

Referred to as "tricones" because of their three resonating discs, the Style 3 was built by National from 1928 to 1941. Their sound is bright and metallic. The metal body is made of a nickel-plated alloy called German Silver. It has large latticework upper bout soundholes, a three-sided coverplate with cutouts with mesh grills, a T-shaped handrest over the bridge, and a metal tailpiece holding the strings.

DOBRO (RIGHT)

The Dopyera family made a cheaper wooden instrument with one internal resonating cone from 1928. Called Dobros to differentiate them from metal body National resonators, these guitars have a softer, more natural, sound, popular with country players in the 1930s. Their sound is established in bluegrass and some American folk music. The guitar featured has a slotted headstock, 19-fret fingerboard, laminated wood body, metal coverplate, and trapeze tailpiece.

Sunburst finish

Nut The guitar can be set up with a high nut for playing slide.

Coverplate The circular metal coverplate has small round soundholes. Many Dobros have more ornate soundholes that form patterns.

ELECTRIC GUITARS

THE DEVELOPMENT OF THE ELECTRIC GUITAR

Manufacturers
Electric guitar making is dominated by Americans. After the Rickenbacker and Gibson models, the Fender Telecaster in 1950 triggered the manufacture of today's classic guitars in the 1950s and early 1960s. These include the Les Paul, 335, Stratocaster, and Flying V.

The electric guitar has become a design icon of the 20th century, instantly recognizable the world over as the mainstay of rock, pop, blues, jazz, and country music. The initial experiments with electric guitars started in the 1920s, and the first full-production guitars were the Rickenbacker electro-Spanish models of 1932. In 1936 Gibson produced the ES-150, sparking a golden age of innovation and design in the 1940s and 1950s.

Fingerboard changes
In 1959 the Stratocaster acquired a rosewood fingerboard, which gives a slightly softer tone. Maple fingerboards returned as an option in the late 1960s.

FENDER STRATOCASTER (BELOW)

Launched in the spring of 1954 as the rock'n'roll era dawned, the Fender Stratocaster is the world's most famous electric guitar. Its aerodynamic shape suggested the advent of the space age. The guitar has been used by the most famous players in rock, blues, and pop, starting with Buddy Holly, Hank Marvin, and Buddy Guy. After the emergence of Jimi Hendrix with his astonishing sounds and inspired playing, the Stratocaster was adopted by leading guitarists, such as Eric Clapton, Jeff Beck, Dave Gilmour and, later, Mark Knopfler, Stevie Ray Vaughan, and Johnny Marr. Its sound ranges from thin, dry, and metallic through to a singing string that soars in the upper register with a colourful tone. Today, the Stratocaster is available in forms ranging from models that follow the look of the classic early series to extravagant "Custom Shop" models.

Bridge and tailpiece Six height- and length-adjustable metal saddles sit on the bridgeplate and tailblock assembly, which tips forwards and backwards as a tremolo unit. It is held by two adjustable anchor posts.

Body The ash body has offset double cutaways, aerodynamic shape, and comfort contouring.

Pickups There are three single coil pickups with white plastic covers with exposed polepieces.

White three-layer pickguard

Finish The body has an ivory-cream seethrough finish with a woodgrain pattern.

Tremolo arm Pressing down the detachable tremolo arm lowers the pitch of the strings. An internal metal block tips back, stretching the springs.

FENDER TELECASTER (BELOW)

The first mass-produced solid-body electric guitar, the Telecaster and its single pickup version the Esquire, were launched in 1950. Initially called Broadcasters, the name Telecaster came in during 1951. It is still a popular classic, particularly favoured by country players and one of the major instruments in pop. Roy Buchanan, Albert Lee, James Burton, Danny Gatton, Keith Richards, Andy Summers, and Jonny Greenwood have all used Telecasters. The guitar has a tonal range from a plangent throaty twang to a cutting and chunky metallic edge ideal for rhythm. The construction of the Telecaster is straightforward. It has a flat solid body made from ash with a single cutaway. The solid maple neck

with an asymmetric headstock and cambered fingerboard has 21 frets and inset black dot markers. The neck is attached to the body with a rectangular metal neckplate held by four screws. A dark "skunk stripe" appears down the back where the neck is routed for a strengthening truss rod. The string scale length is 65cm (25½in). In the 1950s the guitar acquired a lighter cream finish and a white pickguard replaced the black one. In 1959 a rosewood fingerboard was introduced. Maple fingerboards came back in the late 1960s, and today Telecaster models reflect differing 1950s and 1960s classic designs. There was also a 1960s Custom model and a Thinline model from 1968 to 1978.

Construction and finish The ash body has a single cutaway, and is routed for two pickups and controls. The parts are chrome plated with a blonde finish termed "butterscotch" on the early models.

Neck The one-piece maple neck and fingerboard join the body at the 17th fret.

Headstock The asymmetric headstock has the Fender logo and "Telecaster", and Kluson tuners with oval metal buttons.

Coverplate The guitars were produced with a snap-on "ash-tray" coverplate which sits on the bridge baseplate – this is normally taken off, arguably to improve the sound.

Controls Set on a metal control plate are one volume and one tone control with metal barrel-shaped knobs and a three-way selector switch with a black plastic tip.

Pickups There are two pickups. The front one has a metal cover. The back one has exposed pole-pieces and is set at an angle and mounted in the bridge tray.

Headstock The asymmetric headstock has a string retainer holding E and B strings, tuners set in a row with metal buttons, and a truss rod adjustment hole.

Construction The one-piece maple neck and fingerboard join the body just above the 16th fret, attached with a four-bolt metal neckplate with adjustment screw.

Neck The neck has a "skunk stripe" routing covering the internal truss rod. There are 22 frets, and circular black dot markers set directly into the top. The fingerboard has a pronounced curvature (camber). The overall string scale length is 65cm (25½in).

Logo This 2003 American Series model has a silver black-edged Fender logo and the words "Stratocaster" and "Original Contour Body".

Jeff Beck

An inspired player with a magical touch on the Fender Stratocaster, Jeff Beck is a master of melodic invention and fine touches and nuances. Playing harmonics and using tremolo to move pitches with great delicacy, his performances are full of detail with surprising quotes, with the addition of rakes, and accurate string bending. He plays with his fingers, which gives a great range of textures and dynamic control.

Tailpiece The strings are attached to a stud tailpiece held by threaded anchor bolts set into the body.

Finish The book-matched two-piece flame maple top has a sunburst finish.

Pickups This guitar has had its metal pickup covers removed, which was thought to improve the sound. It has Patent Applied For humbucking pickups (PAFs).

Plastic raised pickguard

Body It is 32.5cm (12¾in) wide and 4.5cm (1¾in) deep at the rim.

Bridge The ABR-1 Tune-O-Matic metal bridge is mounted on height-adjustable discs.

GIBSON ES-335 (BELOW)

In 1958 Gibson added a new model with symmetrical double cutaways and a "thinline" shallow body fitted with a solid internal centre block to help sustain and cut feedback. During 1958 and 1959 a whole range of models was introduced based on this design, including the ES-355, ES-345, and the hollow body ES-330. The guitars' powerful reedy tone with depth and sustain is ideal for blues, rock, and jazz fusion. Chuck Berry and B. B. King have played ES-335s during their careers and they have been widely used by, among others, Eric Clapton and John Scofield. Gibson bought the Epiphone company in 1958 and produced a range based on this body outline, including the Epiphone Casino used by John Lennon with the Beatles.

Body The laminated maple hollow body is 4.5cm (1¾in) deep at the rim. The cherry red finish was introduced in 1960.

Neck The ES-335 has a one-piece mahogany neck, with a 22-fret bound rosewood fingerboard with dot inlays. It has an overall 63cm (24¾in) string scale length.

Fittings This ES-335 has standard fittings. There are two PAF humbucking pickups, each linked to its own separate volume and tone controls and a three-way selector switch.

GIBSON LES PAUL (LEFT)

The Les Paul came out in 1952. It was the first solid-body Gibson electric guitar, brought out in response to the growing interest in amplified instruments. The design was entirely traditional. The outline shape and gold finish with cream fittings was based on the ES-295 archtop, and the Les Paul is virtually a scaled-down version of this guitar with a solid body. The guitarist Les Paul had some input on the design and his name was used to endorse the new instrument. During the 1950s the guitar underwent minor changes until it acquired its classic sunburst finish in 1958.

A whole family of Les Pauls was introduced including the black top-of-the-range Custom in 1954. The original series Les Paul has a one-piece mahogany body, maple top, and a single sharp cutaway, routed for pickups and controls. The original series body shape was discontinued in 1960, but a Les Paul was reintroduced by popular demand in 1968. Eric Clapton made the Les Paul famous in the mid-1960s, and after that it was extremely successful. Today it is the icon of rock along with the Fender Stratocaster.

Headstock
The face has the Gibson logo, and "Les Paul" silkscreened in gold lettering. It has a bell-shaped truss rod cover and Kluson tuners with plastic tulip-shaped buttons.

Neck
The Les Paul has a one-piece mahogany neck and 22-fret bound rosewood fingerboard with crown inlays joining the body at the 16th fret, with overall 63cm (24⅜in) string scale length.

Jimmy Page
The Les Paul was taken up by Jimmy Page, who used it extensively for recording and performing, producing a tremendous tensile power. In the studio, he was able to create a wider range of textures. Jimmy Page in his 1970s Led Zeppelin heyday with his low-slung Les Paul is one of the enduring images in rock history.

Body The mahogany body has offset symmetry and sharp incurved double cutaways. Its bevelled edge acts as comfort contouring. A cherry finish covers the body and neck.

Headstock The first models carried a Les Paul endorsement, along with the Gibson logo and crown motif. The headstock has Kluson tuners.

Pickups Two humbucking pickups are connected to four rotary controls.

GIBSON SG STANDARD (ABOVE)

The SG range was brought out in 1961 as a replacement for the Les Paul. This futuristic shallow-body electric guitar with sharp cutaway horns became popular in the 1960s. It was used by many players for a blues-rock sound, including Frank Zappa, Eric Clapton, and Tony Iommi. Frank Zappa made the SG-series guitars his main instrument for a number of years. He played customized models, some with an additional contact pickup placed on the bridge or neck to make an extra range of tones available. Eric Clapton acquired an SG standard after he lost his original Les Paul in 1966.

Painted in psychedelic style, it was modified by removing the vibrato unit. Clapton used it for the "Crossroads" solo, on Cream's 1968 *Wheels of Fire* album.

The 1961 model featured here has a one-piece mahogany neck and a 22-fret bound rosewood fingerboard with crown inlays, similar to the earlier Les Paul. The fingerboard joins the body between the 21st and 22nd frets, giving excellent upper-register access. The early models were fitted with a sideways-action vibrola tremolo unit, which pulled the guitar out of tune. The vibrola was replaced by another design in 1963.

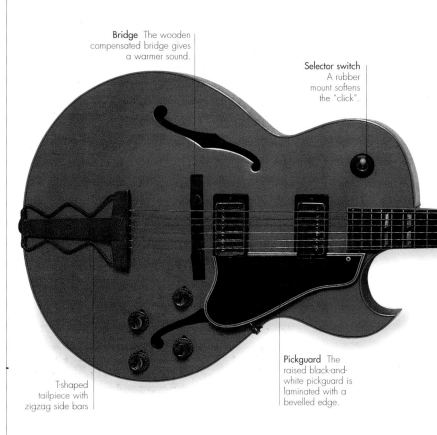

Bridge The wooden compensated bridge gives a warmer sound.

Selector switch A rubber mount softens the "click".

Pickguard The raised black-and-white pickguard is laminated with a bevelled edge.

T-shaped tailpiece with zigzag side bars

GIBSON ES-175 (LEFT)

The Gibson ES-175 was first launched in 1949. After the ES-350, it was the second electric Gibson model with a cutaway and was built as a dedicated electric archtop for the mass market rather than as an acoustic with pickups. It incorporated many Gibson innovations and was given a new-style sharp cutaway. It has always been popular and widely used in jazz by, for instance, Jim Hall, Pat Metheny, and Derek Bailey. Its arched top is made from pressed wood laminate with a maple facing.

The wood gives a bright clear sound. The first models had a P-90 pickup and by 1957 the guitar had acquired its modern fittings and two humbucking picks.

This model from 1960 has a headstock with the Gibson logo and crown inlay, a mahogany neck, and a bound 20-fret rosewood fingerboard with double parallelogram inlays. The neck joins the hollow body at the 14th fret. It has the standard configuration of two PAF humbucking pickups, four rotary controls, and a selector switch. The input jack is on the side.

ELECTRIC 12 STRINGS

Rickenbacker guitars, with 12 strings, have a unique glassy tone. The Rickenbacker became a part of the Beatles sound after George Harrison was given a 360/12 in 1964 when the band were on their first American tour. George Harrison's adoption of this instrument established the electric 12-string sound in pop music. In 1964 the major companies started to produce 12-strings: Gibson an ES-335 and Fender an electric XII model.

Single cat's eye "f" hole

Two "toaster-top" pickups

Neck The 21-fret rosewood fingerboard with triangular inlays joins the body right at the 21st fret.

Headstock The 360/12 headstock has a striped laminate effect and 12 tuners.

Pickguard The two-tier pickguard has four rotary controls, an additional mixer control, and the selector switch.

Body The maple body has double cutaways and a "fireglo" finish.

RICKENBACKER 360/12

The 360/12 has the lower four pairs of octave strings reversed so that the normal string is struck on a downstroke before the upper octave string. This creates a shimmering jangly harmonic effect that can be heard on the opening to The Beatles' *Eight Days A Week*. It was this sound that inspired Roger McGuinn of The Byrds to take up a 360/12. It became an integral part of The Byrds' sound. Rickenbacker produced a new-style 360/12 with a rounded upper-body edge in late 1963.

PRS McCarty (LEFT)

Paul Reed Smith (PRS) became known in the 1980s as a maker of high-quality electric guitars. PRS are now a major force in the guitar world with a large range of models used by, for example, Carlos Santana. The guitars have a full, well-balanced sound with a smooth feel and response. Ted McCarty, the legendary engineer and designer at Gibson, became involved with a new PRS McCarty model, launched in 1994. The guitar featured here is no.48, one of the first batch. The body is mahogany with a two-piece flamed maple top, which has a clear uncoloured wood edge instead of binding. There are two PRS Dragon humbucking pickups with metal covers controlled by one volume and one tone control, which are recessed into the top.

Headstock It has incurved sides and a Paul Reed Smith signature logo with McCarty on the truss rod cover.

Neck The guitar has a mahogany neck, a 22-fret unbound rosewood fingerboard with moon inlays and a 3.5cm (25in) string scale length.

Brown "honey-burst" finish

Volume control To improve the tone, there is no capacitor on the volume control.

Tailpiece The guitar has a compensating wraparound stop tailpiece held by anchor posts.

IBANEZ JEM (LEFT)

Ibanez are a long-established Japanese company who have produced many fine guitar models. They are used widely, and are particularly popular with jazz players and rock musicians, such as virtuoso rock instrumentalists Steve Vai and Joe Satriani. The guitars are easy to play and have a wide range from a fat humbucking to a thinner single-coil sound. The two-octave scalloped fingerboard gives access to a high E, and the guitar is excellent for high-register solos. The Ibanez Jem is a successful modern "Superstrat". Its body is derived from the Fender Stratocaster but with sharper double cutaways and modern tremolo fittings. The guitar has a mahogany neck, a body with double cutaways, two humbucking pickups and one single-coil pickup, two rotary controls, a selector switch, and a clear plastic pickguard.

Headstock The guitar has an asymmetric headstock with Ibanez logo, and a locking nut.

Fingerboard The 24-fret maple fingerboard has blue foliate inlays joining the body above the 16th fret.

Carrying handle cut through body

Exotic blue floral finish

Tremolo fittings The guitar has a combination bridge and tremolo tailblock with tremolo arm, which has micro adjusters.

SYNTHETIC SOUNDS

In the 1970s and '80s guitars were designed to use synthesizer keyboard innovations. During the 1980s, "midi guitars" appeared. The string triggered a midi signal, which controlled digital sounds stored in modules or keyboards. This widened the guitarist's musical palette. Today midi pickups are fitted to guitars. With a pickup conveying the attack and register of the note, any guitar can be linked to any sound. Sound modelling makes it possible to play an electric guitar with a classical sound.

SOLID-BODY ELECTRIC GUITAR CONSTRUCTION

After more than forty years of production, the Telecaster, inspired by Leo Fender's early Broadcaster guitar, remains an industry standard – a tribute to its creator and the excellence of its simple design. The straight-sided, single-cutaway slab body carries the hardware and pick-ups, and the detachable rock-maple neck is secured by four wood-screws. The single-sided headstock allows the strings to run straight over the nut to the machine heads: a *string tree* is required on the 1st and 2nd strings to provide sufficient angle over the nut. The strings are threaded from the back, and pass through the body over the six individual saddles, allowing height and intonation adjustment for each string. Early Telecasters had only three saddles, which led to a compromise on intonation accuracy. The ball-ends of the string rest in six string *ferrules* in the back of the body. There have been many different types of Telecaster produced, including those with humbucking pickups, tremolo arms, and the semi-hollow "thinline" body-style.

Strings

Neck plate and screws

Front strap button

Body The front is made from quilted bookmatched maple, and the back is made from alder.

Rear strap button

Jack plate The jack socket is secured to the jack plate from the inside.

Edge binding

Three-way pick-up selector switch

Electrics The circuitry consists of volume and tone potentiometers, jack socket, and battery connector.

Bridge Six individual saddles make up the bridge assembly.

Control plate

Control knobs

Schaller machine heads

Neck The neck is made from hard rock maple.

Nickel silver frets

Ebony fingerboard

Truss rod

Pick-up

Custom-made guitars
Hand-built instruments can usually be custom-ordered to meet a player's specific requirements. For example, the controls and pickups may be back-routed so that they are set into the body without a mounting plate or a pickguard surround.

"Tortoiseshell" Scratch plate

CONTEMPORARY TELECASTER DESIGN

On this model, produced by Hugh Manson, Telecaster styling is combined with modern refinements that include 22 frets, a compound radius fingerboard, and a graphite nut. The alder body has a maple front with a vintage sunburst finish of hand-polished lacquer. Regular Telecaster pickups are replaced by a set made by EMG which give a low-noise, low-impedence output, and impart harmonic sweetness, to which the ceramic magnets add clear, bright, treble notes. The bridge allows for the adjustment of individual string height and intonation, and the Schaller machine heads facilitate precise tuning. The hardware on this instrument is all chrome-plated.

String tree

Graphite nut

Neck This guitar features neck made from "Bird's-eye" maple.

String ferrules

ELECTRICS

The Telecaster has two pickups – a small single coil unit (*rhythm* pickup), which sits near the end of the neck, and a larger single coil unit (*lead* pickup), set at an angle into the bridge assembly, to balance treble and bass response. This pickup provides the famous cutting treble "tele" sound. The pickups are controlled by a three-way select or switch allowing the use of either or both pickups. There is one volume control and one tone control. When a guitar is fitted with a traditional passive pickup, a treble bleed capacitor is wired to the volume control. This prevents treble being lost as the volume is turned down.

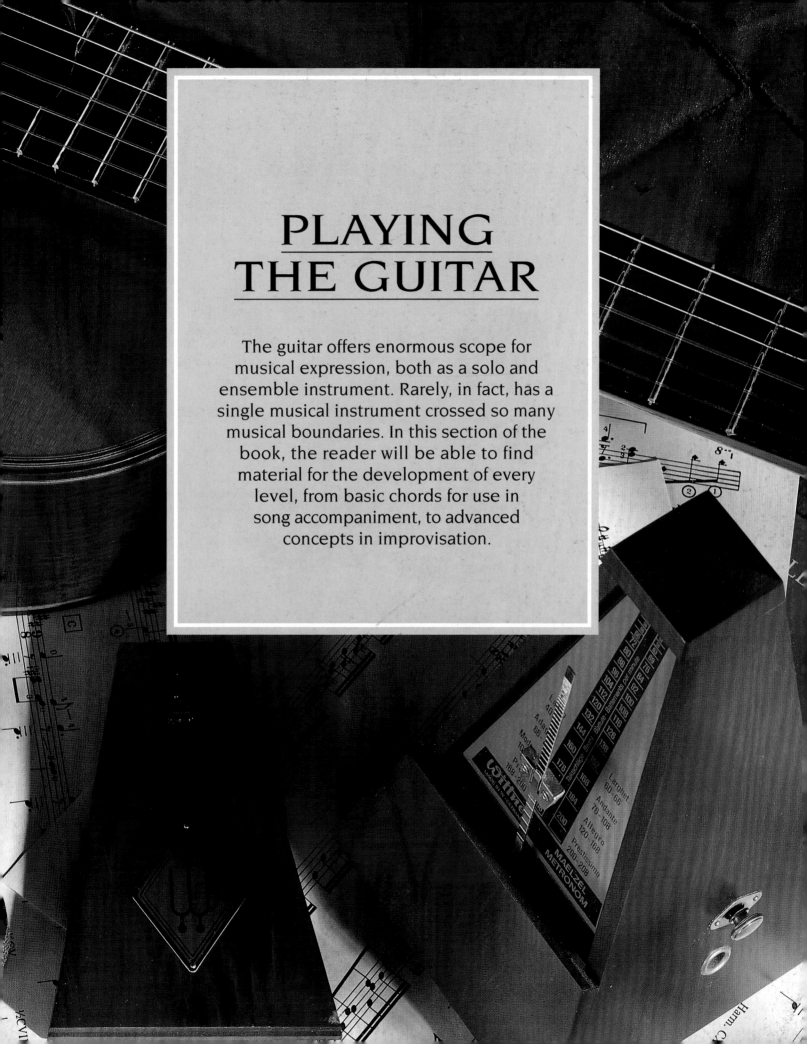

PLAYING
THE GUITAR

The guitar offers enormous scope for musical expression, both as a solo and ensemble instrument. Rarely, in fact, has a single musical instrument crossed so many musical boundaries. In this section of the book, the reader will be able to find material for the development of every level, from basic chords for use in song accompaniment, to advanced concepts in improvisation.

FIRST STEPS

PLAYING YOUR FIRST NOTES ON THE GUITAR

Fingers and plectrums
Classical, flamenco, latin, folk, and some pop guitarists play with their fingers. This gives far more control and variety with music. Rock, pop, jazz, blues, and country players mainly use plectrums with acoustic or electric guitars. Plectrums work well for strumming and fast solos.

All types of guitar have the same positions for locating and holding notes with the left hand. Choose the type of guitar to suit the music you want to play, such as steel-string acoustic or electric for popular styles or nylon-string for

classical. Try different techniques before going in one direction with finger styles or a plectrum. You will need to tune the guitar so that all the strings are at their correct pitch, but at first just strum open strings and pick single notes out.

Begin with fingers
At the start, just use fingers. For virtually all nylon-string playing this is standard. Then, if you want quick results playing pop and rock, try various plectrums. Start with a standard-size plectrum with some stiffness. It draws a smooth response and clarity from the strings.

Holding the guitar It is essential to sit down comfortably to play at first. Practice requires a sitting position. Place the guitar on the right leg close in to the body. For classical playing place the guitar on the left leg.

Looking Tilt the guitar slightly inwards to see the frets on the fingerboard. Bring the neck upwards or closer to the body so that the left hand can reach round to press the strings.

Finger work The first finger is playing a note on the 3rd fret. The other fingers are lifted away from the strings.

Stabilize the guitar Balance the instrument so that both hands hold it lightly.

Getting used to playing
Co-ordinate the hands to play notes on the fingerboard. Try pressing different frets with the fingers of the left hand. Find and hold a note with the first finger of the left hand, then strike the string with the right hand purposefully but not too hard.

SOUNDING THE STRINGS

At first, play with just the right hand to produce a sound from the open strings without pressing down any notes on the fingerboard with the left hand. Look down at the body and place the right hand above the soundhole on an acoustic or the pickups on an electric. With the thumb, play a downstroke across some or all of the strings. Then pick out a single, top or bottom string and pluck it on its own. Now try this with the index (first) finger – in this case you have to pluck upwards, which needs concentration. Repeat single notes with the thumb or first finger and a group of strings together with the thumb.

STRING ACTION

The end of the fingerboard has a nut where the strings are supported to raise them clear so that they do not rattle against the frets. The bridge on the body has the same function. The height of the string, termed the "action", determines how easy the guitar is to play. If the strings are high they need to be pressed hard. Strings can be lowered, and many professionals using electric guitars play with low string action. One slight difficulty at first is that the highest tension on the string is on the first fret next to the nut.

Classical guitar: higher action with thicker strings

Electric guitar: lower action with thinner steel strings

LEFT-HAND POSITION

It is essential to cut the nails extremely short on the left hand so that they do not impede the finger tips from playing notes. Place the thumb on the back of the guitar neck, and use the fingers to press the strings down against the frets. Pressure from the thumb stabilizes the fingers, and lets them exert muscular power. After the right hand has played the required notes, release the pressure of the fingers to stop the notes sounding. The fingers and left hand move freely along the guitar neck for other positions. Stretching and muscular pressure can be difficult at first. Make sure that you do not strain the left hand.

Thumb position
Place your thumb on the back of the neck, just above the centre, and the first finger against a string, pushing it down. The pressure needs to be firm, but the fingers also need to be flexible.

Finger angle
The finger has to go straight down on to the fret so that the tip is holding the string – it does not have to be vertical. The fingers are curved as they bend round to play the notes.

Fret position
Hold notes firmly in the right place so that the strings do not buzz. Press about two-thirds of the way between any two frets, and nearest the fret where the string is being sounded.

Clearance
While fretting the note, ensure the fingers are not muting any other strings which need to sound. For mobility keep the palm of the hand away from the back of the guitar neck.

THE FIRST FOUR NOTES

Try playing a short series of notes on the top string. The "top" string, meaning the thinnest and highest in pitch, is at the bottom of the series of six strings as you look at the guitar. If you play steel-string acoustic or electric guitar the top string has a bright thin metallic sound. On the classical guitar the string is thicker and made of nylon, producing a softer, warm full sound.

Strings The lowest string is called the top string.

Open string With the left hand not in use, the right hand plays an "open string"

1 Right hand only
Play the top string (at the bottom) by resting the right-hand thumb on the string and then sweeping through it in an arc to make the sound. Try this with the right-hand first finger.

2 Left hand on 2nd fret
With the left hand, find the 2nd fret between the first two frets. Press just below the 2nd fret with the first finger. Hold it down while you sound the note with your right thumb.

3 Left hand on 3rd fret
Release the pressure from the left-hand finger on the 2nd fret. Lift the finger just above the string and move it up one fret. Play the next note as before, this time on the 3rd fret.

4 Left hand on 5th fret
Release the pressure from your finger and move up two frets higher to play the note on the 5th fret. Repeat playing the four notes, and try them in a different order.

FUNDAMENTALS

UNDERSTANDING THE GUITAR

Guitar styles
Systems for learning to play the guitar sometimes concentrate on a single style of music or use a specific type of instrument. This book is for players using every type of guitar, from acoustic to electric. It provides the foundation for playing any guitar music and encourages a creative approach.

To play the guitar, you need to understand the fingerboard and recognize note positions. Standard guitars have six strings running along a fingerboard: they provide the means to play notes. Metal frets sit at intervals all along the fingerboard: they divide the

smallest degree of pitch between each note. When you press a string against a fret and strike it with the right hand, it vibrates between the fret and the bridge. The length, thickness, and tension of the string set the frequency of the soundwaves.

Easy learning
Most of the musical examples in this book are in the key of C major and its related minor key. As a framework for memorizing and comparing sections of music C major is one of the simplest keys. As soon as you understand elements in this key, follow the suggestions for repeating the material in all other keys.

NOTES AND SYMBOLS ON THE STAVE

Music is written down using a five-line grid called a stave. Each line and space is used to place a symbol that represents the pitch and time-value of a note. The first seven letters of the alphabet, A to G, are used to name the notes. A stylized letter G

(𝄞) – known as a treble clef – fixes the second line of the stave as the note G. Notes that sit above and below the stave are placed on ledger lines. To make guitar music easy to read, the notes on the fingerboard are written one octave (C to C, for instance) higher than their actual

pitch. Middle C occurs on the 1st fret of the 2nd string, not on the 3rd fret of the 5th string. When reading music not written specifically for the guitar, remember to play it one octave higher. The octave change is particularly apparent if you play melodies too low.

Notes on the treble stave
*Memorize the notes on the treble stave and their positions with simple mnemonic phrases. The notes **on** the stave lines are, from bottom to top, E-G-B-D-F. Remember them by the first letter in each word of the phrases "**E**at **G**ood **B**read **D**ear **F**ather" or "**E**very **G**ood **B**oy **D**eserves **F**avour". The notes in between the stave lines are F-A-C-E, spelling the word "**FACE**".*

The stave and open strings
*The six open-string (using right hand only, with no left-hand fret position) notes on the guitar can be placed on the stave using symbols. The lowest note **E** corresponds to the open 6th string on the guitar. **A** is the open 5th string; **D** the open 4th string; **G** the open 3rd string; **B** the open 2nd string; and **E** is the open 1st string.*

RANGE OF THE GUITAR

The full range of notes available in standard tuning is shown on the stave. The top notes of an acoustic guitar normally range between B and D. Electric guitars have a higher range, which varies from C# to E. On many Fender guitars, C# is the top note. On 22-fret guitars (such as Gibsons) the top note is D. 24-fret electric guitars have a top note of E.

Fret The metal fret determines the pitch of the note. The letter shows the note played when the finger sits below it on the "fret position".

Open strings	1	2	3	4	5
E	F	F#/G♭	G	G#/A♭	A
B	C	C#/D♭	D	D#/E♭	E
G	G#/A♭	A	A#/B♭	B	C
D	D#/E♭	E	F	F#/G♭	G
A	A#/B♭	B	C	C#/D♭	D
E	F	F#/G♭	G	G#/A♭	A

Fret number

SCALE ON THE 5TH STRING

The interval between any 12 chromatic steps on the fingerboard, such as the open 1st string and the 12th fret of the 1st string, is an octave. Each of the 12 steps is called a semitone. An interval of two frets is called a tone. To name every semitonal step, the letters A to G have intermediate names: they are raised by adding sharps (#), and lowered by adding flats (♭). A natural (♮) cancels a sharp or flat. The interval between B and C is a semitone. A tone is twice the interval, such as F to G. Using the 5th string as an example, the order of note names runs from the open string (the note A), through the chromatic series up to the 12th fret, when it is repeated on the octave. The octave here is the note A, which vibrates at twice the frequency of the open string A, giving a higher register of the same pitch.

NUMBERS AND LETTERS

Below is a standard guitar fingerboard with the fret numbers indicated above. Every open string and fret position has its own letter name, corresponding to the 12 chromatic semitones (steps) of an octave on the fingerboard. Every semitone is the musical interval between one fret.

So, each string runs in a chromatic series of 12 semitones from its open note up to the 12th fret. At this point the series is repeated. Playing these notes is one way to ascend through a series of semitones on the guitar. The same notes also occur at other points on the fingerboard, and in higher and lower octaves.

12th fret The series of notes repeat themselves with the open E occurring one octave higher. The same series of notes starts again with F from the 13th fret upwards.

TUNING THE GUITAR

TECHNIQUES FOR ACCURATE TUNING

Tempered scale
The scale length and fret positions on a guitar are constructed to produce a chromatic series of "tempered" intervals. The chromatic scale was tempered during the middle of the 18th century in order to balance the spatial relationship between notes, enabling accurate tuning.

Before any piece of music can be played, the guitar must be tuned correctly. Each of the open strings should be adjusted so that it is in tune with all the others. If the strings are tuned to concert pitch (see below), the guitar can be played with other instruments. The various types of tuning equipment range from familiar aids, such as a piano or tuning forks, to electronic systems that monitor calibrated frequencies accurately for electric and acoustic guitars.

Discord
Accurate tuning of the guitar is vitally important. When the open strings are not perfectly in tune, the guitar produces an unpleasantly discordant and unmusical effect: chords and scales sound wrong, which can often deter the beginner from playing the instrument altogether.

Machine head

Using the machine heads
Each string on the guitar is wound onto a machine head. String tension is adjusted by turning the machine head until the string is in tune. Turning the machine heads anti-clockwise increases string tension and raises the pitch of the strings. Guitar strings may go out of tune as a result of age, string slippage, changes in temperature, or simply the movement from playing.

OPEN-STRING INTERVALS

The fixed series of pitches that run from the lowest to the highest strings are tuned in an ascending order of musical *intervals*. Intervals between notes have a numeric value based on the relationships of those notes within a scale. Each of the open strings is also designated a letter name from the series A to G. The 6th string (E) and the 5th string (A) are separated by an interval of a fourth. This is because there are four tones running from the notes E to A (E-F-G-A). The remaining strings are also tuned in intervals of fourths except the 3rd (G) and 2nd (B) strings, where there is an interval of a *third* (the three notes G, A, and B).

1st string

6th string

TUNING TO A REFERENCE POINT
The guitar is frequently tuned by selecting a single reference note, and tuning a string to that note. For example, a standard tuning fork that provides concert pitch A at 440 Hz on the 5th fret of the 1st string, or any musical instrument playing the note E, equivalent to an open 1st string on the guitar, can be used as the source for tuning at an accurate pitch level. The guitar string is adjusted to match the sound of the note by playing the appropriate open-string or fretted note, then turning the machine head until it has been brought to a pitch level where it matches the reference note exactly. For the beginner, tuning an open string is by far the most straightforward approach. When an open string has been tuned, that string can then be used as a reference point from which all of the other strings on the guitar can also be tuned.

Tuning forks
When struck, a tuning fork vibrates at a specific frequency. Its sound is amplified by placing the base of the fork against the surface of the guitar. The tuning fork shown above emits an A note at a frequency of 440 Hz. The note A on the 5th fret of the 1st string should be at the same pitch.

Electronic tuners
An electronic tuner monitors the frequency of each of the six strings. The guitar tuning is adjusted until the correct reading is given. An electric guitar can be plugged into the tuner. Sound can also be picked up by a built-in microphone; this allows acoustic guitars to be tuned.

Pitch pipes
Pitch pipes are blown, and emit reference notes for each of the six strings. It requires concentration to tune the guitar by matching the strings with these tones. Whilst some people find it easy, for the majority it requires a certain amount of experience and practice.

TUNING WITH A KEYBOARD

The first step in learning to tune the guitar is to find a source for reference tones. Using a piano or other keyboard, the strings on a guitar can be tuned to six keys on the keyboard. The diagram on the right shows the relationship between the keys on the piano and the open strings of the guitar.

E
B
G
D
A
E

BASIC TUNING METHOD

Once the 1st string is in tune, it can be used as a reference point for tuning the 2nd string. Play E on the 2nd string 5th fret, and leave the note to ring. Sound E on the open 1st string so that it rings at the same time, then adjust the 2nd-string machine head until the two strings are in tune. This technique of matching adjacent strings can be used right across the fingerboard.

1 Play E on the 5th fret of the 2nd string, then the open 1st string. Adjust the 2nd string until it is in tune with the 1st string.

2 Play the note B on the 4th fret of the 3rd string, closely followed by B on the open 2nd string. Adjust the 3rd string.

3 Play the note G on the 5th fret of the 4th string, then the G on the open 3rd string. Adjust the 4th string.

4 Play the note D on the 5th fret of the 5th string, then D from the open 4th string. Adjust the 5th string.

5 Play A on the 5th fret of the 6th string, followed by A from the open 5th string. Adjust the 6th string.

TUNING IN OCTAVES

Another common approach to tuning the guitar makes use of octave intervals. To begin with, the open 1st string should be tuned to the note E. When it is in tune, the open 2nd string (B) can be tuned an octave below the B played on the 7th fret of the 1st string. With the 2nd string in tune, the open 3rd string (G) can be tuned to the G an octave above on the 8th fret of the 2nd

string. The open 4th string (D) can then be tuned to the D an octave above on the 7th fret of the 3rd string. Similarly, the 5th and 6th strings may also be tuned using the 7th-fret octaves. All the strings, except the 3rd, should have an interval of an octave between the open string and the 7th fret of the string above. From the 3rd string, though, the octave is heard by playing the 8th fret of the 2nd string.

Tuning the B string
Match the note B, on the 7th fret of the 1st string, with B on the open 2nd string, an octave below.

Octave pairs
Tune the adjacent strings in octave pairs, matching the fretted notes with the appropriate open strings.

TUNING WITH HARMONICS

On certain frets, when a string is played while a finger touches it gently directly over the fret, a *harmonic* is produced. By placing a finger over one of these points, the usual pitch of a vibrating open string is no longer heard. Instead, a related higher-frequency note is sounded. This harmonic

is referred to as an *upper partial*. The technique shown below uses a series of harmonics to tune the guitar. Over the 5th fret, the harmonic occurs two octaves above the pitch of the open string. Over the 7th fret, the harmonic is an octave and a fifth above open-string pitch. Harmonics are explained in more detail on page 114.

Open strings The open strings marked with a circled 4 and 5 are matched with their harmonic counterparts (marked in diamonds).

Matching harmonics The harmonics marked 1, 2, 3, and 6 on different strings are matched.

1 Tune the 6th (E) string, then play the 5th-fret harmonic. Leave this note to ring, and play the 7th-fret harmonic on the 5th string.

2 Adjust the 5th string until the harmonics sounded from the 6th and 5th strings are vibrating together at the same pitch or frequency.

3 Play the 5th-fret harmonic on the 5th string, leaving the note to ring, then follow it with the 7th-fret harmonic on the 4th string.

4 Adjust the 4th string until the harmonics sounded from the 5th and 4th strings vibrate together at the same pitch or frequency.

5 Play the 5th-fret harmonic on the 4th string; while this is still ringing, follow it with the 7th-fret harmonic on the 3rd string.

6 Adjust the 3rd string until the harmonics sounded from this and the 4th string are vibrating together at the same pitch or frequency.

7 Play the 7th-fret harmonic on the 6th string; let it ring, and play the open 2nd string. Adjust the 2nd string until it is in tune with the harmonic.

8 Play the 5th-fret harmonic on the 6th string, and let it ring with the open 1st string. Adjust the 1st string until it is in tune with the harmonic.

PLAYING POSITIONS
ADOPTING THE CORRECT POSTURE FOR PLAYING THE GUITAR

Playing different instruments
The type of guitar affects ease of playing. For example, a classical guitar with large, heavy strings and a high action, and a modern electric with light-gauge strings and a low action require completely different levels of pressure when the notes are fretted.

When playing the guitar, it is essential to adopt a relaxed and comfortable position. For beginners, the sitting positions are easiest. Most guitarists rest the instrument in their lap, supporting it with either the left or right leg for stability and control. Many live performers, though, play standing up, with the guitar supported by a strap. To an experienced electric guitarist this can become the most natural way to play.

Stretching the hand
Nearly all guitar music requires left-hand stretching that initially feels awkward and causes difficulties. As an exercise to prepare the hands for playing, open out the fingers of the left hand, stretching them gently.

POSTURE WITH A CLASSICAL GUITAR
When sitting down, classical players rest the waist of the guitar's body on the left leg. The neck is angled upwards so that the left arm can easily reach the fingerboard. The right arm rests on the edge of the upper rim of the body. The left foot is often placed on a small stool to bring the left leg up to a higher position. In this standard posture, the weight of the instrument is well supported. Some players in other styles use this or a similar position.

Acoustic posture
The standard posture is to rest the guitar on the right leg. This allows the guitarist to sit in a comfortable and relaxed position.

Head Beginners need to look down at the strings.

Head Look ahead or at the strings, whichever is comfortable.

Right arm
Pressure from the right arm holds the guitar steady.

Shoulders
Relax the shoulders.

Right arm
The forearm is parallel to the floor.

Legs Keep legs parallel, feet flat on the floor.

Right leg
Point the right leg out at a comfortable angle.

Footstool
Use an adjustable footstool so you can find the best leg height.

ACOUSTIC GUITAR POSITION
A popular and natural sitting position for playing acoustic guitars is with the instrument resting on the right leg. The inside of the right arm keeps the guitar in place and prevents it tipping forwards or sideways. The right arm is drawn back, resting against the guitar with the forearm diagonal to the strings. The neck is close in to the player's body. This gives a comfortable left-arm position for playing any guitar.

Classical posture
The orthodox classical posture is for the waist of the instrument to rest on the left leg. To achieve the correct neck angle, raise your left foot on a footstool or other support. This raises the height of the guitar, helping the left arm position and your overall posture.

STANDING UP

With the support of a strap, any type of guitar can be played in a standing position. It is important to let the instrument hang from the strap, with its weight against the body and a good centre of gravity. This leaves the hands and arms free for easy access and comfortable movement. With many modern pop players it is fashionable to place the guitar in a low position. Although this may be visually desirable, it makes the instrument harder to play and is not recommended for beginners.

Arm The right arm is crooked to form a triangle.

Strap support Standing up should feel comfortable when the guitar is supported by a strap.

Thumb You can place the thumb on the upper edge of the neck for some playing positions.

Legs Keep the weight on both feet when standing still.

Electric guitar posture
All electric guitars are designed primarily for a performance-style standing position. For a practical left-hand position, tilt the neck upwards. The posture should feel comfortable when a strap supports the electric guitar.

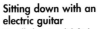

Sitting down with an electric guitar
Small electric solid-body guitars have a low playing position, close in to the body. Larger electric guitars with acoustic proportions are played with a more normal posture. You may need a strap even when sitting down to support and balance the weight of the guitar.

PLAYING LEFT-HANDED

For the many left-handed musicians, it is entirely acceptable to play with the guitar the other way around. Try the guitar both ways round because some left-handers prefer to play right-handed. It is a matter of which way feels instinctively correct and which gives easier control and hand co-ordination. If you play a symmetrical acoustic guitar or a right-handed electric guitar upside down, change the strings. The thinnest, high-pitch strings must be at the bottom.

Moving the guitar
Tipping the neck upwards can make it easier to play notes higher up.

Tremolo arm Use the tremolo arm or "whammy bar" to move the pitch of notes.

Standing posture
There are guitars designed specially for left-handed people. They are made and strung so that they are mirror images of right-handed guitars. Whether left- or right-handed, standing up with the guitar can give a creative feeling of freedom and rhythmic movement. There is nothing wrong with playing "air guitar" with the real thing.

Express yourself
Many players find it exciting and inspiring to move around with an electric guitar.

Mirror image
*The chord below is the chord of E minor for the left-handed player looking down at the fingerboard. It is a mirror image of the chord on the right, which is a right-*hander's view of E minor. Throughout the book, left-handers should treat all images of guitar necks, chord boxes and superimposed scale patterns as mirror images.

STARTING TO PLAY

Numbering
The fingers on the left hand are given numbers from one to four, starting with the index finger. The diagrams for playing include numbers that represent the fingerings used for playing chords and single notes. The numbers are shown inside circles, which are positioned just below the fret. Circles without numbers, over the nut, represent open strings.

When two or more notes are played at the same time, the effect is called a *chord*. One of the simplest ways to begin playing is to construct basic chord shapes on open-string positions. The strings are tuned so that standard chords can be produced when the fingers are placed in certain set patterns. *Harmony* is the term used for the arrangement of notes and chords in a musical structure. It is very easy to produce chordal harmony by brushing the right-hand fingers across the strings. The left-hand fingers press strings against the fingerboard to create fretted notes. This action will make the fingertips sore at first, but the problem will soon pass; with practice, the skin will harden and the muscles of the left hand will become stronger.

First notes
Play the individual guitar strings by picking one string at a time. Without playing any fretted notes or chords, pick the 1st string with the index finger of the right hand. Pick each string from the 1st to the 6th, and as each open-string note is plucked, try not to hit any other strings.

INTRODUCTION TO FINGERING

Chords are formed by using one or more fingers to press the strings down on a fretted position. With *open-string* voicings, the fretted notes are combined with open strings. The fingers must remain in the correct position behind the fret so that the notes ring clearly without buzzing. Forming chords tends to stretch the hand and fingers into uncomfortable positions at first. Depending on the size of the hand, reaching some notes can be difficult. On many of the chord shapes, the fingers may feel rather bunched together. The third and fourth fingers will have less strength than the first two; extra practice and patience are needed to develop accuracy in using them. The fingers must hold the pressure on the notes after they are played to keep them ringing.

1 Play an A on the open 5th string. Put the second finger on the 2nd fret of the 5th string and play the note B.

2 Add the third finger next to the second finger, placing it on the 2nd fret of the 4th string to play the note E.

3 Holding the two notes down firmly, strum across all six strings with the first or second finger of the right hand.

Forming an E minor chord

Before attempting to play the full E minor chord, build up to the chord shape by playing each fretted element separately. Pick the open A on the 5th string carefully either with an upstroke of the first or second finger of the right hand, or with a downstroke of the thumb. Place the second finger of the left hand on the 2nd fret of the 5th string, forming the note B. Play this note and then take *the finger off the string. Now place the third finger of the left hand on the 2nd fret of the 4th string, forming the note E, and play this with the right hand. Take the third finger away. Place both the second and third fingers back on these note positions at the same time and strum all six strings with a downstroke. This is a full E minor chord. With practice, you will be able to place the fingers of the left hand on a chord position as one movement.*

TABLATURE

The tablature system is widely used when writing down guitar music, and is often included as a complement to the stave. Tablature indicates the positions for playing notes and chords, as well as the order in which they are to be played. Some systems add symbols to indicate time, rhythm, and techniques. The guitar strings are depicted as six horizontal lines running from left to right. Numbers placed on the lines show the fret positions. For example, the number 3 on the top line represents the 3rd fret of the 1st string. A group of numbers running along the lines indicates a series of notes that are to be played one after the other in sequence.

Chords in tablature

The lines and numbers shown on a tablature diagram correspond to the individual strings and the fret numbers found on the fingerboard. Whenever the numbers are shown in a vertical line, play all the notes indicated at the same time; i.e., play them as a chord.

Arpeggios in tablature

Whenever numbers in tablature are written from left to right, play the notes one after the other, in sequence. The tablature diagram below shows an E minor chord with each of the notes sounded separately. This way of playing a chord is termed an "arpeggio".

Single-note movements

It is also possible to indicate single-note movements in tablature by writing the numbers from left to right. In the sequence shown below, begin by playing an open A, followed by B on the 2nd fret, C on the 3rd fret, and an open D. These movements constitute a simple four-note scale.

Chords Tablature in a line indicates that the notes are played together.

Arpeggio Staggered tablature indicates that the notes in the chord are played separately.

Single notes These positions indicate a four-note scale played on the 5th and 4th strings.

INTRODUCING CHORDS

Using only a small number of chord types, it is possible to develop a basis for playing with other instruments or accompanying songs. Each of these chords should be learnt, both visually and by name. At first, building a chord one note at a time is useful, but eventually the chord has to be formed by placing the fingers accurately in position at the same time. Every note in the chord should ring clearly: notes must not buzz against the frets, and open strings must not be muffled by adjacent fingers.

Chord charts
The chord notation system used in the book features a fingerboard photograph, a diagram that shows fingering positions, a small block of tablature, and the notes of the chord on a traditional stave. Circled numbers on the diagram show which fret to play on, and which finger to use when playing notes on the fingerboard.

Chord fingering The photograph shows how an E minor chord is played.

Stave The notes played are E, B, E, G, B, and E.

Tablature The 2nd fret of the 4th and 5th strings, and the open strings, should be played.

E MINOR The E minor chord shape consists of the notes E, B, E, G, B, and E. All six strings should be played at the same time.

E MAJOR The E major chord shape consists of the notes E, B, E, G♯, B, and E. All six strings should be played at the same time.

A MINOR The A minor chord shape consists of the five notes A, E, A, C, and E. The 5th to the 1st strings should be played.

D MAJOR The D major chord shape consists of the four notes D, A, D, and F♯. The 4th to the 1st strings should be played.

PLAYING A CHORD SEQUENCE

The exercises on the right show the chords learned above linked together in a short musical sequence. In each case, voicings and names should be memorized. To begin with, chord changes should be practised slowly, and speed built up gradually. The first movement simply changes an E minor to an E major by adding the first finger to the shape. Once this change can be made smoothly, the second chord change – to an A minor – should be tried. This shape is the same as E major, with the E fingering simply moved across onto the 2nd, 3rd, and 4th strings. The final chord change – from A minor to D major – requires the biggest jump in technique, and should be practised separately. A common mistake when first playing D major is to strike the 5th and 6th strings, which are not part of the chord, but this will be remedied by practice.

E minor
Place the second finger on the 5th string 2nd fret, and the third finger on the 4th string 2nd fret. This forms E minor. Strum the chord gently downwards with the right hand.

E major
While still holding down the E minor chord, change it to E major by adding the first finger to the 1st fret of the 3rd string. Again, strum the chord downwards with the right hand.

A minor
Take the three fingers away from the E major position and move this shape across from the 3rd, 4th, and 5th strings onto the 2nd, 3rd, and 4th strings, to form the A minor chord.

D major
Take the fingers away from the A minor shape. Place the first finger on the 3rd string 2nd fret, the second on the 1st string 2nd fret, and the third on the 2nd string 3rd fret.

SCALES AND TIMING

AN INTRODUCTION TO FORMING SCALES AND UNDERSTANDING TEMPO

Introducing scales
Melody and harmony are based on the organization of individual notes into an ordered succession. This sequence is termed a *scale*. Most scales used in western classical music are made up using a pattern of seven notes, with fixed intervals within an octave.

Having linked together a series of chords, the next step is to pick out individual notes and play them as scales. To play any sort of scale structure, or *melody*, it is important to develop the ability to play notes evenly, and build up timing control. To play a scale, the left hand must be able to pick out each individual note clearly. To be effective, the right hand must be co-ordinated with the left. These skills are vital in laying the foundations for playing correctly.

Scale positions
The guitar is constructed in such a way that the same notes can be played in different positions on the fingerboard. The same scale can be played by moving along one string or across different strings. This choice can lead to difficulties in positional thinking.

FINGERING ON ONE STRING
The first step towards developing single-note technique is to play a five-note chromatic scale on the top string of the guitar. For this exercise, each finger is used for a fret. As each new note is played, any previous note held is released.

Fingering technique
The scale on the left is composed of semitone intervals running from the open top E string to the G♯/A♭ on the 4th fret. This series of intervals is not melodic but provides an ideal starting point for the development of technique by building towards an equal facility with each finger of the left hand. Break the scale down to a one-note movement between each of the fingers.

E   F   F♯   G   G♯   G   F♯   F   E

C MAJOR SCALE
The major scale is the primary order of tones and semitones. Each note is termed a *degree* of the scale, the first note of the scale being the first degree, or *key note*. The major scale always has the following ascending order of tones and semitones: tone-tone-semitone-tone-tone-tone-semitone. This sequence of intervals can be repeated in any octave. A major scale pattern can be built from any note on the fingerboard. The notes in the C major scale have letter names without sharps (♯) or flats (♭) – they are the same as the white notes on a piano keyboard. These notes occur in all registers of the fingerboard. To play a C major scale on the guitar, the lowest C – the 3rd fret of the 5th string – must be located. The seven-note scale ascends from this point.

The C major scale
The scale is played as a descending order of notes from the key note C on the 1st fret of the 2nd string.

C   D   E   F   G   A   B   C

MELODY EXERCISES
By varying the sequence of notes in the C major scale, a series of patterns and melodies may be created. Two passages are shown as examples on the right. After carefully picking them out, you should try to create your own single-note lines.

RHYTHM AND TIMING

Rhythm and time is the framework within which the notes are placed to define their character and effect. Up until now, chords and scales have been played as a sequence of movements without any sort of strict time value. However, virtually all music is played or written down using an ordered system for the duration and position of musical sounds. Once the left hand has become reasonably comfortable when forming the E major and A minor chord shapes, the next logical step is to develop smooth and even movement between

chords, creating a basic rhythmic structure. With practice, co-ordination between the hands will gradually improve, paving the way for playing chord changes in a set period of time.

TEMPO AND CROTCHET SPEED

As the beat in music can vary in speed, the amount of time between each beat changes: this is referred to as the *tempo*. The *crotchet* is often used as a reference point for tempo. A crotchet written down with a number next to it indicates how many are played during each minute. For

example, if a crotchet is marked as ♩=60, the rate of movement in the music is one crotchet beat per second.

METRONOMES AND SOUND SOURCES

Using a source to provide an even beat can be of great help when trying to acquire basic rhythmic co-ordination. The "click" from a metronome, or a regular beat from a drum machine or sequencer can be adjusted to provide a comfortable speed to strike chords and individual notes. This will help to develop the ability to coincide right-hand movement with the beat.

Playing in time

Play the eight crotchet beats slowly and evenly, counting to four seconds between each chord. Still counting at the same speed, play a chord every two seconds – this doubles the tempo. Working up to playing a chord every second requires practice. Playing along with a metronome or drum machine will ensure accuracy.

Crotchets
This bar contains four crotchets. It represents the note A played four times with an equal lapse of time between each note.

Time signature of four beats to the bar.

Four-second count between chords.

Two-second count between chords.

One-second count between chords.

BAR LINES

Repeating the eight chords and playing the first downstroke on each chord change with a greater volume gives an accent to each group of four beats. Each of the accented groups is separated by a bar line that denotes its overall rhythmic length and structure. The two numbers at the beginning of a bar show the *time signature* – a grouping of four crotchet beats is 4/4 (*four-four*) time. Groups of three notes (3/4), and two notes (2/4) can also be played.

Time signature of 2/4
The top figure (2) represents the number of beats in the bar, and the bottom figure (4) represents crotchets, or quarter notes.

Time signature of 3/4
There are three crotchets per bar, implying a structure with three beats. This time signature is termed "waltz" or "triple" time.

PLECTRUM TECHNIQUE

DEVELOPING RIGHT–HAND PLAYING TECHNIQUE

Plectrum types
Plectrums are produced in a wide variety of shapes, sizes, and materials. The shape of a plectrum can influence your technique and movement. The size and thickness of a plectrum affects the tone and colour produced from contact with the strings. Try the various types available. Acoustic players often favour a thin plectrum, whereas thicker rigid types are usually preferred for soloing on an electric guitar.

The standard plectrum, or pick, is a flat, triangular piece of plastic held between the first finger and thumb. The majority of electric and steel string acoustic guitarists use plectrums. Many of the sounds and styles in popular music stem from the use of the plectrum, which lends itself naturally to the block chords and solos associated with blues, jazz, and rock. Its use is essential for fast soloing and achieving the texture, nuances, and tone on an electric guitar. The plectrum is also used to create tightly played, percussive, rhythmic chordal patterns. As the point of contact with the strings, playing with a plectrum produces a strong, clear, and even tone.

Plectrum direction
The key to developing a good plectrum technique is mastering the upstroke and downstroke. In the diagrams shown throughout the book, plectrum directions are shown below the stave and tablature. The symbol "⊓" represents a downstroke, and "V" represents an upstroke. A passage of notes can be played using different combinations of pick strokes depending on the desired effect or musical context.

HOLDING THE PLECTRUM

Accurate plectrum movement with a relaxed position is essential for playing with any degree of control and for eliminating tension. Guitarists tend to play by swivelling the wrist and forearm, and moving the joints of the thumb and fingers. Plectrum technique uses a combination of these elements to varying degrees.

Plectrum position
The plectrum must be pointed directly down, towards the body of the guitar. It is important that you do not allow it to turn round as you use it to pick the strings. Keep the flat body of the plectrum in line with the strings in order to ensure free movement and control.

Gripping the plectrum
Hold the plectrum between the side of the top joint of the first finger and the bottom of the first joint of the thumb. Your grip should be firm enough to stop the plectrum moving out of position as it strikes the strings. The second, third, and fourth fingers should be curved inwards.

Stability
Rest the inside of the right arm on the guitar, keeping the right hand away from the body to give free movement to the arm. Alternatively, to give more stability, rest the side of the hand or fingers on either the body, pickguard, or the bridge. Take care to avoid accidentally muting strings.

Striking the string
Play the top E string with a downstroke. The tip of the plectrum should touch the strings evenly, and make just enough contact with the string to produce a full tone. If you hit the string with too much body, it can impede movement when passages of notes are being played.

Parallel position
Ensure that the tip of the plectrum is parallel to the strings. This produces a clear attack on the note, and makes pick movement easier to control during fast passages. Turn the pick to an angled position in relation to the strings to produce a fuller sound with more colour.

PLECTRUM DIRECTION

To control plectrum technique properly it is important to be able to play a series of single notes on the guitar using all types of directional movement. Fast passages of notes are played much more economically by using alternate strokes – an upstroke after a downstroke as a single movement. Speed and fluency are developed in this way to achieve a high level of control for playing scales, melodies, and improvised solos. The ability to play a series of repeated downstrokes or upstrokes is also necessary for controlling tone, rhythmic phrasing, and other advanced playing techniques. The exercises on the right are designed to develop a thorough grounding in plectrum control. At this stage, simple downstrokes, upstrokes, and then more advanced combinations of both are played on an open string.

Downstrokes
Play four downstrokes, using similar volume and attack for all of them. As you position the plectrum for the repeat downstroke, avoid hitting the string.

Upstrokes
Play four upstrokes with a similar level of volume and attack. The upstroke movement is important for balancing the overall control of the plectrum.

Alternating
Pick a downstroke, then an upstroke. Repeat, using an even motion. Passages are usually played with alternating strokes for economy of movement.

Directional control
Play two downstrokes followed by two upstrokes. Using different directional movements is important when single notes are played across the strings.

PICKING A SCALE

A short succession of notes, such as part of a scale or a melody, can be played using a combination of alternate pick movements on a single string. When moving from one string to another, it is helpful if the plectrum is on the correct side of the string just played, ready to play the next adjacent string.

Extending C major

The C major scale on the right has been extended to cover all the notes on the open string position. Play up and down this extended scale with the plectrum. Take small sections of two- and three-note movements from any position and work on achieving a smooth, comfortable action. If possible, play these scale movements against a drum machine or metronome. This will help you to develop an accurate, balanced technique.

C major The scale is built on the four middle strings only.

Picking C major

Play C and D as downstrokes, then E and F using alternate picking. Play the open G as a downstroke followed by A as an upstroke. Play the open B as a downstroke, and complete the movement with an upstroke on C.

C major The scale runs from the open E to G on the top string.

CHORD STRUMMING TECHNIQUE

Some of the basic principles of movement for playing single notes with a plectrum are applied to strumming. The plectrum should be parallel to the strings, and the arc of movement should not take the hand too far away when a stroke has been played. The hand should not rest against the face of the guitar. The inside of the forearm can rest on the edge of the body, but the hand and forearm must be free to make a sweeping movement across the strings.

The downstroke

Downstroke technique is important for strumming chords: a fast downward sweep, playing every note, is the main method of playing vertical harmony with a plectrum. Play a full downstroke across the open strings, followed by the E major chord.

E major down The order of notes when E major is played with a downstroke is E, B, E, G♯, B, and E.

Downstrokes The E major chord is played as a series of four downstrokes.

The upstroke

Play an upstroke, using a movement similar to the downstroke. Build up control by playing the same series of single note directional exercises shown on the previous page. Start with loose alternate strumming and then move on to disciplined strokes.

E major up The order of notes when E major is played with an upstroke is E, B, G♯, E, B, and E.

Upstrokes The E major chord is played as a series of four upstrokes.

Alternating strokes

Play four downstrokes followed by four upstrokes. Reduce this to two of each, moving back to alternate strumming. Now play E to A minor, first using downstrokes, then with upstrokes, and finally with alternate movements.

E major Play all the notes of the E major chord on both the downstroke and the upstroke.

Alternating E major is played as a downstroke followed by an upstroke.

FURTHER TECHNIQUES

Move the plectrum slowly across the E major chord, so that each note can be heard separately. This sound is called an arpeggio – a succession of chord notes. Variations can be played by picking out individual notes to form patterns of arpeggios. The first exercise below is based on a pattern on the E major arpeggio.

Arpeggio on an E major chord

Using a series of downstrokes, play the 6th, 4th, and 3rd strings. Repeat the 4th string, this time as an upstroke. Pass over the 3rd string and play the 2nd string as a downstroke. Finally, play an upstroke on the 3rd string. This style of breaking a chord into single notes can be used to develop a number of melodic variations.

Bass notes with a chord

Using a downstroke, play the 6th string, then pass over the 5th string and strum the top four strings together with a downstroke. Then, using a downstroke, play the 5th string, and then strum the top four strings together with a downstroke. Repeat this sequence, trying to keep even time. This style of playing is commonly heard in country music, or as an accompaniment to popular ballads.

BASIC CHORDS

EXTENDING YOUR CHORD VOCABULARY

Chord vocabulary
The following group of twelve chords should be added to the four shown on page 47, giving a total vocabulary of sixteen chords. These include many of the basic open-string chords, and provide the player with a framework for trying out a large number of sequences. The group shown here includes three chords that do not use open strings: F major, B major, and B diminished.

Chords can be constructed with two or more notes using any combination of positions on the guitar. Every chord has a letter name and a short definition of its harmonic structure. Most guitar chords are named from the root, which is usually the lowest pitched note. The root is the reference point from which a chord is built. The open-string position forms an initial area for playing where basic chord types can be formed, using fretted notes and open strings. A small group of chord types are commonly used in guitar music, primarily the major, minor, and dominant seventh chords.

Learning chords
Memorizing the available string positions for these chords is the first stage in assembling a comprehensive vocabulary. A comparison can be made between different shapes using open strings or fretted positions for the root, and how many strings are played. Four chord types are used here: major, minor, dominant seventh, and diminished chords.

C MAJOR Built from the notes C, E, G, C, and E, this chord uses three fretted and two open strings. Only the top five strings are played.

D MINOR This consists of the notes D, A, D, and F, using three fretted notes and one open string. Only the top four strings are played.

D DOMINANT SEVENTH Formed from the notes D, A, C, and F♯, this uses three fretted notes with one open string. Only the top four strings are played.

E DOMINANT SEVENTH The notes for this chord are E, B, D, G♯, B, and E, played on two fretted and four open strings. All six strings are used.

F MAJOR This chord is formed from the notes F, A, C, and F. All of these notes are fretted. The first finger holds the 1st and 2nd strings.

G MAJOR The notes that make up this chord are G, B, D, G, B, and G. All the strings are used; three of them are fretted, and three are open.

G DOMINANT SEVENTH This chord consists of the notes G, B, D, G, B, and F, using three fretted and three open strings. All six strings are played.

A MAJOR Formed from the notes A, E, A, C♯, and E, this chord uses three fretted and two open strings. Only the top five strings are played.

A DOMINANT SEVENTH This consists of A, E, G, C♯, and E, played on two fretted and three open strings. Only the top five strings are used.

B DIMINISHED The chord is formed from the notes B, F, B, and D. Only the four middle strings are played, and all of the notes are fretted.

B DOMINANT SEVENTH B, D♯, A, and B, on the four middle strings, are used for this chord. Three of the strings are fretted, and the other is open.

B MAJOR This chord is made up from the notes B, F♯, B, and D♯, using four fretted strings. Only the four middle strings should be played.

MOVING A SHAPE ACROSS THE FINGERBOARD

Every chord has a distinctive shape, made from its constituent notes, which forms a pattern referred to as a voicing. When a chord with a fixed voicing is moved, for example from a 6th-string to a 5th-string root, it cannot retain the same shape. This is because the 2nd string has a smaller tuned interval – the open strings on a guitar are tuned with intervals of a fourth between each, except for the 3rd and 2nd strings, where the interval is a major third. The chord shape has to alter in order to compensate for this smaller interval, and the note on the 2nd string moves up by one fret. Similarly, when a 5th-string chord shape is moved across the fingerboard to a 4th-string root, the note on the 2nd string is shifted up by one fret.

MOVING A SHAPE UP THE FINGERBOARD

When chord shapes are moved up and down the fingerboard, they retain their voicings, but the finger positions change as fretted notes are used instead of open strings. One shape can be used to play the same chord type on each fret. The root name changes on each position.

E major, A major, D major
The E major chord built from the 6th string has the same type of voicing as A major on the 5th string and D major on the 4th string. The A major chord uses only the top five strings, and D major only uses the top four strings.

E MAJOR · A MAJOR · D MAJOR

G major, C major, F major
The chord shapes for G major, C major, and F major have the same type of structure on the fingerboard. The chord voicing for G major has a set order of notes in relation to the root. The C major chord with the root on the 5th string and F major on the 4th string share the same order of notes in relation to their roots.

G MAJOR · C MAJOR · F MAJOR

D major, E♭ major, E major
The D major chord shape can be moved up and down the fingerboard. When D is moved up one fret to E flat, the new fingering can be used to play any of the ascending major chords. For example, holding the shape and moving it one fret up forms E major.

D MAJOR · E♭ MAJOR · E MAJOR

SONG SEQUENCES

PUTTING CHORDS TOGETHER

Count and strum
At first try to get used to counting the numbers under the chords and playing them at the same time. You can lightly emphasize 1, the first beat. Count and play evenly and rest on the point where it states 1 & HOLD. To play the strings, either pluck them with the fingers or strum them with the thumb. With a plectrum play downstrokes.

One of the primary roles of the guitar is to accompany songs. To set you on your way to playing an accompaniment, learn how to put the most common sentences of chords together. This section introduces formulas for songs and full sequences that shape or underlie innumerable pieces. The easiest way for the beginner to play chord sequences and understand how they work is to learn a basic vocabulary of related chords in C major. This section will build up to six standard chords in C major with a series of additional chords. Simple movements start with playing just pairs of chords.

Building sequences
Use these chords to make songs as well as learning to busk round simple sequences for backing songs in one key. It will be necessary to learn many further chords and other keys to build up a practical vocabulary of chords. Songs in C often use various chords with notes outside the scale, such as D major, which uses an F#, or F minor, which uses an Ab.

NUMBERING CHORDS

Roman numerals (**I-VII**) often denote the position of a chord in relation to the first note, **I** (one). So, 5 is **V**, still called "five".

C	D	E	F	G	A	B	C
I	II	III	IV	V	VI	VII	I
1	2	3	4	5	6	7	1

BASS NOTES

Learn names and fingerboard positions for C, D, E, F, G, A, and B. The lowest position of each note is the chord bass note. So, the lowest C is on the 3rd fret of the 5th string and matches the C note in the chord voicing. Use open D above for the D minor chord. Drop down to the bottom open string for E minor. Move up through F, G, A, and B for the other bass notes.

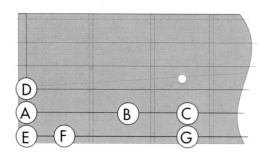

F major
In the sequences below a full F major chord is written out in the chord box. The full chord requires the use of a "barre" with the first finger, which is covered on pages 90-94. For now, try this simpler version.

C MAJOR (I) TO G MAJOR (V)

Start by just moving from the C major chord to the G major chord and back to C. Practise this in your own time without trying to rush the change to the following chord at first. If you find C and G are difficult as full shapes, simply hold as many of the upper string notes as you can. Later on try playing the full chord.

C MAJOR	G MAJOR	C MAJOR
1 2 3 4	1 2 3 4	1 & HOLD

C MAJOR (I) TO F MAJOR (IV)

Now move from C major to F major. At first play F as a chord on the top four strings only if you find the shape difficult, or start building from the bass note upwards. Practise it slowly and keep going – F major is an important chord and it is essential to persevere with it.

C MAJOR	F MAJOR	C MAJOR
1 2 3 4	1 2 3 4	1 & HOLD

I-IV-V-I and I-IV-I-V

Combine C, F, and G chords in short sentences, practising a smooth transition between them. Count and play C, F, G and a return to C in the first exercise; C to F, C to G in the second exercise. Notice that the G sounds unresolved and needs to go back to C.

C MAJOR	F MAJOR	G MAJOR	C MAJOR
1 2 3 4	1 2 3 4	1 2 3 4	1 & HOLD

C MAJOR	F MAJOR	C MAJOR	G MAJOR
1 2 3 4	1 2 3 4	1 2 3 4	1 & HOLD

I-V-IV-I

This sequence is light and jaunty. It moves round the chords in another direction and is in 3/4: each bar has three beats instead of four. Strum each chord evenly three times, emphasizing the chord on the number 1.

C MAJOR	G MAJOR	F MAJOR	C MAJOR
1 2 3	1 2 3	1 2 3	1 & HOLD

THREE-CHORD SONGS AND SEQUENCES

With three chords you have a basis for playing a three-chord 12-bar blues and simple rock sequences. Many simple folk and popular songs are also based on combinations of three chords in various keys. Chuck Berry's *Johnny B. Goode*, James Brown's *I Got You*, and the Carter Family's *Wildwood Flower* all use harmony based on various versions of three chords in different keys. Listen for the chord changes in songs to develop an ear for basic chord movements. The three **I**, **IV**, and **V** chords occur in all 12 keys. For example, in G major the notes are G (**I**), A (**II**), B (**III**), C (**IV**), D (**V**), E (**VI**), F# (**VII**). Therefore, the three chords are those on the the first, fourth, and fifth degrees (a degree is a step of the scale). In G major they are G major (**I**), C major (**IV**), and D major (**V**). G major is one of the most common keys for all types of music played on the guitar. In this key it is possible to play the three full chords without using a barre.

Auld Lang Syne

This famous Scottish song played on New Year's Eve can be supported with just three chords of C, F, and G. Play two or four strums in the bar. The chord structure is eight bars, repeated.

Amazing Grace

Written in England in the 18th century, this song can be played with the three basic chords. It is in 3/4. Try strumming three downbeats in the bar. Repeat the entire 16-bar structure.

Blues in C

These sequences are three of the basic versions running over 12 bars: they are all "12-bar blues". At first just get used to the rate of change between the three chords before trying a rhythmic feel.

INTRODUCING MINOR CHORDS

With the three major chords of C, F, and G mastered, it is time to add the three minor chords in C major. They are A minor on the sixth (**VI**) degree of the scale, D minor on the second degree (**II**), and E minor on the third degree (**III**). This practical group of chords widens your palette of colour and mood and lets you play more sequences. Try the first example of C major (**I**) to A minor (**VI**).

C MAJOR				A MINOR
1	2	3	4	1 & HOLD

Adding D minor

Move from C major (I) to D minor (II), and down to G major (V). Resolve the sequence by moving back to C major (I). The movement from D minor (II) to G major (V) back to C major (I) is a common chord movement.

C MAJOR				D MINOR				G MAJOR				C MAJOR
1	2	3	4	1	2	3	4	1	2	3	4	1 & HOLD

Adding E minor

Move from C major (I) to A minor (VI). Drop down to the low six-string E minor (III) chord and rest on it. Notice how it has a dark, sad quality.

C MAJOR				A MINOR				E MINOR
1	2	3	4	1	2	3	4	1 & HOLD

Major with minor chords

Here the three major chords already encountered, together with the three new minor chords, are combined in common four-bar sequences that form the introduction, or part, of many songs. The first sequence I-VI-IV-V and the variant I-VI-II-V, sometimes referred to as "turnarounds", are common as endings that lead back to the beginning of a song. The third sequence I-VI-III-V has a more sombre sound, while the last sequence I-V-VI-IV is uplifting.

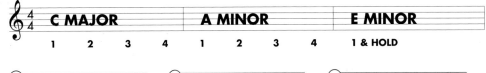

C MAJOR				A MINOR				F MAJOR				G MAJOR
1	2	3	4	1	2	3	4	1	2	3	4	1 & HOLD

C MAJOR				A MINOR				D MINOR				G MAJOR
1	2	3	4	1	2	3	4	1	2	3	4	1 & HOLD

C MAJOR				A MINOR				E MINOR				G MAJOR
1	2	3	4	1	2	3	4	1	2	3	4	1 & HOLD

C MAJOR				G MAJOR				A MINOR				F MAJOR
1	2	3	4	1	2	3	4	1	2	3	4	1 & HOLD

Two-chord vamp

Sequences can start on any chord in C major and function without the C major chord. D minor (II) to G major (V) is repeated as a rhythmic "vamp" that can go round and round behind a solo.

D MINOR	G MAJOR	D MINOR	G MAJOR
1　2　3　4	1　2　3　4	1　2　3　4	1　2　3　4

Step movements

Without strumming the four beats in the bar, move up the scale with chords. Go from C major to D minor then, rather than going up to an E, drop an octave for the E minor and up to F. In the second example, go from C up to G major then resolve back to C major.

C MAJOR	D MINOR	E MINOR	F MAJOR

C MAJOR	D MINOR	E MINOR	F MAJOR	G MAJOR	C MAJOR

Cycle movements

Natural chord cycles, moving in fourths up or fifths down, can be used for all six chords. Count the bass notes as four notes up or five notes down. The first example uses four chords and the second all six.

A MINOR	D MINOR	G MAJOR	C MAJOR

E MINOR	A MINOR	D MINOR	G MAJOR	C MAJOR	F MAJOR

USING THE B BASS NOTE

The seventh degree, B (**VII**), has a diminished chord with the notes B, D, and F. As a simple chord voicing this can sound dissonant and so has been left out for the moment. However, it is a highly important chord and is fundamental in jazz. Simple pop song sequences often use one of the existing chords with a B in the bass, called an inversion and written as a "/" chord, for instance, G major/B.

The first example uses an inversion of G major with B in the bass to link C major with A minor. The second sequence shows C major moving down to E minor with B in the bass, which acts as another link to A minor. Play both sequences the other way round, too, as A minor going up to C major via the two inversions.

C MAJOR	G MAJOR/B	A MINOR
1　　　　2	3　　　　4	1 & HOLD

C MAJOR	E MINOR/B	A MINOR
1　　　　2	3　　　　4	1 & HOLD

The scale in chords

Both sequences have a bass movement, the first going down the scale and the second up. A different chord inversion is used in each for the B bass note.

C MAJ	E MIN/B	A MIN	G MAJ	F MAJ	E MIN	D MIN	C MAJ

C MAJ	D MIN	E MIN	F MAJ	G MAJ	A MIN	G MAJ/B	C MAJ

THE MINOR SYSTEM

The notes or chords from A to A in C major are also a harmonic system with Roman numerals. A minor, the 6th chord (**VI**) of C, is the pivotal home note one (**I**) chord.

A	B	C	D	E	F	G	A
I	**II**	**III**	**IV**	**V**	**VI**	**VII**	**I**
1	**2**	**3**	**4**	**5**	**6**	**7**	**1**

A MINOR TO D MINOR

In the first example, the A minor (**I**) chord moves to the D minor (**IV**) chord. Practise the chords until the transition is smooth.

A MINOR	D MINOR	A MINOR

A MINOR TO E MINOR

In the second example, practise moving smoothly from the A minor (**I**) chord to the E minor (**V**) chord.

A MINOR	E MINOR	A MINOR

A MINOR TO E MAJOR

The E minor (**V**) chord is often altered by adding a G# to make it an E major (**V**) chord, giving a **V-I** release.

A MINOR	E MAJOR	A MINOR

THREE MINOR CHORDS

Play A minor (**I**), move up to D minor (**IV**), and play two bars of E minor (**V**). Move smoothly from one to the next.

A MINOR	D MINOR	E MINOR	E MINOR

MINOR BLUES

Blues is essentially a minor-scale music. The minor chord system has its own 12-bar blues sequences based around **I**, **IV**, and **V**. The first example below has an outline movement that is similar to major chord rock-blues sequences. As a variation, it can be played with an E minor chord in the tenth bar instead of a D minor chord. The second sequence uses E major chords as the (**V**) chord in bars nine and ten. There are other movements of chords using minor chords. Try this interesting alternative sequence with a different order of minor chords, retaining the distinctive blues feeling: A-A-E-E-A-A-D-D-A-E-A-A.

A MIN	A MIN	A MIN	A MIN	D MIN	D MIN	A MIN	A MIN	E MIN	D MIN	A MIN	A MIN

A MIN	A MIN	A MIN	A MIN	D MIN	D MIN	A MIN	A MIN	E MAJ	E MAJ	A MIN	A MIN

Mixing minor and major chords

Bring major chords into the minor framework. The three majors C, G, and F function as chords revolving around A minor. This turns the chords into a system with its own harmonic flavour.

A MINOR	G MAJOR	A MINOR

A MINOR	C MAJOR	G MAJOR	A MINOR

A MINOR	G MAJOR	F MAJOR	G MAJOR

A MINOR	G MAJOR	F MAJOR	E MAJOR

F MAJOR	E MINOR	A MINOR	A MINOR

PENTATONIC ROCK SYSTEM

Rock, blues, and pop use a hybrid minor system with major chords. Take five chords, **I**, **II**, **III**, **IV**, and **V**, in the minor system and play them as a blues-style pentatonic (five-note) scale. Below this.system (right) are all five as major chords. Major and minor chords in various mixtures can follow pentatonic bass lines. This open harmonic interchange is not strict or fixed.

A MINOR	C MAJOR	D MINOR	E MINOR	G MAJOR	A MINOR
I	**III**	**IV**	**V**	**VII**	**I**
1	3	4	5	7	1

A MAJOR   C MAJOR   D MAJOR   E MAJOR   G MAJOR   A MAJOR

ROCK MOVEMENTS

Powerful chord sequences can be put together using the combination of minor and major chords with an outline pentatonic movement or framework. With this way of approaching harmony, major chords can replace any minor chord.

Such sequences are sometimes presented as a type of major system. A major (**I**) is the major home chord and the rest are C major

(♭**III**) instead of C# minor, D major (**IV**), E major (**V**), and G major (♭**VII**) instead of G# diminished. In other words, there are the three fundamental **I**, **IV**, and **V** chords in A major with C major as a flattened third (**III**) chord and G major as a flattened seventh (**VII**) chord. In fact, it is not a proper major system but a type of hybrid blues-scale minor system. Coincidentally, these five chords are

often used as a beginner's system for learning the five open-string major shapes with the acronym "**CAGED**" to remember the group.

The sequences below show a number of common rock movements. All the examples have an instantly recognizable blues-rock sound. Try chords with just two notes, using the root and fifth note as chords – they are neither major nor minor.

Three chord moves
*Run up and down three major chords: A (**I**), C (**III**), and D (**IV**). The 2/4 beat helps the rhythm.*

A MAJOR	C MAJOR	D MAJOR	C MAJOR	A MAJOR
1 2	1 2	1 2	1 2	1 & HOLD

Three chord I-IV-III-I
*In 4/4, go from A major (**I**) up to D major (**IV**), and down through C major (**III**) to A major (**I**).*

A MAJOR	D MAJOR	C MAJOR	A MAJOR
1 2 3 4	1 2	3 4	1 & HOLD

Four chord IV-III-I-VII-I
*From the D major (**IV**) chord, go down to C (**III**), pause on A (**I**), then down to G (**VII**). Emphasize the final A major (**I**) chord.*

D MAJOR	C MAJOR	A MAJOR	G MAJOR	A MAJOR
1	2	1 2	1	2

Three chord I-VII-IV-I
*Catchy and memorable – go from A (**I**) down to G (**VII**) to D (**IV**) before returning to A major (**I**).*

A MAJOR	G MAJOR	D MAJOR	A MAJOR
1 2	3 4	1 2	3 4

Three chord I-IV-V
Treat this three-chord sequence as a major or minor blues movement.

A MAJOR	D MAJOR	E MAJOR
1 2 3 4	1 2 3 4	1 & HOLD

CHORD AND MELODY RELATIONSHIPS

The A minor pentatonic scale can be used as a framework for movements of major chords or a mixture of chords for three-chord or pentatonic-type rock

sequences. In this case, the "one" (**I**) chord, whether it is a simple A major, A7, or A minor, relates melodically to the minor scale called the Dorian mode (scale). It is the A minor scale (called the

Aeolian mode) with the F raised a semitone to F#, creating the Dorian mode notes A, B, C, D, E, F#, G, A. This also applies to blues where the Dorian mode and blues scales can be combined.

House of the Rising Sun
This famous traditional bluesy minor song has major chords added, including F. Strum it in 3/4 and also play it 6/8. The dots at each end are repeat signs.

A MIN	C MAJ	D MAJ	F MAJ	A MIN	C MAJ	E MAJ	E MAJ
A MIN	C MAJ	D MAJ	F MAJ	A MIN	E MAJ	A MIN	E MAJ

PLAYING RIFFS

REPEATING SHORT, CATCHY PHRASES WITH THE GUITAR

Varying riffs
The examples below are in simple downbeat crotchet form. Try doubling to quavers or even semiquavers, and add upbeats with certain notes. Bluesy dotted quavers and triplets also work well.

Riffs are greatly enjoyable to play on the electric guitar, particularly with distortion and effects. As catchy introductions and motifs, they recur in breaks to uplift and strengthen the music. Riffs are usually based around pentatonic-type scales, rhythmically propelled and emphasized by down- and upbeats. Short and focused, riffs can run over just two bars.

Control and expression
To control staccato, quickly release the left-hand pressure on the notes. The outer edge of the palm of the right hand can rest on the strings just near the bridge to mute the sound, which can give a strong and effective texture.

Pentatonic and blue note
Move up the pentatonic scale playing A-C-D-E-G-A, then down playing A-G-E-D-C-D. Give the notes an emphatic dynamism for a blues-rock sound. Break the notes into groups of three and four, starting from any note, and try making up riffs. Now play the same scale, adding an E♭. This is a strong "blue note", sometimes called a flat five. Experiment with short phrases using the new note. Now try to play all of this material starting on A on the 5th fret of the bottom string and staying in the middle of the fingerboard.

Phrases
Try playing the ascending phrase as even notes. The fall from the top E to C and A gives it a rock-blues character. Now try the ascending phrase that answers it. The move from E up to the note G complements the first phrase. The two work together as a call and response. Give the phrases a strong rhythmic framework, turning them into a long riff. In the four-bar example the first two notes are repeated and there are now 16 notes on the beat.

Double-stopped riffs
Now try the A pentatonic scale from the first, top example, with a note a fourth underneath it. Each note has an additional one on the same fret four steps lower. The technique is sometimes called "double stopping" from violin terminology, where two notes are held by the left hand.

Fourths above
Now try a completely different sound, the pentatonic scale with fourths above. This means an additional note four steps above each note. The notes are on the same fret position apart from the top two, G with C and A with D.

Fifths above
Try the same idea with fifths above. It is harder to control with open-string positions. Once you are used to fretting one pair of fifths on adjacent strings, move up and down the lower strings as a fixed pattern with the left hand.

RIFFS WITH DROPPED TUNING

A particularly popular and effective approach to playing pairs of double-stopped notes is to tune the bottom string down a tone or two half steps to D. Play the open D 4th string and detune the bottom E string until the notes resonate together smoothly as an octave D pair. Alternatively, tune down until the note on the 7th fret of the bottom string matches the open A. This gives a powerful, exciting effect, and it is instantly possibly to play the entire series of pentatonic double-stopped notes up and down the bottom two strings. These pairs of notes, which are in fact two-note chords, can be made into bigger chords by playing or fretting across all three bottom strings to give D5, F5, G5, and the other chords ("5" means the chord is roots and fifths only).

Free movement
Try playing up and down, strumming open lower strings and fretting notes on the pentatonic with one finger. Instant rock sequences come out. Try other frets such as the 2nd or 9th to give different chords and movements.

CHORD RIFFS

Another way to approach riffs is to apply some of the above ideas to playing chords. Short pithy chord movements, sometimes with muting and rhythmic emphasis, are termed chord riffs if they are used to give a song a particular flavour. Simple harmonic movements within chords are also sometimes thought of as riffs. Try experimenting with two-note and three-note chords, using the low bass note and the adjacent note, and try two- and three-chord movements. These can be played on any guitar. The use of distortion and effects on electric guitars thickens the texture and enhances sustain, both of which can dramatize the chord riffs.

Chord riffs G to E
Play G and B with the first and second finger. Lift off the second finger to sound the open E with the B. This is one of the simplest chord riffs based on G major and an E5 voicing.

This has simplified fingering.

Open strings
Strum open strings and hammer fretted chords such as E major while the notes are ringing. Play the open string and quickly press down the E major on an emphatic downbeat.

Chord extension
Similar in outline to the open-string riff idea, chord extensions are more practical musically. Hold the A major chord and play an extension with two notes to give it a melodic movement. You can resolve the extension back down to the major chord.

Suspended note
This example starts with a major chord with the addition of a D "suspended" note, written as A sus 4 or A sus 11. The suspended note creates a strong need to be resolved down to the C#. Try playing all the examples over a metronome, drum machine, or computer sequencer.

PLAYING MELODIES

STARTING TO PLAY SONGS AND MELODIES

Note lengths
The crotchets are one beat. Hold the minims for two beats. Hold the dotted crotchets over to the first half of the next beat and play the quaver note on the upbeat.

Songs and melodies are appealing and memorable sentences of notes. When written down as music they should be phrased and interpreted sensitively. The three well-known English folk songs here are sung and played traditionally and have also been arranged as melodies for orchestra by the British composers, Ralph Vaughan Williams and Frederick Delius.

Technique
Play with a finger per fret. Play all 1st fret notes with the first or index finger, all 2nd fret notes with the second or middle finger, and all 3rd fret notes with the third or ring finger. Tablature fret numbers coincide with finger numbers.

BRIGG FAIR

Like all good melodies, this 16-bar folk song is characterized by attractive groups of notes, which form phrases that make up the song. Brigg Fair has an opening four-bar phrase and succeeding phrases. It uses the notes of C major in 3/4, running throughout a one-octave range from C to C. The tune starts on an A and ends on a D and has a tendency to pivot around D. C is not the "tonal centre", although it is written with C major notes. Brigg Fair has a D Dorian modal flavour – the series of notes from D to D within C major acts as a mode (scale) with its own shape. The song has been moved down to an easier position and so is played lower than normal. The rhythm has been slightly simplified.

LOVELY JOAN

This also uses the notes of C major. Lovely Joan is a lively eight-bar folk song in 4/4, which runs throughout a range from C to D. It starts on D and ends on a D. As with Brigg Fair, C is not the tonal centre, although it is written with C major notes. It is in the minor mode of D Dorian. At the beginning a pair of notes lead into the first bar, called an anacrusis. To play the anacrusis, count four beats. On the fourth beat, play the two notes on the downbeat and upbeat. Lovely Joan is also simplified rhythmically and moved on to the lower strings and positions.

GREENSLEEVES

This well-known melody is 16 bars long and has been written in 6/4 instead of the standard 6/8 to make it easier to read. *Greensleeves* has a range of notes running from E on the 2nd fret of the 4th string to G on the 3rd fret of the 1st string. It is in A minor Dorian as well as A minor with the use of an

F# and G# and G natural. It starts on A as an anacrusis (lead-in), similar to *Lovely Joan*, and ends on an A. The melody has an F# on the 4th fret of the 4th string, which should be played with the fourth finger. As in the previous two examples, tablature fret numbers are the same as finger numbers. Chord

symbols have been placed underneath so that the melody can be played in a duo, or solo fingerstyle. To learn *Greensleeves* as a piece with chords, start by adding just the bass note under the melody note. Fill out with chord notes. Where there is one chord in the bar, you can play it twice, on the first and fourth beats.

FINGERSTYLE

THE TECHNIQUES USED IN CLASSICAL AND NYLON-STRING PLAYING

Naming the fingers
The fingers of the right hand have letters derived from their Spanish names. The thumb is **P** (pulgar); the first, or index finger is **I** (índice); the second or middle finger is **M** (medio); and the third or ring finger **A** (anular). The little finger, when used, is **X** (or **E**). **PIMA** notation is used to direct fingering for playing all types of scales, chords, and arpeggios. **PIMA** directions are written above the stave.

The guitar has evolved mainly as a chordal instrument, played with the thumb and fingers of the right hand. Using the fingers opens up the entire vocabulary of musical movement on the guitar. Chords can be played with arpeggiated variations, bass movements, or melody lines. Two or more parts can also be played simultaneously. Classical guitar playing is based entirely on a fingerstyle approach that has developed to a point where it has become standardized. Flamenco playing, and some of the steel-string styles of music based on fingerpicking, each have their own distinctive techniques and traditions. The classical right-hand technique shown here can provide the basis for stylistic variations. Fingerstyle also enables chord sequences to be played without imposing technical limitations.

Nails with steel strings
Guitarists do play on steel-string acoustic and electric instruments with right-hand fingernails. However, the main problem is simply that nails are easily damaged by regular contact with metal strings, and they wear down quickly. Playing with nails on nylon-string guitars is important for producing a good tone. The composition and tension of the steel strings make this kind of tone control difficult.

RIGHT-HAND NAIL TECHNIQUE

In the past, a number of outstanding classical instrumentalists have played without fingernails. However, nowadays virtually all nylon-string players use them. Fingernails must be maintained at a shape and length that provide optimum playing control and tone production. Guitarists cut and file their nails in a number of different ways – some use a rounded nail shape, whereas others prefer a straighter edge, where the nail plucks the string. However, the preferred length of nail varies greatly. Many guitar players have badly formed or weak nails that split or break. Wear caused by playing on nylon strings with a high level of attack exacerbates the problem. To overcome such difficulties, false nails are sometimes used.

Arm position
Rest the inside of the forearm on the upper edge of the guitar, keeping the hand at an angle to the strings. The shoulder and arm should be relaxed, and the hand in a position to reach all of the strings comfortably.

Hand height
Your hand should not touch the soundboard or the bridge. If it is too close to the strings, the movement of the fingers is impeded. Your wrist should be about 7cm (2.75in) above the strings. This will enable the fingers to move freely.

Playing action
Move the thumb downwards to play the bass strings, and the fingers upwards to play the middle and top strings. The fingers should be curved slightly inwards. Strike the notes with a flowing movement through the strings.

Using PIMA
The arrows show the playing direction of the thumb and fingers. The circles indicate the order in which the fingers move. For clarity, the points at which the strings are played in relation to the soundhole are exaggerated. The correct positions are shown on the left.

LEARNING TO PLAY PIMA

When playing, the thumb is referred to as "**P**", the first finger as "**I**", the second finger as "**M**", and the third finger as "**A**". In the following exercise, **P** plays the 6th string, and **I**, **M**, and **A** play the 3rd, 2nd, and 1st strings respectively. The fingernails strike the strings, over the soundhole towards the side closest to the bridge. The strings should be sounded with a *downward* movement of the thumb, and an *upward* movement of the three fingers. After striking the notes, the fingers and thumb should move up and away without hitting or resting on any of the other strings. This action is termed *free stroke movement*. Once the exercises have been played on the open strings, they can be repeated using chord shapes.

Playing PIMA
*Begin by playing the 6th string using the thumb (**P**), followed by the 3rd, 2nd, and 1st strings with the **I**, **M**, and **A** fingers.*

Playing PAMI
*Play the 6th string with the thumb, the 1st string with the **A** finger, the 2nd string with the **M** finger, and the 3rd string with the **I** finger.*

Playing PIMI
*Play the 6th string using **P**, the 3rd string using **I**, the 2nd string using **M**, returning to play the 3rd string with **I**.*

Playing PIMAMI
P Plays the 6th string, I the 3rd, M the 2nd, and A the 1st. Return to the 2nd and 3rd strings using M and I.

PIMA WITH CHORDS

Hold down an E major chord hand and play the first set of open string **PIMA** variations. Take the left hand away from the E major chord, and hold down an A minor chord. Repeat the same set of variations, this time playing the bass note on the 5th string with the thumb. Keep the finger movements on the right hand as even as possible. Play these exercises accurately, gradually increasing the tempo.

PIMA using E major

The notes on the 4th and 5th strings should not be played. Try playing E major with the 1st finger of the left hand holding G♯ and the 2nd and 3rd fingers removed.

PIMA using A minor

Play the A minor chord with a different fingering. The 1st and 2nd fingers hold down the notes C and A, and the 3rd finger is removed. In these exercises, the note on the 4th string is not played.

PIMA VARIATIONS

The following variations are all based on the E major chord. They will help to build flexibility of movement and the control of arpeggiation. There are many variations with the **I**, **M**, and **A** fingers. Play the exercises and then work on the **IMA** part of each one without the bass note. In these examples **I** always plays the 3rd string, **M** the 2nd string, and **A** the 1st string.

Alternatives

*Repeat the exercises in A minor with **P** playing the 5th string, and **I**, **M**, and **A** repeating on the 3rd, 2nd, and 1st strings.*

MOVING THE THUMB

Thumb movement is a vital part of right-hand technique. To begin with, it is useful to play the exercises using only the open strings of the guitar. Using **P**, play an open 6th string followed by open 5th and 4th strings. Move back and forth across the three lower strings, building up alternate movements between the 6th and 5th, 5th and 4th, and the 6th and 4th strings. The exercises on the right should be played holding a standard open string E major chord, moving **P** from the open 6th string to the other strings. Play the **IM** and the **IMAMI** arpeggio with **P** moving from the 6th to the 5th, and then to the 4th strings. Independent thumb movement is built up in this way, using arpeggio patterns with the bottom notes played individually by the thumb on the lower strings.

IMA and IM exercises

*In the first bar, play the 6th string followed by **IMA**, and the pattern from the 5th string: **PIMA** is played twice. In the second bar, play the 6th string followed by **IM** and then the pattern from the 5th and 4th strings: **PIM** is repeated three times.*

PIMAMI exercise

*In the third bar, play the 6th string followed by **IMAMI** and then the pattern from the 5th and 4th strings. The sequence **PIMAMI** is repeated three times. Play each pattern as a continuous cyclical movement.*

FURTHER THUMB MOVEMENT

The thumb can be used to play more than one note in a five-note arpeggio. Play the first *and* second notes with the thumb. Complete the arpeggio using the **I**, **M**, and **A** fingers. The thumb can also be used to move across from the bass strings to play notes usually played by the fingers.

PIMA alternatives
*There are many variations possible using **PIMA** technique – the thumb and fingers may be interchanged. In the second example, showing a movement of **PPIPMP**, the standard right-hand movement is more often played as **PIMPAI**.*

POSITION ON CHORD CHANGES

It is important to maintain control during chord changes. In this exercise, when E major is changed to A minor, ensure that the thumb hits the correct bass string as the chord changes. Play **P** on the 6th string followed by **IMA**, then **P** on the 5th string followed by **IMA** as the chord changes.

CHORD MOVEMENTS

This exercise will develop overall stability, and independence of the thumb. Play the **IMAMI** finger sequence continually as the chord changes. To perform this exercise well, the chord changes must be made quickly. To improve speed and control, practise **P** and **IMA** independently.

ARPEGGIO WITH THUMB SCALE

The thumb can also be used to play scales and melodies *below* arpeggios. In this exercise the thumb is used to play notes from the G major scale against a pattern on the open top strings. Play **IMA** on its own before adding the scale that ascends from the 3rd fret of the 6th string.

STRUMMING WITH PIMA

When a chord of more than four notes is played quickly with the fingers of the right hand, the thumb (**P**) is used to play more than one string. For example, when an E major chord is played on the bottom five strings, in order to sound all the notes together, **IMA** plays the 4th, 3rd, and 2nd strings, and the thumb strikes the 6th and 5th strings at the same time. Similarly, with a full six-string voicing, the **I**, **M**, and **A** fingers play the top three strings and the thumb plays the bottom three strings.

Block chord exercise
*Further control of the thumb and fingers can be developed with the four variations on the right. Chords can be broken up into sections and played with different bottom notes. The thumb can be used to play bass notes and the **I**, **M**, and **A** fingers to play a section of the chord. Try playing all chords in sections.*

Voice movement
"Oblique motion" refers to a note being held while a second moves in relation to it. Repeat an A while playing the scale ascending from B to E. Then repeat E while playing the bass notes descending from A to E.

Contrary motion
Play the two scales that ascend from B to E and descend from D to A.

Parallel motion
Play the two ascending scales at the same time. They run from B to G, and from G to E.

STRUMMING WITH THE THUMB

Mastering a combination of downstrokes and upstrokes with the thumb enables the player to develop an important element of control for playing rhythms with a relaxed and loose wrist. In the thumb exercise below, combinations of strokes are used. Strumming with the side of the thumb may also be used as an alternative technique.

STRUMMING WITH THE INDEX FINGER

When strumming with the index finger, the movement should be made by the finger itself, rather than by the entire wrist. In the exercises below, when using alternating strokes, care should be taken to prevent the nail from catching the strings and impeding movement on the upstroke. The exercises can also be played with the **M** finger.

TREMOLO TECHNIQUE

The **I**, **M**, and **A** fingers can be used to play a continually repeating pattern on one note. This is known as *tremolo*, and is widely used in classical and flamenco styles. Try playing tremolo slowly on the top string while playing the open 6th or 5th string below with the thumb. When these notes are brought up to a fast level, the effect should have an even, rippling sound.

AMI movement
Play the open E string, with **A**, **M**, *and* **I**. *Repeat the sequence slowly and evenly. Build up speed, and play as a continuous pattern, eventually connecting each* **AMI** *movement without stopping between the* **I** *and* **A**.

RIGHT-HAND SCALE TECHNIQUE

Acquiring a good scale technique is one of the most important priorities in learning the guitar. There are different approaches to playing scales with the right-hand fingers on a nylon-string guitar. Most players alternate

the **I** and **M** fingers. An alternating **IMA** technique for some passages may also be used. Play the passages below with both combinations of fingers. Ascending and descending passages sometimes use different combinations of fingers.

The use of **IM** and **IMA** depends on the number of notes on a string. For example, with a five-note scale, two notes on a string will be played by **IM** or **MI**, and three notes on an adjacent string will use **IMA** or **AMI**.

IM technique
The scale above is a two-octave modal scale that uses fifteen notes in C major, starting on the bottom E and ascending to the E on the top string. Play this scale starting with the **I** *finger, and play the next note with the* **M** *finger. Play the entire scale alternating right-hand fingers. The scale should then be played starting with the* **M** *finger, alternating the fingers the other way.*

Scale order The chart above shows which right-hand fingers play the notes held down by the left hand.

IMA technique
The scale shown above is a shortened version of the E scale. Use the **A**, **M**, *and* **I** *fingers to play groups of three notes on the 6th, 5th, and 4th strings. Then strike the notes in reverse using the fingers in* **IMA** *sequence. Because of the length of the* **M** *finger, playing with* **IMA** *or* **AMI** *on the lowest strings of the guitar may be rather difficult to begin with.*

IMA sequence The chart above shows which right-hand fingers play the notes held down by the left hand.

Thumb scales

The thumb is often used to play scales. Play the lower part of the C major scale shown below.

Rest stroke using IMA

The rest stroke is used to play notes with greater volume and a fuller tone. When a note is struck, the finger plays down towards the body of the instrument and completes its movement by resting on an adjacent string.

Rest stroke using the thumb

The thumb can also be used to play rest strokes. Play with a downward movement, resting on the adjacent string after the completion of the stroke. Rest strokes can be played with considerable volume.

LIGADO

The ligado technique is used to give the impression of smooth, flowing movement. After a note has been struck, the left hand plays by hammering on and pulling off further notes. Play an ascending ligado line from the open E string: strike the open string, and quickly place the first finger on the 1st fret, causing the note F to ring. Similarly, move F to G by striking F, and hammering on G. Play a descending ligado by striking F on the 1st fret and, as you take the finger away, pull it down slightly to sound the open E.

The following note
Play ligado between the pairs of notes E-F, F-G, and G-A. Descend with A-G, G-F, and F-E.

Full scale position
These two exercises move across the fingerboard, using all the notes to play both ascending and descending ligados.

Three-note variations
Play three-note variations by hammering on and pulling off two succeeding notes.

PREPARED ARPEGGIOS

A system of setting the hand down into position, touching the notes that are about to be played, is sometimes used to stabilize the right-hand position.

Arpeggio exercises
Play the first exercise (far left), placing the thumb (P) on the 6th string, and the IMA fingers on the 3rd, 2nd, and 1st strings. For the downward-moving arpeggios (left), place the P and A fingers on the outer voices only.

TREMOLO EXERCISE

Keep the **AMI** fingers on the 1st string. The thumb (**P**) plays a scale from the 5th to the 4th string and on to the open 6th.

MALAGUENA

A traditional flamenco theme, Malaguena is based on the chords E major and A minor. The **M** finger plays top E throughout the piece and the thumb (**P**) plays the melody below, over the chords. The piece ends with a rasguedo on the E major chord and uses compas accents (see page 66).

Playing Malaguena
Hold G# on the 1st fret of the 3rd string with the first finger, and E on the 2nd fret of the 4th string with the second finger. Play the notes E, G#, and B with the thumb, while the middle finger plays an E on the first string. Move the second finger to A on the 2nd fret of the 3rd string, and the first finger to C on the 1st fret of the 2nd string, to play the notes A and C, then B and A. Take the second finger off to play an open G. Play the note F on the 3rd fret of the 4th string with the third finger. Repeat these movements from bar five to bar eight.

STUDY NO 1 IN A MINOR

This relatively easy piece, *Study No 1 in A minor*, is by Dionisio Aguado (1784-1849), a Spanish virtuoso guitarist. The piece comprises two 16-bar repeating sections. It is helpful for developing thumb movement and building independence between the thumb and fingers. Play the lowest note of each arpeggio with the thumb and the upper three notes smoothly and evenly with the index and middle fingers. In the first bar the thumb plays an open A string, the index finger plays the fretted C note, the middle finger plays the open E note and the index finger plays the C note again. Throughout the piece the thumb plays a series of bass notes and melodic links while the index and middle fingers play simple variations. Work out the easiest and most sensible fingering positions.

FLAMENCO

SEQUENCES, SCALES, AND TECHNIQUES IN THE FLAMENCO STYLE

Technique

Fingernails are used for power and attack. The thumb rests on the 6th string as an anchor and plays powerful downstrokes. It is also used for up- and downstrokes from the wrist – termed *alzapua*. The fingers often sit in prepared positions on the strings to play rest strokes.

A traditional Spanish folk music, flamenco can be used to accompany singers and dancers, or developed as a virtuosic instrumental style for group and solo. Its evolution and sound are closely linked with the guitar.

Flamenco is based around a framework of strict rhythms, characterful scales, and chord sequences, and the use of unique techniques. The music varies in style from set forms through to open improvisation.

Sounds

Players tap the top to make percussive sounds termed *golpe* with the A finger. Upstroke "harp" arpeggios with the A finger are played near the bridge. Fast tremolo techniques are different from the classical approach – the movement is PIAMI or the variant PMAMI.

COMPAS

Count and memorize these repeating 12-beat cycles with the accents marked **bold**. A five-stroke *rasgueo* is often started on beat 9 and finishes on beat 10.

BULERIA

Play with the compas accents. Rest the thumb on the 6th string and strum downstrokes on each beat with the index finger. Double each beat to quavers, counting "1 and 2 and 3 and...". Play the downstroke as you count and the upstroke on "and".

PHRYGIAN SCALE

The main scale is the Phrygian mode with an added note. For example, in F major the scale runs from the third note, A, using F major notes with a C# as well as a C natural. Phrygian starting from E and F# are also used. Play the scale with picado technique, alternating the **I** and **M** fingers, using rest strokes to the string below.

A Bb C C# D E F G A Bb C C# D E F G A

Open 5th string up to 1st string

Improvise, following the shape of the harmony and rhythm.

STRUMMING

The burring and percussive chords of *rasgueo* are at the heart of flamenco. With the thumb lifted from the 6th string, the fingers strum evenly and lightly. The wrist and forearm may pivot so thumb and fingers strum up and down.

Five-stroke rasgueao
Unfurl the fingers as downstrokes, starting with the little finger X followed by A, M, and I. I adds the upstroke effortlessly.

Four strokes
Start with the A (ring) finger followed by M and I. Bring the I finger back up to play the final upstroke.

Three strokes
This shorter rasgueao is simpler with A, M, and I downstrokes.

Three strokes
Start the percussive three-stroke pattern with M, followed by I and finishing with I as the upstroke.

Three strokes
Lift the thumb and pivot with the wrist. Play a P (thumb) upstroke, then an M downstroke and a P downstroke.

Three strokes
Lift the thumb and pivot with the wrist. Play a P upstroke, an A downstroke, and an I downstroke.

MUSIC EXAMPLES

Flamenco forms are often derived from songs of differing mood and intensity. *Cante jondo* (deep song), from which *solea*, a "mother chant", springs, is full of soul and yearning. A less intense form is *cante medio* (middle song), from which *taranta* is derived, and the lighter *cante chico* (light song) is the basis for the buleria. These examples are by flamenco guitarist Rafael.

BULERIA (FROM JEREZ)

The buleria follows the 12-beat rhythmic compas cycle. This is played *por medio* (middle register) around an A Phrygian modal framework with both a C and C#. It ends with a five-stroke rasgueo on an A major chord with an added A# (B♭). There is a *golpe* tap on the soundboard.

SOLEA (FROM TRIANA, SEVILLE)

Following a compas, this mother chant is slower and more mournful than a buleria. It is based on the E Phrygian mode, but with a G and G# (A♭). On the third and sixth beats, the thumb plays a two-note chord while the ring finger taps a *golpe*. It ends with an ascending arpeggio.

TARANTA (FROM ALMERÍA)

Dark and ruminative with a Moorish flavour, the taranta is played around the F# Phrygian mode with A and A# (B♭). It expresses rhythmic freedom but with an underlying pulse. It uses sombre chords, dissonance, and voicings with augmented fourth and minor second intervals.

ALTERNATIVE PICKING

COMBINING PLECTRUM WITH FINGERS AND USING A THUMBPICK

Handling the plectrum
When not using the plectrum, you can put it down or tuck it in the right hand, but this restricts finger movement. Try hybrid picking – combining plectrum with fingers.

There are various ways to use a plectrum for playing chords on a steel-string acoustic or electric guitar. Many guitarists, particularly in folk and country, combine plectrum use with fingers to play bass notes with chords, counterpoint, arpeggios, and chordal variation. Such techniques widen your options.

Fingerstyle
Nails break easily, so steel-string players use the hard flesh on the ends of fingers. They use a combination of thumb and fingers to strum and pluck chordal variations.

Picking G major
With the plectrum, pick the full G major shape from the lowest note on the 6th string to the highest on the 1st. Use downstrokes on the ascent and upstrokes on the descent. Now try the exercise below breaking the chord into groups of three notes.

Jumping strings
With the plectrum, play the three lower notes, then the bass note and successive pairs of upper notes by jumping over strings. In the second exercise, jump from the bass note to each string. It requires concentration and control. Plectrum direction determines down- and upstrokes.

Scales with G note
With the plectrum, play an F against an open G and move down the scale. Try ascending using a G major scale with an F# and ending with two G notes. The exercises develop speed and control between two adjacent strings.

HYBRID PICKING
The technique combines a normal plectrum position with the middle and ring fingers. Use the plectrum for bass notes, the lowest notes in a chord or arpeggio, or a solo. Use the fingers in an upward picking movement for chords, arpeggiation, or fast flourishes.

THUMBPICK WITH FINGERS
Fitting a thumbpick over the thumb gives free movement to the fingers. Use them in the normal way, similar to classical technique. The extended shape of the thumbpick gives cutting, incisive bass notes, and can be used for scalar passages as well as strumming.

Hybrid picking

Thumbpicking

HYBRID PICKING EXERCISES

In Exercise 1, use the plectrum to play the G chord bass note and alternate it with other parts of the chord as three notes and two pairs of notes. Now play the same notes using the plectrum with the middle and ring fingers for comparison. In Exercise 2, fill out a three-note chord as a four-note chord by using the middle finger to play a pair of notes or the little finger to play the top note. Exercise 3 has tenths with a melodic effect. Develop use of both the middle and ring fingers to play the upper line. In Exercise 4, play a series of ascending three-note chords quickly, like banjo rolls. In Exercise 5, play a series of simple arpeggio variations, moving from G to C.

Thumbpick variations

You can use the thumbpick to create a wide variety of chordal control. Follow the examples on the right. First, block chords: play the bass note with the thumb and the other three notes with the index, middle, and ring fingers. Now separate the bass note from the other chord notes and break them into pairs. In the second exercise play simple arpeggios with the thumbpick and fingers.

Country bass line

This country-style approach, simplified by removing bar lines, uses a thumbpick to play chords with a linking bass line. The bass line goes up to C major, alternated with G and the upper chord notes. It moves to the G major chord with G and D in the bass.

TUNINGS AND SLIDE

DIFFERENT WAYS TO TUNE THE GUITAR

String tension
Most tunings use detuned notes lower than the standard open strings, which makes the strings looser.

The open strings can be altered from the EADGBE tuning to create alternative tunings that give interesting voicings and chord progressions as well as drone effects. Using slide, it is possible to move the pitch of notes and chords freely.

String sound
With loose tension, strings can be pushed out of position and even rattle. This can add atmosphere.

E
B
G
D
A
-2 D

DADGBE
Tune the bottom 6th string down two semitones (a tone) to a low D: release tension on the 6th string until it is an octave below the open D 4th string.

-2 D
-2 A
G
D
A
-2 D

DADGAD
Now tune the top two strings down two semitones. This creates an attractive open tuning for fresh chord voicings, used in folk and crossover styles.

-2 D
-2 A
-1 F#
D
A
-2 D

DADF#AD – open D major
Move to DADF#AD: tune the 3rd G string down a semitone. The resulting D major voicing is the same shape as an open E major chord, used for slide.

-2 D
B
G
D
-2 G
-2 D

DGDGBD – open G major
From DADGBE, tune the 5th and top string down two semitones to a G major chord, the same shape as open A major. Use for slide, and to fret and extend chords.

F#
D
A
D
A
D

DADGBE – D major chord
Low D can act as a drone note underpinning chords and melodies. It can also create a bigger sound for a chord such as this D major voicing.

D
C
G
F#
A
D

DADGAD – D11 chord
This D11 chord, with its bass with fifths and two pairs of close-voiced notes, is a shape that can only be easily created using an open tuning such as DADGAD.

F
C
A
F
C
F

DADF#AD – F major chord
Place the first finger across the 3rd fret to form an F major shape. This tuning is good for fretting simple barre chords and chord extensions in rock.

F
D
B♭
F
B♭
F

DGDGBD – B♭ major chord
Place the finger across the fret to form a B♭ major chord with F in the bass. Sometimes the bottom string is removed for this tuning to give it focus.

USING A CAPO

Short for *capodastra*, the capo is a device that raises the pitch of the open strings. It has various mechanisms to lock it over any fret. Its function is similar to that of the nut or a first-finger barre (see page 78).

Third fret capo
The capo is positioned just below the 3rd fret. It must be fitted firmly so the strings do not buzz. With the device in place, you can play a range of higher-pitched chords, dictated by the capo position, using the new series of open strings.

G
D
B♭
F
C
G

Open strings
On the third fret, the capo gives open notes a minor third higher: G, C, F, B♭, D, and G.

G major open voicing
With a capo on the third fret, use your fingers to hold down the open string chord shape for E major. The capo now makes this an open string G major shape with the notes G, D, G, B, D, and G. Experiment with the new higher-pitched chords.

USING A SLIDE FOR BLUES

Slides are tubular cylinders made of metal or glass, used to move the pitch of notes expressively. They fit over the ring or little finger. The index or middle finger can be placed behind the slide to stop unwanted string noise. The slide itself needs to be lightly placed across the strings and vertically in line with the frets so that the strings are in tune with each other.

Glass slide on ring finger

Metal slide on little finger

Open D and G tunings

In the first exercise, play the open D major tuning. Place the slide at the 3rd, 5th, 7th, 10th, and 12th frets to play a pentatonic D scale in chords. Try playing single lines and pairs of notes. With the D tuning the pairs of notes on the two top strings and the 4th and 5th strings can be used to play the same phrases an octave apart. Try sliding among all the different elements. Hold the slide on the string, sustaining the note, and move it up and down.

In the second exercise, try the open G major tuning with the same positions.

Repeat this series of positions in the higher octave.

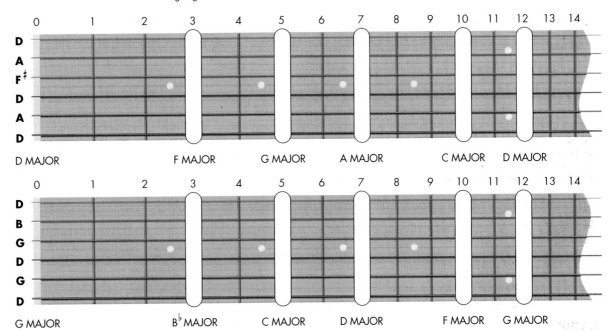

SLIDE VARIATIONS

The slide technique is often called bottleneck because it is derived from the use of an actual bottleneck. Glass, in various shapes, has a warm sound, while brass or chrome-plated metal is brighter and metallic. With slide, it is possible to achieve microtonal nuances between notes. Try moving the slide up from the 3rd fret (right) or down from the 4th fret to play a flattened third blue note that sits between the frets. Now try playing a scale on the top string using notes on other frets, such as the 2nd, 6th, and 9th. This creates a fuller blues scale of open, 2, 3, 5, 6, 7, 9, 10, and 12. Experiment with single-note slide with standard tuning as well.

FURTHER TUNINGS

Open E
Tune the 3rd string up by a semitone and the 4th and 5th strings up by two semitones to form the open-string fretted shape of E major. This adds tension to the strings.

Open C
Tune the 2nd string up by one semitone, the 4th and 5th strings down by two semitones, and the 6th string down by four semitones. This gives a powerful low C major tuning.

Open D minor
Tune the 1st, 2nd, 3rd, and 6th strings down by two semitones to give a D minor chord voicing with a distinctive minor flavour. Experiment with more open tunings.

THE MAJOR SCALE

UNDERSTANDING THE INTERVALS THAT MAKE UP SCALES

The "sol-fa" system
Each note of the major scale has a sol-fa series of note names. They are *do*, *re*, *mi*, *fa*, *sol*, *la*, and *ti*. These one-syllable words can help the player to memorize the sound of intervals. A useful exercise is to sing each note as it is played on the guitar. This helps the ear to recognize notes and melodies.

The major scale is formed from a series of fixed intervals, and provides the framework for many harmonic and melodic structures. Every note on the scale is assigned with a name that denotes its relationship to the first note (*tonic*). These names label the seven notes in the major scale system both as individual tones and as roots for chords. Interval names are also used to label the number of tones and semitones between two points. For example, an interval of three tones and a semitone from a note is referred to as a *perfect fifth*.

Naming major scale notes
The formal name of a note on the major scale describes its relationship to the **tonic** (root) and the **dominant** (fifth). The **supertonic** is the note above the tonic. It is followed by the **mediant** (midway between the tonic and the dominant), **sub-dominant**, **dominant**, **sub-mediant**, and **leading note**.

DO	RE	MI	FA	SOL	LA	TI	DO
C	D	E	F	G	A	B	C
TONIC	SUPER-TONIC	MEDIANT	SUB-DOMINANT	DOMINANT	SUB-MEDIANT	LEADING NOTE	TONIC

INTERVALS ON THE MAJOR SCALE

The intervals on any scale occur between individual notes. The series of tone and semitone steps on the major scale are termed *major seconds* and *minor seconds*. For example, C to D is a tone or a *major second*, and E to F is a semitone or a *minor second*. Larger steps between notes of the major scale also have an interval name to identify the number of scale notes and the size of the space between them. Compare the names used to determine the interval between individual notes and the root note of the scale. For example, C to E is a *major third* and C to F is a *perfect fourth*.

THE SCALE OF C MAJOR

There are several ways to play a scale from its root to its octave note. The C major scale is usually played across the strings. To illustrate the intervals from the root, the C major scale is shown here played on the 5th string.

C major shape
Compare the arrangement of the notes in C major both on the 5th string and in the standard position. The scale on the 5th string shows the relationship of the notes as a series of tone and semitone steps.

| C TO D (MAJOR 2ND) | D TO E (MAJOR 2ND) | E TO F (MINOR 2ND) | F TO G (MAJOR 2ND) | G TO A (MAJOR 2ND) | A TO B (MAJOR 2ND) | B TO C (MINOR 2ND) |

| C TO D (MAJOR 2ND) | C TO E (MAJOR 3RD) | C TO F (PERFECT 4TH) | C TO G (PERFECT 5TH) | C TO A (MAJOR 6TH) | C TO B (MAJOR 7TH) | C TO C (OCTAVE) |

FURTHER SCALE POSITIONS

The C major scale has already been played from the 5th string to the 2nd using a combination of open strings and fretted notes (see p. 48). However, it can also be played from several other positions. One of the most widely used standard patterns starts on the 3rd fret of the 5th string and moves across the fingerboard to the higher octave C on the 5th fret of the 3rd string. This pattern is played using the fourth finger to fret notes. The fingering pattern can also be moved to start the scale on the 8th fret of the 6th string, and extended across the fingerboard to an upper octave.

CHROMATIC INTERVALS

The diagram on the right uses the note C as a fixed point, and shows a one-octave chromatic scale that includes all seven notes of the major scale as well as the five unused notes outside the scale. The notes are shown on the 5th string from the 3rd fret to the 15th fret, along with the names for all the intervals. There are twelve chromatic intervals before the octave is reached. It should be remembered that an interval may have more than one name.

Major scale intervals
The C major scale is shown ascending the 5th string. The intervals, labelled with their relationship to the root, are found on the 5th, 7th, 8th, 10th, 12th, 14th, and 15th frets.

OCTAVE
MAJ 7
MAJ 6
PERF 5
PERF 4
MAJ 3
MAJ 2

FURTHER MAJOR INTERVALS

All the different types of interval occur in the major scale when other notes are used as a reference point. For example, in the key of C major, the intervals running from the note A are major, minor, and perfect. The intervals from the note B are all minor, perfect, or diminished.

Intermediate intervals
These five notes are the remaining intervals in the octave. They occur on the 4th, 6th, 9th, 11th, and 13th frets, between the frets for the major scale intervals.

MIN 2
MIN 3
AUG 4/DIM 5
MIN 6
4MIN 7

A TO B (MAJOR 2ND) · A TO C (MINOR 3RD) · A TO D (PERFECT 4TH) · A TO E (PERFECT 5TH) · A TO F (MINOR 6TH) · A TO G (MINOR 7TH) · A TO A (OCTAVE)

B TO C (MINOR 2ND) · B TO D (MINOR 3RD) · B TO E (PERFECT 4TH) · B TO F (DIMINISHED 5TH) · B TO G (MINOR 6TH) · B TO A (MINOR 7TH) · B TO B (OCTAVE)

CHORD THEORY

The chords used so far have been built using a combination of notes from scales in different keys. Building chords from the notes within a single scale will provide an understanding of the way most chords are constructed. Major, minor, and other triads contain a root, from which the chord takes its name, a third, three notes above the chord root, and a fifth, five notes above the root. Because of this three-note structure, the chords are called *triads*. Each note on the C major scale is used as a root from which a triad can be built following a pattern of intervals. In C major, a triad is constructed starting from the note C. The note E is a major third above C, and the note G is a minor third above E and a

perfect fifth above C. Because of the shape of the major scale, with differing third and fifth intervals from each note, triads built from each note are either major, minor, or diminished types. The seven degrees of the C major scale and the triads

built from each of them are shown on this page. Guitarists do not often use triads alone – chords are usually expanded by doubling notes. However, understanding triads is an important step in developing a knowledge of chord theory.

Playing the C major triad To form the triad, C is held in position, E is placed on the 2nd fret of the 4th string, and G is played on the open 3rd string. The three notes are then played together.

C major
The interval between the root and the third, C to E, is a major third. The interval between the third and the fifth, E to G, is a minor third. The interval between the root and the fifth, C to G, is a perfect fifth.

D minor
The interval between D and F (the root and the third) is a minor third. The interval between the third and the fifth, F to A, is a major third. The interval between the root and the fifth, D to A, is a perfect fifth.

E minor
There is a minor third between E and G (the root and the third). The interval between the third and the fifth, G to B, is a major third. The interval between the root and the fifth, E to B, is a perfect fifth.

F major
Between the root and the third, F to A, is an interval of a major third. The interval between third and fifth, A to C, is a minor third. The root to fifth, F to C, is a perfect fifth.

G major
Between G and B (the root and the third) is a major third. The interval between third and fifth, B to D, is a minor third. The root to fifth, G to D, is a perfect fifth.

A minor
A minor third comes between the root and the third (A and C). The interval between the third and the fifth, C to E, is a major third. The interval from the root to the fifth, A to E, is a perfect fifth.

B diminished
There is a minor third between B and D (the root and the third). The interval between the third and the fifth, D to F, is also a minor third. The interval between the root and the fifth, B to F, is a diminished fifth.

G dominant seventh
The interval between the root and the third, G to B, is a major third. The interval between the third and the fifth, B to D, is a minor third. The interval between the fifth and seventh, D to F, is a minor third. The root to fifth is a perfect fifth, and the root to seventh is a minor seventh.

Tonic major (I)
Major triad

Supertonic minor (II)
Minor triad

Mediant minor (III)
Minor triad

Subdominant major (IV)
Major triad

Dominant major (V)
Major triad

Submediant minor (VI)
Minor triad

Leading note diminished (VII)
Diminished triad

Dominant seventh (V7)
with a seventh in addition to the root, third, and fifth

C major chord voicing

The root, third, and fifth can all be doubled by adding extra octave tones. This enlarges the basic triad and gives a fuller-sounding chord. The standard C major triad – C, E, and G – is shown with an additional C and E in a higher octave.

C D E F G A B C D E

C major chord voicing
This chord has a doubled root note (circled "1" on the diagram), doubled third (3), and a single fifth (5).

A minor chord voicing

The root, third, and fifth can all be doubled by adding extra octave tones. In this voicing, an extra octave root (A) and fifth (E) have been added. In this voicing of the chord, the third (C) only appears in the higher octave.

A B C D E F G A B C D E

A minor chord voicing
This version of A minor has a doubled root note (1), a single third (3), and a doubled fifth (5).

THE DOMINANT SEVENTH CHORD

The fifth chord on a major scale is termed the *dominant* chord. In the scale of C major this chord is G major. In addition to the standard G major, built from the notes of the triad G, B, and D, it is often extended to a G dominant seventh; i.e., the seventh note from the root is added to the chord. Moving from the root (G), the scale has the following notes: G-A-B-C-D-E-F. When voicing chords on the guitar, the seventh often replaces an existing note in a basic chord. In this case, the high G on the 3rd fret of the 1st string is moved down to F on the 1st fret of the 1st string.

G dominant seventh

This dominant seventh voicing has the root (G), third (B), fifth (D), an additional "doubled" root note (G) and third (B), and a seventh (F). This uses notes from G to F on the major scale in C.

G A B C D E F G A B C D E F

G dominant seventh voicing
This chord has a doubled root note (1), a doubled 3rd (3), a fifth (5), and a seventh (7).

CHORDS ON THE MAJOR SCALE

There are twelve major scales, each with a different keynote. Every major scale has a set order of tone and semitone steps from the keynote. All have the same major scale shape and construction, which provides a structure for building chords. For example, in the key of G major the notes ascending from the keynote are G-A-B-C-D-E-F#. The open string chords G major, A minor, C major, D major, and E minor occur as chords in the key of G, made up from thirds built on scale notes in the same way as C major. B minor and F# diminished complete the seven chords. The two major scales C and G are closely related – they share the same notes, apart from F/F#. With six scale notes in common, both keys share certain chords as well. These are G major, A minor, C major, and E minor.

G major scale fingering
The G major scale starts on the 3rd fret of the 6th string, which is the lowest-pitched keynote on this major scale. A, B, and C are played on the 5th string, D, E, and F# on the 4th string, and G on the open 3rd string. All the notes are naturals, i.e., without sharps or flats, except for F#. Here, F natural (♮) on the 3rd fret has been moved up a semitone, one fret to F#.

CHORDS AND SCALES

CHORDAL VARIATIONS USING NOTES FROM THE MAJOR SCALE

Chords from scales
The chords based on the seven degrees of the C major scale can be viewed in relation to the other notes in the scale. They are shown below, with the C major scale superimposed, using black dots for the notes that are not part of the chord. Each chord can be seen as a shape within C major, and altered by adding scale notes to create chordal variations.

Any chord on the fingerboard can be visualized as a shape which consists of a group of notes sitting within a scale position. The majority of players look at the fingerboard and relate chord shapes to scale positions. It is important to understand this relationship. The first step towards acquiring these skills is to work on the guitar using chords and a scale position in one key. This enables the player to add melody, extend harmony, and move around the fingerboard, combining single notes and chords. Linking notes with chords paves the way for playing solo pieces and developing a grounding for the development of composition and improvisation.

Building chords
Triads are extended by using extra notes from related scales. One of the most common additions to a major or minor chord is the seventh. These additions have already been encountered with the dominant seventh (see p. 62). In the first octave, fourths and sixths are often added. In the second octave, ninths, elevenths, and thirteenths may also be used.

C MAJOR The notes taken from the C major scale are C, E, and G.

C MAJOR 7TH The note B, a major seventh above the root, is added.

C MAJOR 6TH The note A, a major sixth interval above the root, is added.

D MINOR The notes taken from the C major scale are D, F, and A.

D MINOR 7TH The note C, a minor seventh above the root, is added.

D MINOR 9TH The note E, a major ninth interval above the root, is added.

E MINOR The notes taken from the C major scale are E, G, and B.

E MINOR 7TH The note D, a minor seventh above the root, is added.

E MINOR 7TH The note D, an extra seventh, is added on the 2nd string.

F MAJOR The notes taken from the C major scale are F, A, and C.

F MAJOR 7TH The note E, a major seventh above the root, is added.

F MAJOR 6TH The note F, a major sixth interval above the root, is added.

G MAJOR The notes taken from the C major scale are G, B, and D.

G DOMINANT 7TH The note F, a minor seventh above the root, is added.

G MAJOR 6TH The note E, a major sixth interval above the root, is added.

A MINOR The notes taken from the C major scale are A, C, and E.

A MINOR 7TH The note G, a minor seventh above the root, is added.

A MINOR 9TH The note B, a major ninth interval above the root, is added.

B DIMINISHED The notes taken from the C major scale are B, D, and F.

B MINOR 7 FLAT 5 The note A, a minor seventh above the root, is added.

B MINOR 11TH FLAT 5TH The note E, an eleventh above the root, is added.

ADDITIONS WITHIN ONE OCTAVE

Adding a note a third above the fifth on every triad using the C major notes creates a seventh chord on every degree. On the C major chord, for example, C, E, and G have the note B added, a third above G and a major seventh above C. This is similar to adding the minor seventh on the dominant chord (see p. 62). Each triad on the C scale has an seventh added. When the sixth is added to a triad, the major sixth on the three major chords C, F, and G, and the major sixth with the D minor chord are the most common harmonic additions. A suspended fourth can be used with C major and G major: this type of chord is constructed without a third in order to balance the voicing.

Adding sevenths

*The chords shown below, constructed as triads on each degree of the major scale, can all be extended by adding a seventh. This is placed a third above the fifth of each chord – this is seven notes above the root. In C, the seventh on the chords of C major (**I**) and F major (**IV**) are major seventh intervals from the root. The seventh on D minor (**II**), E minor (**III**), G major (**V**), A minor (**VI**), and B diminished (**VII**) have a minor seventh from the root.*

Adding sixths

*The four chords shown below, constructed on the major scale, can be extended by adding a sixth. In C, the sixth on the chords of C major (**I**), F major (**IV**), and G major (**V**) are major sixth intervals from the root. The sixth on the chord of D minor (**II**) is also a major sixth.*

Suspended fourths

*The two chords shown below – C major (**I**) and G major (**V**) – can have a perfect fourth added. Do not play the major third.*

COMPARING SEVENTHS

There are four main types of seventh chord on the major scale. The *major seventh* is a major triad with a major seventh addition. This occurs on the first (**I**) and fourth (**IV**) degrees of the scale. The *dominant seventh* chord is a major triad with a minor seventh that occurs on the fifth (**V**) degree of the scale. The *minor seventh* chord is a minor triad with a minor seventh addition, built on the second (**II**), third (**III**), and sixth (**VI**) degrees of the scale. The *minor seventh flat five* chord is a diminished triad with the addition of a minor seventh built on the seventh (**VII**) degree of the scale. The structure of the major scale determines the shape and combination of the intervals in a seventh chord on each degree.

C major seventh

This chord is composed of a major third between the root and the third, a minor third between the third and the fifth, and a major third between the fifth and the seventh. The two major sevenths on the C major scale are C major 7 and F major 7.

C MAJOR 7

THIRD

FIFTH

SEVENTH

C major

The C major seventh chord is composed of the first, third, fifth, and seventh notes.

G dominant seventh

The dominant seventh chord is composed of a major third between the root and third, a minor third between the third and the fifth, and a minor third between the fifth and the seventh. G7 is the only dominant seventh on the C major scale.

G DOMINANT 7

THIRD

FIFTH

SEVENTH

C major from G

The G dominant seventh chord is composed of the first, third, fifth, and seventh notes.

D minor seventh

This chord has a minor third between the root and the third, a major third between the third and the fifth, and a minor third between the fifth and the seventh. The three minor sevenths on the C major scale are D minor 7, E minor 7, and A minor 7.

D MINOR 7

THIRD

FIFTH

SEVENTH

C major from D

The D minor seventh chord is composed of the first, third, fifth, and seventh notes.

B minor seventh flat five

This chord has a minor third between the root and the third, a minor third between the third and the fifth, and a major third between the fifth and the seventh. There is only one minor seventh flat five chord in the C major scale: B minor 7♭5.

B MINOR 7♭5

THIRD

FIFTH

SEVENTH

C major from B

The B minor seventh flat five chord is composed of the first, third, fifth, and seventh notes.

CHORDAL VARIATIONS

The development of the technical skills in arpeggiation with chords, and the control of harmonic structure, can be achieved by breaking chords down and separating out their voices. Upper extensions of melody and harmonized passages can be put together over basic chords and roots. The examples shown below are written for the right-hand fingers using **PIMA** directions above the music, and plectrum directions below. Both methods can be tried. A practical way to acquire these techniques is to take individual chords and play them in sections, using the fingers or plectrum to play melody notes. A considerable number of possible variations can be played on a single chord. Changing from one chord to another opens up further variations and is a first step towards melodic and harmonic movement.

Chords and Arpeggios

Play the C major chord above as a block chord (in one movement) and as an arpeggio. If the individual notes are played separately, an arpeggio based on the chord can be used for fingerstyle or plectrum variations. Each note can also be played in a melody. Play a melody that descends from E on the 1st string. Pick out fretted notes, then take the fingers off each: play C then open B, E then open D. Repeat as a series: top E, C, open B, G, E, open D, and C. Also try this with the G chord.

Chords and scales

Play the C major and G major chords with their arpeggios and scales. The C scale runs from the C root up to E on the first string, and the G scale in C major runs from the G root to G on the 1st string. Play both scales ascending and descending. Play a scale to link G to C in the following way: hold the G chord down and strum across all six strings.

Take the fingers off the chord and play a descending scale from the note F on the 1st fret of the 1st string. This moves down in the sequence F-E-D-C-B-A-G-F-E-D. Play the G major chord again and use this scale to move to C major. Repeat the G major chord and descend from the note F to the note D on the open 4th string, then play the chord C in place of the final scale note.

ADDING MELODIES TO CHORDS

The top note of a chord tends to stand out as a natural melody note. Melodies can be played by simply strumming through a group of different chords. Play all the chords used so far and compare the top notes. Now, using a C chord shape, pick out the melody notes on all the strings from the root. Try playing a scale melody by strumming the open 1st to 3rd strings, and place the fingers on the 2nd fret (F♯), 3rd fret (G), 5th fret (A), and 7th fret (B). Play C to G major, picking out the top notes. Try using the top two notes as melody notes: play the C chord, with the top note as a melody, then the note on the string below, before moving to the G chord: play the top note and the note on the string below as melody notes. Next, play a chord with a fretted note as the first melody note, followed by an open string or another fretted note. Repeat this with the next chord. For example, play G major with G on the 1st string, then E on the same string.

Harmonizing melody notes on one chord

Play C major using the 1st to 5th strings. Play the chord with the top E string, then with C on the 1st fret of the 2nd string, as the top note. Take the 1st finger off C and play B as the top note of the chord, followed by D on the 3rd fret. Play the three lowest notes of the chord together, using the

open G as a melody note. As a variation, rather than resolving on the root note, end the sequence with the note E on the 2nd fret of the 4th string. Now play the C major chord by holding the three lower notes of the chord and play the previous melody as a series of single notes. Try playing the five melody notes after the chord as **I-M-A-M-I.**

Adding a melody to three chords

Strum C major using the 5th to 2nd strings. Play D on the 3rd fret, 2nd string, then B on the open 2nd string. Play A minor from the 5th to the 2nd strings, then 1st string open E, and 3rd fret, 2nd string D. End with an E minor chord from the 6th to 2nd strings with an open B melody note.

Melody notes supported by chords

A melody note can be harmonized using a large range of chords. On the right is an example of the note E on the 1st string as the top note in four different chords. The first chord is F major 7, the second chord is C major, the third chord is A minor, and the fourth chord is E minor. The note E can be heard all the way through the four-chord progression. It can be left ringing as a sustained tone while the four chords are played underneath. The descending bass line composed of the roots F, C, A, and E can also be heard. Play the chords with plectrum downstrokes or downstrokes with the thumb.

Alternative melody note

In the second example, shown on the right, the note G on the 3rd fret is played over the four chords F major 7, C major 7, A minor 7, and E minor. The supporting voices differ in this example because the two middle chords, C major and A minor, have been changed to seventh chords. The note G can be heard ringing over the chord changes, creating a different, slightly brighter sound on all the voicings. The descending bass line is the same as the first example: F, C, A, and E. Play the chord with plectrum downstrokes or downstrokes with the thumb.

DIVIDING CHORDS

There are many ways of breaking a chord into smaller vertical blocks of notes. The first example uses the four lower notes of E major, then the four middle notes and the four top notes. The second example uses the three bottom notes, three from the 3rd to the 5th string, three from the 2nd to the 4th, and the three top notes. The third example breaks the chord into pairs of notes on adjacent strings.

Finger variation
Try playing the third example using PI, IM, IM, IM, and IM fingerings. Using this method keeps the thumb in place and, at the same time, prevents the hand moving away from its position.

THIRDS AND FOURTHS

A melody using a series of intervals can be played over a chord or a single note. These examples have the top melody harmonized with a third or fourth, over the root note. In the first example the notes B, C, D, and E are supported by thirds, on a C major chord. The second example shows a series of thirds in A major, and the third example has fourths in D major. Both are played over a sustained low E note.

Bass notes
On both the second and third examples, play the root note under the thirds and fourths both as a sustained note (pedal tone), and as a single note under every element.

MELODY NOTE WITH CHORDS, ARPEGGIOS, AND DESCENDING BASS

The first example on the right shows the high E note supported by a series of chords and a descending bass line. The chords are: F major 7, E minor, D minor 9, C major, E minor over a B root, and A minor. Each of these should be played as block chords. The bass line drops from F on the 3rd fret, 4th string, to E on the 2nd fret, to the open D, to C on the 3rd fret, 5th string, to B on the 2nd fret, and A on the open string. The second example repeats this sequence using arpeggiated chords. The top E note is still played throughout, but the lower E note on the 2nd fret of the 4th string on each of the last three chords has been left out.

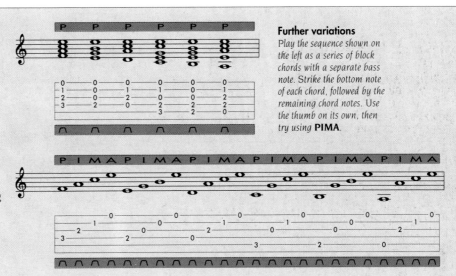

Further variations
Play the sequence shown on the left as a series of block chords with a separate bass note. Strike the bottom note of each chord, followed by the remaining chord notes. Use the thumb on its own, then try using PIMA.

RIGHT-HAND TECHNIQUES
All the examples of chordal variations and melodies that are shown on this page can be played using either a fingerstyle or a plectrum technique.

PLAYING WITH FINGERS
A wide range of approaches can be used; there are often different ways of playing the same passage with **PIMA**. To give the effect of a block chord, with all the voices sounding together, the **IMA** fingers are used to play the top notes of a chord, while the thumb plays between one and three notes in the bass as a fast movement synchronized with the fingers. The thumb is used, in folk and flamenco styles, to play arpeggiated chord notes or melody notes, on the higher strings. The fourth or little finger, marked **X** (or **E** in some systems), is used for strumming, playing *rasguedos*, and block chords. A strummed chord, marked with **P** on the examples above, can be played using the thumbnail, or with the flesh on the side of the thumb to produce a mellower sound.

PLAYING WITH PLECTRUMS
The standard plectrum held between the thumb and the first finger is generally used to play chords, mainly with downstrokes, and melodies with alternating strokes and combinations. Thumb and fingerpicks can be used instead of nails to arpeggiate and strum chords using a fingerstyle technique. A technique using the **IMA** fingers to arpeggiate and play block chords, with a thumbpick fitted over the thumb to play bass parts, is used in American country guitar styles. Where **P** is marked, the exercises above can be played with a thumbpick. Chords can also be played with a fingerpick on each finger. These can be used in a similar fashion to nails. Thumb-picks and fingerpicks can be used with a high level of attack in order to generate a great deal of volume on steel-string acoustic instruments.

MAJOR SCALE SEQUENCES

AN INTRODUCTION TO CHORD MOVEMENTS WITHIN THE MAJOR SCALE

Other keys
The Roman numeral system is used in every key with the same order of major, minor, and diminished chords. The major scale is constructed below from A and D, using two sharps in D major and three in A major.

Chords are constructed on the major scale using each note as a separate root. These *scale tone* chords are each assigned Roman numerals. For example, the key of C major has the scale-tone chords

C major (**I**), D minor (**II**), E minor (**III**), F major (**IV**), G major (**V**), A minor (**VI**), and B diminished (**VII**). Many common sequences are built around the tonic (**I**), subdominant (**IV**), and dominant (**V**) chords.

The perfect cadence
The term **cadence** describes a movement between melody notes or chords. The **perfect** cadence is a movement from the dominant **V** chord to the tonic **I** chord. It is often used as a "full close" at the end of a section or a piece of music.

C MAJ	D MIN	E MIN	F MAJ	G MAJ / G DOM 7	A MIN	B DIM	C MAJ
I	**II**	**III**	**IV**	**V / V⁷**	**VI**	**VII**	**I**

PRIMARY MOVEMENTS IN C

The three primary major chords that are built on the first, fourth, and fifth degrees of the major scale have a close musical relationship to each other, and are often used together to form chord sequences

and progressions. Each movement from chord to chord has an effective sound and harmonic quality. In the key of C major, the chords are C, F, and G major. G major is often modified with an added seventh when playing a movement from **V** to **I**.

C MAJ	F MAJ	G MAJ	C MAJ
I	IV	V	I

C MAJ	F MAJ	G7	C MAJ
I	IV	V⁷	I

C MAJ	G MAJ	F MAJ	C MAJ
I	V	IV	I

Movements in C
Play each of the three movements shown on the left. Play them using both the G dominant 7 chord and G major.

C MAJOR

G DOMINANT 7

G MAJOR

F MAJOR

G MAJ	A MIN	B MIN	C MAJ	D MAJ / D DOM 7	E MIN	F# DIM	G MAJ
I	**II**	**III**	**IV**	**V / V⁷**	**VI**	**VII**	**I**

MOVEMENTS IN G

The type of movement shown above in the key of C major can be played in other keys. In G major the primary chords are G major (**I**), C major (**IV**), and D major (**V**).

The chord progression C-F-G-C (**I-IV-V-I**) in the key of C major therefore becomes G-C-D-G (**I-IV-V-I**) in G major. These progressions may easily be transposed to D major and A major by writing out the major scales and

using the three primary major chords in each key. All of these sequences can be played in other keys by using the major scale and selecting the three primary major chords in that particular key.

Movements in G
The movements in the key of C major are played in G major, with voicings that use the open strings of the guitar.

G MAJ	C MAJ	D MAJ	G MAJ
I	IV	V	I

G MAJ	C MAJ	D7	G MAJ
I	IV	V⁷	I

G MAJ	D MAJ	C MAJ	G MAJ
I	V	IV	I

D MAJOR

D DOMINANT 7

D MAJ	E MIN	F# MIN	G MAJ	A MAJ / A DOM 7	B MIN	C# DIM	D MAJ

A MAJ	B MIN	C# MIN	D MAJ	E MAJ / E DOM 7	F# MIN	G# DIM	A MAJ
I	**II**	**III**	**IV**	**V / V⁷**	**VI**	**VII**	**I**

FURTHER TRANSPOSITION

The progressions that are used in C major and G major can be constructed in D major and A major. For example, the progression **I-IV-V-I** in C major becomes D-G-A-D in the key of D and A-D-E-A in the key of A.

A MAJOR

A DOMINANT 7

E MAJOR

E DOMINANT 7

C MAJ	D MIN	E MIN	F MAJ	G MAJ / G DOM 7	A MIN	B DIM	C MAJ
I	II	III	IV	V / V⁷	VI	VII	I

Adding the relative minor in C

On the major scale, the submediant minor chord positioned on the sixth degree (**VI**) is known as the relative minor. This is the most important of the secondary chords. In C, the relative minor chord is A minor. A minor has a close harmonic relationship to C major. Both chords have the notes C and E in common.

Adding A minor

The addition of A minor to the three primary major chords extends the range of progressions and movements. One of the most widely used progressions is **I-VI-IV-V**: C major, A minor, F major, G major.

The A minor (**VI**) links C major (**I**) to F major (**IV**).

A minor (**VI**) links G major (**V**) and F major (**IV**).

Compare A minor with C major. They share notes and are often combined in chord movements.

Further secondary minor chords in C

The secondary minor supertonic and mediant chords are found on the second (**II**) and third (**III**) degrees of the scale. In C these are D minor and E minor. They are used to extend and vary sequences. The **II** chord is frequently used before the **V** chord, as **II-V-I**, in a further development of the perfect cadence. The III chord often moves to **VI**, and is used in the progression **III-VI-II-V-I**. The **II** and **III** chords move up the scale in the movement **I-II-III-IV**. Play through the following sequences in C using the scale tone chords.

Using secondary minor chords

In the first bar (top stave), the **II** chord links **I** and **V**. In the second bar (top stave), the **VI** chord links **I** to **II**. In the third bar (middle stave), the **II** and **III** chords link **I** and **IV**. In the fourth bar (middle stave), the movement **III-VI-II** leads to **V**. In the fifth bar (bottom stave), the **II** chord links **IV** and **V**. In the sixth bar (bottom stave), the **III** chord links **I** and **IV**.

D minor and E minor can be used as related minors in combinations with the other chords.

The diminished chord in C

The diminished chord, **VII**, is built on the major scale leading note. In C this is the note B. Diminished chords often resolve to the tonic. They have a dissonant sound with the interval between the root (B) and the diminished fifth (F). The diminished chord sometimes replaces the dominant **V**, in this case G or G7. B diminished **VII** completes the series of chords on the major scale.

Adding B diminished to a movement

In the first bar (top stave), the **VII** chord resolves to the **I** chord linking **II** and **I**. In the second bar (top stave), the **VII** chord links **VI** and **I**. In the third bar (bottom stave), the **VII** chord replaces **V** in the sequence **I-VI-II-V-I**.

B diminished; the triad contains B, D, and F which are the 3rd, 5th, and 7th of G dominant 7.

REPEAT SIGNS, D.C., D.S., AND CODA

Music is often written down with repeat signs. Abbreviated signs are also used to direct the player to different sections. The signs are shown on the right; a chord sequence demonstrating their use is shown below.

Playing a standard sequence

Play the "intro" chord and the first twelve bars. On seeing the repeat sign at the end of the "first-time" bar, return to the repeat sign at the beginning and play the first eleven bars through to the "second-time" bar and the middle section. At the D.S. "al coda" sign, go back to 𝄋 and play until you reach ⊕. Move to the coda section ending with "fine".

Repeat signs

A repeat sign faces in the direction of the two dots. A section of bars is repeated between the dots.

"Da Capo" (D.C.)

When the D.C. letters appear, the music is played through again from the beginning. Da Capo is Italian, and means "from the head".

"Dal segno" (D.S.)

D.S. directs the player back to the point where the D.S. sign (𝄋) appears. Dal Segno means "from the sign".

"Al coda"

The ⊕ sign indicates that the music moves on to a section marked by another ⊕ sign. Al coda means "to the tail".

TIME VALUES

UNDERSTANDING THE SYMBOLS USED FOR RHYTHM

Sustaining notes
When a note on a crotchet beat in 4/4 is kept ringing over the next beat, doubling its length, a minim is used as the symbol. A semibreve is a note that lasts four crotchet beats – equivalent to a bar of 4/4. This system for notation and timing is extended by using dots and ties. Time signatures use various symbols to represent the beat. For example, in 2/2, a minim represents the beat, and a semibreve two beats.

Virtually all styles of guitar playing are based around the use of rhythm and timing. Music is normally structured by playing pitched sounds in relation to a beat with a regular tempo. Rhythmic effects are created by playing combinations and patterns of accented notes and beats, with spaces of differing lengths. In "Scales and Timing" (see p. 48), the chords are played on each crotchet beat of a bar with time signatures of 4/4, 3/4, and 2/4. This is a simple way of putting music to a steady beat. When playing in any time signature, louder or implied accents are often related to bar lengths. Musical phrases also relate to bars of music in this way. Groups of beats are put together to create a number of different types of time signature. When music is written down on a stave, a system of symbols is used to represent the position where notes are played in relation to the beat, the time signature, and their duration.

Subdividing notes
A crotchet can be subdivided into two notes which are termed quavers. The value of a quaver is exactly half the length of a crotchet. Similarly, a quaver can be split further into semiquavers, which can be broken down into smaller divisions – demi-semiquavers and hemidemi-semiquavers. A crotchet can also be divided into groups of three equal beats. These are referred to as triplets.

SUBDIVISIONS OF TIME

Symbols are used to denote the duration and position of musical sounds in relation to a pulse or beat. A note or a chord can be played so that it sustains for different lengths of time. For example, in a bar of 4/4, a chord sounded on the first beat and left to ring over the remaining beats is written down using a specific symbol (•) known as a *semibreve*. A chord or note could also be played evenly eight times within a bar – twice on each beat. Symbols that show a subdivision of the beat are then used (♪). These are called *quavers*. Timing is usually broken down by writing symbols that split lengths of space by twos and threes. The diagram shows time value subdivisions over a bar of 4/4. The right-hand column shows time values in 3/4. A *hemidemi-semiquaver* is double the maximum subdivision shown. However it rarely occurs in guitar music. The widely used American system for names is shown as well as classical terminology.

SEMIBREVE (WHOLE-NOTE)

MINIMS (HALF-NOTES)

CROTCHETS (QUARTER-NOTES)

QUAVERS (EIGHTH-NOTES)

SEMIQUAVERS (SIXTEENTH-NOTES)

DEMI-SEMIQUAVERS (THIRTY-SECOND-NOTES)

TIME SIGNATURES WITH CROTCHETS

All timing has so far been written down using a crotchet to denote the beat. In the examples shown, a crotchet with the same length and value is written as the lower part of the time signature. The twelve beats are played over the same length of time and written with the accent and bar line separating them into groups with three different time signatures – 4/4, 3/4, and 2/4. The bars and accents should be compared over the twelve beats.

TIME SIGNATURE OF 4/4

TIME SIGNATURE OF 3/4

TIME SIGNATURE OF 2/4

RESTS

Whenever a space is required in music, a rest symbol is used to signify its length. For example, in a time signature of 4/4, when nothing is played on the second crotchet beat, the note is replaced by a crotchet rest symbol in that part of the bar. Rest symbols with a greater value can be written to replace more than one note or beat, and rests with shorter time values subdivide notes or beats. Rests are also used to mark out bars in which nothing is played. They can be used to direct the player to remain silent for any length of time, from a fraction of a beat to a number of bars. When playing music, space and silence are of great importance to the structure. They provide the definition that gives the sounds both rhythmic and musical structure. Rests are often used to displace and shift notes against the beat to create musical effects within a rhythm.

TIME SYMBOLS

Different symbols are used in music to represent notes and rests. The table on the right shows the seven different types of note value accompanied by their equivalent rests.

SEMIBREVE	SEMIBREVE REST
MINIM	MINIM REST
CROTCHET	CROTCHET REST
QUAVER	QUAVER REST
SEMIQUAVER	SEMIQUAVER REST
DEMI-SEMIQUAVER	DEMI-SEMIQUAVER REST
HEMIDEMI-SEMIQUAVER	HEMIDEMI-SEMIQUAVER REST

Semibreve rest | Minim rest | Crotchet rest | Quaver rest | Semiquaver rest

Demi-semiquaver rest | Hemidemi-semiquaver rest

RESTS, DOTTED NOTES, AND TIES

The following examples show the use of rests, dots, and ties in bars of music. While working through the exercise, it may be useful to think of the bars as an outline grid on which time values are written. The first row illustrates the impact of different types of rest within a piece of music. Each bar should be counted, paying attention to the value of each type of note and rest. The length of time for which a note is played is altered in notation by the addition of *ties* and *dots*. A note is sustained when a tie is used to link it with succeeding notes: its duration is sustained for the value of the note it is tied to. A dot placed after a note adds half the value to a note, and a second dot adds half the value of the first dot. As the examples on the bottom row show, the same musical phrase can be written by using either dots or ties.

Crotchets In the first bar, crotchets are only played on the first and third beats. In the second bar, they are only played on the first and fourth beats.

Dotted semibreve A dot added to a semibreve lasts for a bar of 6/4.

Tie Two semibreves are "tied". This sustains the note throughout the following bar.

Equal values A dotted minim is the same length as a crotchet tied to a minim.

Extended minim in 4/4 A dotted minim and a crotchet tied to a minim have the same value.

Extended crotchet A dotted crotchet and a quaver tied to a crotchet have the same value.

Double dot A second dot adds half the value of the first dot to a note.

Dotted rest A dot on a minim rest has the same value as a minim rest followed by a crotchet rest.

UNDERSTANDING TRIPLETS

In all the examples above, the lengths of notes and beats have been halved or doubled. A beat is also frequently divided in three, creating a triplet. Any note with a time value can be divided in this way. Minims, crotchets, and quavers are the main note lengths that are commonly divided. Triplets can easily be understood by comparing a bar of 3/4 or 4/4, containing quaver triplets under the crotchet beats, with bars of 9/8 and 12/8.

9/8 and 12/8

The middle bars are in 9/8 and 12/8. The number at the bottom indicates that the bar consists of quavers. With two quavers making up a crotchet, each bar is one and a half times as long as the others. For triplet comparison, play in the same duration as the 3/4 and 4/4 bars.

PLAYING A RHYTHM

ADVANCED PLECTRUM TECHNIQUE FOR RHYTHM AND TIMING

Using the exercises
To allow concentration on following the right-hand plectrum directions, the exercises should be played with the left hand holding a single note or chord. At first, a metronome can be used as a guide to the rhythms. With firm control over the beats and their subdivisions, the examples can then be repeated using simple scale and chord changes.

Developing the ability to play time and rhythm accurately is essential for playing chord sequences, single line melodies, and solos. This skill requires an understanding of rhythm and the development of more advanced plectrum techniques. The time values shown on previous pages are here converted into exercises where chords and single notes are played with a variety of different strokes. In all types of music, notes are sustained over a number of beats or played as subdivisions of a beat. Awareness of the position of a chord or note within a rhythm is, therefore, extremely important.

Grey panels
The grey shading on the staves is a guide to timing and note duration. On page 73 they indicate the length of the note over the beat. The exercises should first be played as shown, using only one note. When time values are understood, and the right hand is moving accurately, the exercises must then be applied to chord sequences or scales.

COUNTING BARS

Counting groups of bars is an important skill. Being able to think of the position of beats in groups of bars is partly a matter of acquiring a musical feel from listening to recordings, and an awareness of accents, and timing patterns. Stabilizing right-hand technique, and thinking in time, leads to faster overall development. This enables the player to concentrate on left-hand vocabulary. The examples show four time signatures: 4/4, 3/4, 2/4, and 6/8. Play them while counting the beats and bars. Note that the duration of a beat in each time signature can be of any time length.

PLAYING SUSTAINED NOTES

A sustained note normally lasts longer than a single beat of the bar. In these exercises, the beats should be counted, and notes sustained for the length shown by the grey panels. For example, the first bar consists of two notes played on the first and third beats, both of which are two beats long.

DAMPING THE STRINGS

The hands are often used to dampen the strings during silent passages, or to control rests. When a fast chordal rhythm requires short rests, the fingers on the left hand can quickly release pressure from the strings in order to mute them when plectrum strokes are used. For certain styles of music – rock and pop, for example – a plectrum stroke played on deadened strings is often used as part of the guitar sound. The right hand may also be used to mute the strings. This is frequently used while playing an electric guitar at a high volume.

Damping exercise
*Sustain a note over the first bar. Repeat, stopping the sound on the second beat by taking the left hand **off** the strings, or resting the right hand **on** the strings.*

Left-hand damping
The first finger of the left hand can be used to mute the strings. A chord can be muted by leaving the fingers in place but at the same time releasing the pressure.

Right-hand damping
Placing the right hand across the strings is an effective mute. Greater control is possible by resting the hand on the bridge and muting the strings to varying degrees.

CROTCHET SUBDIVISIONS

Each one of the four crotchet beats in a 4/4 bar can be subdivided by playing two quaver notes of equal value in the space of one crotchet beat. For example, when a crotchet beat is counted as "one" on the first beat of a bar, the same crotchet beat when subdivided into two quavers can be played evenly as "one, two" over the same length of time. The quavers can be further divided into semiquavers.

Playing quavers
Begin by playing the exercise using downstrokes. When playing at a faster tempo, practise using alternate strokes.

Playing semiquavers
Play the semiquavers by doubling quavers and subdividing the beat into four even notes.

SYNCOPATED RHYTHM

When a downbeat is not played, and the rhythm is mainly on an accented subdivision of a beat, it is referred to as *syncopation*. This is extremely important in virtually all areas of music. Play a pattern of alternate strumming on an even quaver beat. Count the crotchet beat as "one, two" on every beat, with "one" as the beat which is *not* played, and "two" as the upbeat which *is* played. Try this with semiquavers.

Syncopated playing
On the first bar, count each beat as "one, two", playing the off-beat on "two". This rhythm is often used in popular music. On the third bar, play the semiquavers as two strokes on the off-beat. Note that on the fourth beat you should leave out the first three semiquavers.

DOTTED QUAVER RHYTHM

This rhythm is widely used in all types of music. The dotted quaver is played and held over until the last semiquaver of the beat. This rhythm is often played either with accuracy or a looser type of feel.

Dotted quavers
Play this rhythm slowly. In each bar, sustain the downbeat for half the time of the off-beat.

TRIPLET RHYTHM

When the crotchet beat is subdivided into three even notes, it is referred to as a *triplet*, and written as three quavers covered by a triplet symbol. This can be thought of most simply as three notes of equal value played over a beat. When triplets are played using an alternating strumming technique, the downbeat on every group of three switches from a downstroke to an upstroke on every other beat.

Playing triplets
Play the triplet rhythm as twelve even beats in the bar. Use downstrokes as well as alternate strokes. The triplet on each beat is often played with the downbeat quaver held over the second quaver. Hold the downbeat until the third triplet quaver, just after the off-beat.

RHYTHM EXERCISE

Play through this exercise using single notes and chords. It is important to build rhythmic control and right-hand technique when playing any style of popular music. Rock, blues, and jazz use rhythms based on variations of the beat such as quaver *eights*, syncopation, and dotted quaver and triplet rhythms. The beat is frequently subdivided into semiquavers. Syncopated patterns are often used in funk and reggae.

PLAYING THE BLUES

THE MUSICAL FORM AT THE HEART OF POP AND ROCK MUSIC

Blues expression
There are many approaches to playing the blues. Using rhythmic accents and moving strings to alter pitch are both common practices. Blues has always relied heavily on an expressive playing technique.

Blues music originated in the southern states of America. It evolved from a heritage of African folk music that was introduced to North America in the 18th century via the slave-trade. Vocal chants, rhythms, and work songs mixed together with European influences and church gospel to forge a highly expressive musical form. The blues still underlies a great amount of today's popular music.

Accents
The green ribbon beneath the stave indicates notes or chords that are stressed, or played with an accent.

MINOR PENTATONIC SCALE
The starting point for learning to play the blues is a familiarization with the minor pentatonic scale. This structure contains five notes that are constructed using minor and perfect intervals.

E minor pentatonic
The notes in the scale are E, G, A, B, and D. Play them slowly, both ascending and descending.

THE THREE BLUES CHORDS
Blues harmony revolves around the use of three chords. These primary chords may be major or minor, and are built on the first (**I**), fourth (**IV**), and fifth (**V**) degrees of any named key. The root note of the first chord is equivalent to the first degree of the corresponding pentatonic scale and key. The harmony moves in a **I-IV-V** pattern. Blues melody played over these chords creates a major/minor sound that breaks the standard rules of harmony, producing an expressive vocabulary. With a key note of E, the chords E major (*top*), A major (*centre*), and B major (*bottom*) provide a structure for development and variation. Minor and dominant seventh chords are also frequently used.

TWELVE-BAR STRUCTURE
The three blues chords above are played as a chord progression within a repeating twelve-bar cycle that follows a standard series of movements. The sequence shown on the right is commonly referred to as the *twelve-bar* format.

BLUES RHYTHMS
A number of different rhythms can be used for playing blues. On the right, the top two staves show a complete twelve-bar cycle played in 4/4 time. Below them are two other examples of rhythm and accenting.

Rhythm exercises
Begin by playing the twelve-bar sequence in 4/4 time. Practise accenting the first beat of each bar. Follow this by slowly strumming the 12/8 pattern (bottom left), playing three chords on every beat. Now leave out the middle beat of each group of three chords, playing two chords in the space of the beat. This rhythm is similar to a bar of 4/4 with tied triplets (bottom right). A rhythm can be created in relation to the beat by splitting a crotchet into four semiquavers. Hold the chord over to the last semiquaver. Although they are written in this way, rhythms are not necessarily based on accurate subdivisions.

ADDING EXTRA NOTES

The minor pentatonic scale provides the basic framework for playing the blues. However, further notes are used to add melodic flavour and contrast, creating a sound associated with a wide range of styles, from folk to rock and roll and modern pop music. The most important addition is the flattened fifth which creates the classic "blue note" sound. The addition of a major third comes from combining major harmony with the minor scale. When a major second and a major sixth are added, the pentatonic minor scale acquires a more flexible vocabulary. This can be used to play melodies and solos with a wide range of colour over twelve-bar blues. Major, dominant seventh, and minor chords can also be altered with the selective addition of extra notes.

Major third

Major thirds from the major chord can be added to the scale. The positions are marked by black dots on the diagram.

E PENTATONIC SCALE WITH ADDED MAJOR THIRD

Flattened fifth

The flattened fifth is added between the perfect fourth and perfect fifth. Scale positions are marked by black dots on the diagram.

E PENTATONIC SCALE WITH ADDED FLATTENED FIFTH

Major second/sixth

Adding a major second and major sixth creates a full seven-note scale. The positions are marked by black dots on the diagram.

E PENTATONIC SCALE WITH ADDED MAJOR SECOND AND MAJOR SIXTH

Adding melody to E dominant 7th

The first chord has the note G played on the top string. Although the chord already uses a G♯ as a major third, the G♮ from the blues scale works perfectly well as a melodic addition. Play D♯ as a doubled seventh on the 2nd string and combine this with G♯. C♯ as sixth or thirteenth can also be used on the 2nd string.

E7 WITH ADDED G♮   E7 WITH ADDED D   E7 WITH ADDED D AND G♮   E7 WITH ADDED C♯

Adding melody to A dominant seventh

The first chord has a doubled seventh (G♮) added on the top string. A fourth or eleventh (D) can be combined with a G♮, and a sixth/thirteenth (F♯) can be added on the 1st string. Play the chords with the top-string melody notes, take the fingers off, and strum as a standard seventh to create movement on the chord.

A7 WITH G♮   A7 WITH ADDED D   A7 WITH ADDED D AND G♮   A7 WITH ADDED F♯

Adding melody to B dominant seventh

The first chord has the note D played on the 2nd string. Although B dominant seventh already uses D♯ as a major third chord tone, the D♮ from the blues scale works well as an addition. The other melody notes on the fretted positions on the 1st and 2nd strings can also be used as melodic additions in combination with the open strings.

B7 WITH ADDED D   B7 WITH ADDED G   B7 WITH ADDED C♯   B7 WITH ADDED F♯

SEQUENCES WITH VARIATIONS

Major chords, dominant sevenths, and minors can all be used to play the blues. Chord sequences played with carefully selected additional voices give an impression of flowing continuity. Try playing this twelve-bar variation, which incorporates added melody notes on the top strings. Experiment with fingerstyle and plectrum techniques: both can be used as an approach to arpeggiation and rhythm. You may also work on variations of this sequence by using the added note shapes shown above but keeping to the fundamental chord changes.

Playing open strings A chord consisting of open strings is played leading to a dominant seventh. This is a common blues device.

THE CYCLE OF KEYS

UNDERSTANDING THE RELATIONSHIPS BETWEEN RELATED KEYS

Modulation and transposition
Two terms are widely used to describe movements between keys. "Modulation" occurs when a passage of music moves into another key. A melody in C that moves into a section containing F♯, has "modulated" to the key of G major. The second term, "transposition", refers to a section or piece of music repeated at a different pitch, retaining its form and structure.

Major scales are built on each note of the twelve chromatic degrees. Each scale is formed with a fixed pattern from the key note on which it is based: the sequence of intervals is the same for all twelve keys. When major scales start from notes other than C, sharps (♯) and flats (♭) are used to adjust letter names and intervals so that they conform to the major scale pattern. Sharps and flats are shown on the stave at the start of a bar. C major has two modal scales, on the fourth and fifth degrees (F and G), similar in shape to major scales. One note in each may be changed to form a new major scale.

Learning key signatures
Key signatures can be read quickly to find the correct key note by looking at the sharps and flats at the beginning of the bar. With a group of sharps, the symbol on the far right is the leading note of the key: the key note is one semitone above. With a group of flats, the symbol second from the right is on the line or space which is the key note.

C MAJOR TO G MAJOR

The scale ascending from the dominant fifth note of C major runs from G to G. It has the following order of intervals: tone-tone-semitone-tone-tone-semitone-tone. The seventh degree needs to be raised a semitone with the addition of a sharp to form the major scale of G.

In the first octave of C major, the interval from E to F is a semitone, and F to G is a tone.

C MAJOR TO F MAJOR

The scale running from F to F, which ascends from the sub-dominant, fourth note of C major, has the following order of intervals: tone-tone-tone-semitone-tone-tone-semitone. In order to form the major scale of F, the fourth degree must be lowered a semitone with the addition of a flat.

In the C major scale, the interval from A to B is a tone, and B to C is a semitone.

MIXOLYDIAN

The scale running from G to G in the key of C is termed *Mixolydian*. It shares the same notes as a G major scale, except for the seventh degree, which is an F natural.

LYDIAN

The scale running from F to F in the key of C is termed *Lydian*. It shares the same notes as F major, except for the fourth degree, which in the Lydian mode is a B natural.

G MAJOR ROOTS

From the note C, at any level of pitch, there are two adjacent positions at which the first note of a G major scale can be found. G major can start either five notes above C, or four notes below. The G roots are a perfect fifth above, or a perfect fourth below C.

F MAJOR ROOTS

From the note C, at any level of pitch, there are two adjacent positions at which the first note of an F major scale can be found. F major can start either four notes above C, or five notes below. The F roots are a perfect fourth above, or a perfect fifth below C.

SHARP AND FLAT KEYS

Each of the major scales has two modal patterns which can be adjusted with the addition of a sharp (♯), flat (♭), or natural (♮) to form related major scales. The two major scales built from modal scales of C – G major with one sharp, and F major with one flat – can each in turn be modified to build a further major scale. C major moves to F major with one flat a fourth away.

F major, in turn, moves to B♭ major with the addition of the extra flat, or it can return to C major with a natural. The movement of fourths, using flats, runs in the following way: C-F-B♭-E♭-A♭-D♭-G♭-C♭. C major moves to G with one sharp a fifth away, and G major in turn changes to D major with the addition of an extra sharp. The movement of fifths, using sharps, runs in the following way: C-G-D-A-E-B-F♯-C♯. Each major scale

can move either backwards or forwards, through the cycle. By forming new keys, a scale can be transposed using all twelve keynotes, forming a cycle which finally returns to the original key. The cycle of keys moving in fifths continually raises the seventh degree of the new scale by adding a sharp. The cycle of keys moving in fourths adds a flat by flattening the fourth degree of the new scale.

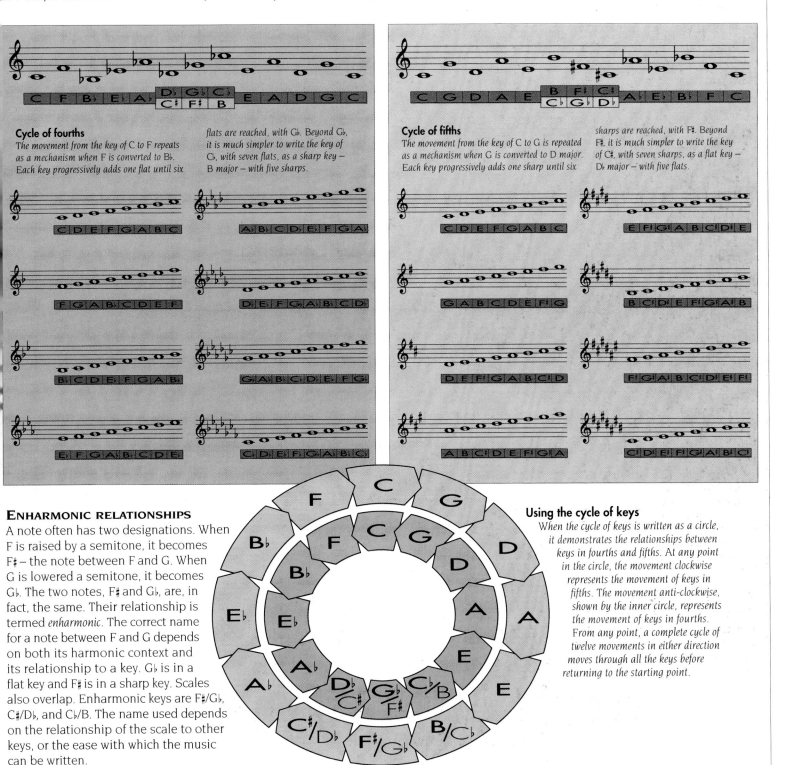

Cycle of fourths

The movement from the key of C to F repeats as a mechanism when F is converted to B♭. Each key progressively adds one flat until six

flats are reached, with G♭. Beyond G♭, it is much simpler to write the key of C♭, with seven flats, as a sharp key – B major – with five sharps.

Cycle of fifths

The movement from the key of C to G is repeated as a mechanism when G is converted to D major. Each key progressively adds one sharp until six

sharps are reached, with F♯. Beyond F♯, it is much simpler to write the key of C♯, with seven sharps, as a flat key – D♭ major – with five flats.

ENHARMONIC RELATIONSHIPS

A note often has two designations. When F is raised by a semitone, it becomes F♯ – the note between F and G. When G is lowered a semitone, it becomes G♭. The two notes, F♯ and G♭, are, in fact, the same. Their relationship is termed *enharmonic*. The correct name for a note between F and G depends on both its harmonic context and its relationship to a key. G♭ is in a flat key and F♯ is in a sharp key. Scales also overlap. Enharmonic keys are F♯/G♭, C♯/D♭, and C♭/B. The name used depends on the relationship of the scale to other keys, or the ease with which the music can be written.

Using the cycle of keys

When the cycle of keys is written as a circle, it demonstrates the relationships between keys in fourths and fifths. At any point in the circle, the movement clockwise represents the movement of keys in fifths. The movement anti-clockwise, shown by the inner circle, represents the movement of keys in fourths. From any point, a complete cycle of twelve movements in either direction moves through all the keys before returning to the starting point.

BARRE CHORDS

EXTENDING CHORD VOCABULARY USING THE BARRE TECHNIQUE

Physical problems
Acquiring barre technique is a difficult stage in learning to play the guitar. The strings dig into the joints and the softer parts of the first finger causing discomfort. With practice, this will soon pass. It is important to keep the barre straight, and ensure that the first finger applies even pressure across the strings.

The *barre* is a chord technique where the first, or other left-hand fingers, hold down adjacent strings across the fingerboard. It enables chord types to be built on any fret by providing a base from which the second, third, and fourth fingers can be used to form chord shapes. When the first finger is used to form a barre across the strings, it is possible to move a chord to every chromatic degree of the scale. Six of the open string shapes shown on page 56 are used to form the basis for major and minor barre voicings. They are shown below, three with roots on the 6th-string, and three with roots on the 5th-string. With the first finger holding a barre position, open string chord shapes need to be played with different fingerings.

The importance of the barre
The barre provides a platform to build chords in all positions. The barre is widely used to play chords with added melody notes in virtually every style of music. The second, third, and fourth fingers also form half-barre shapes, thus enabling the player to hold down a wide range of chord voicings on the guitar in all keys.

BARRE TECHNIQUE

In this example, an open string chord shape is moved up on to the 3rd and 5th fret positions using the barre. The first finger replaces the equivalent of the open string chord notes, and the 3rd and 4th fingers hold the remaining notes. The open string chord voicing of E minor is moved up to G minor on the 3rd fret, and A minor on the 5th fret. This type of minor barre chord can be moved up and down the fingerboard giving all twelve root chords in a standard voicing. The chord retains the same overall shape as it is moved to all other fret positions.

Second and third fingers form the open string shape.

When the first finger forms the barre, the third and fourth fingers are used to complete the barre voicing.

The same shape, moved up two frets, forms the A minor chord.

E MINOR   G MINOR   A MINOR

MOVING E MAJOR TO F MAJOR To form F major, the notes in a standard E major voicing are raised by a semitone. The first finger is pressed down across the strings on the first fret and the second, third, and fourth fingers complete the major shape.

E MAJOR

F MAJOR

MOVING E MINOR TO F MINOR To create F minor, the notes from a standard E minor voicing are raised by a semitone. The first finger is pressed down across the strings on the first fret and the third and fourth fingers complete the minor shape.

E MINOR

F MINOR

MOVING G MAJOR TO A♭ MAJOR To create A♭ major, the notes from a standard G major voicing are raised by a semitone. The first finger is pressed down across the strings on the first fret and the second, third, and fourth fingers complete the voicing.

G MAJOR

A♭ MAJOR

MOVING A MAJOR TO B♭ MAJOR The 5th-string major shape has a full voicing using five notes, including the note on the 1st string. A number of players use the second finger to hold down both the 4th- and 3rd-string notes, leaving the third finger (instead of the fourth) to hold down the 2nd string. Many electric and steel string guitars have narrow necks with close string spacing, which makes the full (barre) fingering including the first string difficult to play. It is important to be able to use this chord.

A MAJOR

B♭ MAJOR (WITH ALTERNATIVE FINGERING)

Alternative fingering

In the example on the right, B♭ major is played on the four middle strings only. The bass note is held by the first finger, and the 2nd, 3rd, and 4th strings are held by the third finger which is used as a half-barre.

MOVING A MINOR TO B♭ MINOR To create B♭ minor, the A minor open string shape is moved up by a semitone. The first finger forms a barre on the 1st fret across the first five strings. The second, third, and fourth fingers complete the minor shape.

A MINOR

B♭ MINOR

MOVING C MAJOR TO D♭ MAJOR To create D♭ major, the C major open string shape is raised by a semitone. The first finger forms a half barre on the 1st fret across the first three strings, and the second, third, and fourth fingers complete the major shape.

C MAJOR

D♭ MAJOR

Root positions

Barre chords with 5th- and 6th-string roots can be constructed on the fret positions shown on the right. Every major or minor chord can be played in more than one position. Barre chords can be moved above the 12th fret, depending on the type of guitar.

FORMING THE BARRE

Forming barre chords is physically difficult for the beginner. The first finger must be pushed down across the strings with extra pressure coming from the thumb. The addition of the remaining fingers when completing chord shapes may pull the first finger out of position and place strain on the left hand. Pressing notes down with the second, third, and fourth fingers might feel awkward, because a certain amount of additional stretching is necessary at first. The player will also encounter the added problem of keeping the barre stable. When barre chords are moved around the fingerboard it is very important to relax the left hand and release the tension from the thumb and fingers. There are three different approaches that can be taken to help develop a good barre technique. Work through each one of them very slowly in order to build up physical strength and barre stability.

"Half-barre" position

Between two and five strings are played across the fingerboard. Start off by holding two strings with the first finger, and continually add a string at a time until the full barre is achieved. This is a very useful exercise when you begin practising barre technique.

Barre on the 1st and 2nd strings.

Barre on the 1st, 2nd, and 3rd strings.

Barre on the 1st, 2nd, 3rd, and 4th strings.

Barre on the 1st, 2nd, 3rd, 4th, and 5th strings.

FURTHER BARRE TECHNIQUES

The second and third methods use the first finger to hold a full barre over all six strings. To begin with, the full barre position can be rather uncomfortable, and differing approaches can assist in the development of this technique. The examples below show how to build the fingering for an F major

chord in stages. In the first example, the chord is formed by adding notes to the first finger barre. When the first finger is placed across a fret, strumming all the notes clearly is a helpful exercise for checking the position. In the second example, the other fingers are stabilized *before* the barre is added. It is worth noting that the

1st fret is a difficult position on which to play barre chords. At this position on the fingerboard, fret spacing is at its widest, and there is also considerable string tension next to the nut. Moving the chord shape half way up the fingerboard can be easier when first practising barre technique.

Full barre position
Begin by placing the first finger across the 1st fret of the fingerboard. Strum all six strings as a chord. Gradually add the other three fingers to form the major chord shape, and play all six strings. When you are comfortable with this technique, try playing on other fret positions.

1 Begin by holding the barre firmly and evenly across the 1st fret of the fingerboard.

2 Start to form the chord shape, placing the second finger on the 3rd string.

3 Continue building the chord by placing the third finger on the 5th string.

4 Complete the major chord by placing the fourth finger on the 4th string.

Adding the barre to a chord
The remaining technique for forming the barre is, first, to play an open E major shape with the second, third, and fourth fingers. Move the basic shape one fret up the

fingerboard. When the fingers feel comfortable and stable, add the barre to the 1st fret with the first finger. This chord movement is sometimes used in Spanish flamenco music.

Basic E major chord shape with the first finger clear of strings.

Only place the first finger barre when the other fingers are comfortable.

E MAJOR   **F MAJOR OVER E**   **F MAJOR**

1 Begin by playing an E major chord with the second, third, and fourth fingers.

2 Move the shape up a fret and play the chord using the six fretted and open strings.

3 Add the barre to the 1st fret, converting the chord to an F major barre shape.

BARRE SEVENTH CHORDS
The major seventh, dominant seventh, and minor seventh chords can also be played on the main barre positions simply by adding the seventh note to major and minor chord shapes. With the addition of these new seventh shapes, the guitarist has a much larger vocabulary of chords available. Using the barre positions with the root on the 6th string, the major and

minor chords are converted to sevenths by removing the fourth finger. When this finger is moved from a note that doubles the root, the seventh note in the chord is held by the first finger on the barre. The major seventh can be played by refingering the barre chord. The doubled root on the major shape is replaced by the seventh a semitone below. Using the root on the 5th string, the doubled octave note is

removed, and the seventh in the chord is held by the barre. This applies to all of the shapes apart from the first example, where the B♭ major chord is converted to B♭ major 7th and refingered with the seventh held by the second finger. Practising the movement of major and minor chords to sevenths is an effective way to learn new shapes. The standard barre shapes are shown below with their seventh voicings.

F DOMINANT 7TH   F major is converted to a dominant 7th by taking the fourth finger away from the 4th string. The 7th is held by the barre on the 1st fret of the 4th string.

F MINOR 7TH   F minor chord is converted to F minor 7th by removing the fourth finger from the 4th string. The 7th is held by the barre on the 1st fret of the 4th string.

B♭ MAJOR 7TH B♭ major is converted to a B♭ major 7th by replacing the second finger with the third, and placing the second finger on the 2nd fret of the 3rd string.

B♭ DOMINANT 7TH B♭ major is converted to a B♭ dominant 7th by placing the third finger on the 3rd fret of the 4th string. The 7th is held by the barre on the 3rd string.

B♭ MINOR 7TH B♭ minor is converted to a B♭ minor 7th by taking the fourth finger away from the third string. The 7th is held by the barre on the 1st fret of the 3rd string.

D♭ MAJOR 7TH D♭ major is converted to a D♭ major 7th by taking the second finger away from the 2nd string. The 7th is held by the barre on the 1st fret of the 2nd string.

CHORD POSITIONS

The same chord voicing can be played in different places. For some players this can be confusing when it comes to choosing chord positions. Below are three ways of playing D major with the chord notes at the same pitch. The three chords contain exactly the same notes. Each chord has a distinct tonal colour from its position on the fingerboard, and this creates a varied musical effect. The choice of chord position depends on technical requirements or the context in a sequence. Learning all the positions for a chord voicing enables chord sequences to be played in different areas of the fingerboard. With a full barre chord vocabulary, sequences can be played in any register without having to move the left hand more than four frets in either direction using the 5th and 6th string roots.

D major extended

The two higher shapes have extra chord voices available. The D major chord with the root on the 5th fret of the 5th string has the extra 1st string available. A doubled fifth note (A) can be added on the 5th fret of the 1st string if a barre is placed across the 5th fret. The D major chord with the root on the 6th string has both the 1st and the 2nd strings available for the addition of chord notes. The doubled 5th (A) can be played on the 10th fret of the 2nd string, with the extra D on the 1st string if a full barre is placed across the 10th fret.

Open D major
Here, the root is on the open 4th string, the 5th on the 3rd string, the octave root note on the 2nd string, and the 3rd on the 1st string.

Root on the 5th string
This chord has the root on the 5th string, the 5th on the 4th string, the octave root note on the 3rd string, and the 3rd on the 2nd string.

Root on the 6th string
In this chord the root is on the 6th string, the 5th on the 5th string, the octave root note on the 4th string, and the third on the 3rd string.

MOVEMENTS ON THE CYCLE OF KEYS

The cycle of keys is an ideal aid to the development of chord technique and movement. Any chord type can be played in every key with all twelve root notes, creating a full and balanced vocabulary. Chords frequently move in fourths or fifths: one of the most commonly used groups is C, G, and D major when playing in the key of G. The chords C, G, and D are related harmonically, and can be found either side of G in the cycle of keys. By playing around the cycle each chord is placed next to its related chords an interval of a fourth or fifth away. Acquiring the technique of moving from any chord to an adjacent shape on the cycle of keys is important for playing all types of music.

Major chord movements in fifths

You can play the twelve major chords using two shapes: a major voicing from the 5th string root, and a major voicing from the 6th string root. There are a number of combinations of fret positions for moving on the cycle of fifths. Play the first example, changing position from C to G on the third fret, and move up the fretboard, two frets at a time, to C on the 15th fret. The second example follows the same movements through to B major, then goes to F♯ major on the 2nd fret and moves up the fingerboard, ending with C major on the 8th fret.

Major chord movements in fourths

The cycle can now be played moving round the other way in fourths. The first example uses the change of position from C on the 3rd fret to F on the 1st fret and moves around the fingerboard before returning to C on the 3rd fret. The second example starts with C on the 8th fret, moving to F on the 8th fret. This movement in chord position descends two frets at a time, until B is reached on the 2nd fret. B moves up to E major on the 7th fret and the cycle descends from E, down the fingerboard, ending with C on the 3rd fret.

Minor seventh movements in fourths and fifths

Every chord type may be played around the cycle of keys in both directions. Following the exercises on the right, play a series of minor seventh shapes around the cycle in fifths, starting with the C minor seventh with its root on the 3rd fret of the 5th string. Starting from the same position, play around the cycle of keys in a movement of fourths. Playing the cycle of fifth positions in reverse order provides an alternative route for the cycle of fourth positions. Now play through the cycles and movements, beginning with C minor seventh with its root on the 8th fret of the 6th string. The cycle of chords moving through each of the keys may be started off from any point. Finally, try playing a complete series of dominant seventh chords through the cycle of fourths, starting from the A chord. The sequence A7-D7-G7-C7-F7-B♭7-E♭7-A♭7-D♭7-G♭7-B7-E7-A7 makes up the complete movement. Play this sequence in fifths.

Playing through exercises based on the cycle of keys is also a highly effective way to learn all the roots for chord shapes and their positions. This can be achieved by playing the different chord types – majors, minors, and sevenths – encountered so far in movements of fifths and fourths around the cycle. There are various possible routes for the same sequence of chords: playing a sequence from C major in fifths or fourths can use a number of different positions. This gives alternative voicings for many of the chords.

POSITIONAL PROBLEMS

One of the most important things to remember is that a movement from one chord in one position, using the cycle movement, may appear confusing because of the position of the next root step in relation to the frets and strings. This may lead to a series of similar-sounding names being used for movements and positions. For example, when C major is moved from a 3rd fret position on the 5th string to F major, using the cycle of keys in fourths, the next chord (F) is a fourth *above* the C chord with roots on either the 5th or the 4th string. The F shape is also a fifth *below* C with the root on the 6th string. When C major is moved from its 3rd fret position on the 5th string to G major, using the cycle of fifths, the next chord (G) is a fifth *above* C major on the 5th or 4th string. The G shape is also a fourth *below* C with the root on the 6th string.

CYCLE OF KEYS IN FIFTHS

CYCLE OF KEYS IN FOURTHS

FIFTHS

FOURTHS

Enharmonic equivalents

In the cycle of fifths, the two minor seventh chords in the middle are labelled F♯ and C♯. In the cycle of fourths, the chords can use the enharmonic equivalents of G♭ and D♭. *When they are treated as a relative minor chord, or as a minor on the second degree of the scale (see p.69), C♯ minor seventh and F♯ minor seventh are the correct scale note names.*

TRANSPOSING CHORDS

PLAYING CHORD MOVEMENTS IN DIFFERENT KEYS

Roman numerals
The Roman numeral system for naming scale degrees can be used for chordal movements. In each major key, the numerals I to VII are written as a shorthand method to indicate the position and movement of chords. The same chord can be assigned different numerals depending on the key. For example, C major is a I chord in the key of C major, a IV chord in the key of G major, and a V chord in the key of F major.

A piece of music may be moved from one key to any other key; this is referred to as *transposition*. This is used for vocal ranges and instrumentation, or it may occur as part of a piece of music. Each key has the same type of structure: a scale and a group of chords that are based on a fixed system of harmonic relationships. As we have seen on page 70, each of the seven degrees of any key is labelled with a Roman numeral, from I to VII. In the scale of C major, C major is the I chord and G major is the V chord. Therefore, if a piece of music is transposed from the key of C major to the key of G major, the I chord beomes G major, and the V chord becomes D major.

Cycles of transposition
C major is the starting point for the cycle of transpositions in fifths using sharps and the cycle of fourths using flats. In the chart below, the chords line up vertically, enabling the player to compare the same type of movement in each of the keys. The chart below is divided into two sections: a partial cycle of fifths that moves through the sharp keys, and a partial cycle of fourths that moves through the flat keys.

TRANSPOSITION IN FIFTHS

In the key of C major, the sequence I-VI-II-V consists of the chords C major, A minor, D minor, and G major. This movement can be repeated in the key of G major by transposing all roots and chord types by a perfect fifth. This is repeated when G is transposed to D, and for all succeeding key movements in fifths.

CYCLE USING SHARPS

The movement in fifths using sharps can continue beyond F♯ major using flats to complete the full cycle of twelve keys: D♭-A♭-E♭-B♭-F-C.

TRANSPOSITION IN FOURTHS

The relationship between the chords in the key of C major is repeated in the key of F major by transposing all the note names and the chord types by a perfect fourth. The I chord, C major, becomes F major, and the other elements also move by a fourth. When F major is transposed to B flat major, the transposition by a fourth is repeated. All the succeeding movements through the keys are the same.

CYCLE USING FLATS

The movement in fourths using flats continues beyond G♭ major using sharps to complete the full cycle of twelve keys: B-E-A-D-G-C.

	I - V		I - IV		I	VI	II	V
C MAJOR	C MAJ	G MAJ	C MAJ	F MAJ	C MAJ	A MIN	D MIN	G MAJ
G MAJOR	G MAJ	D MAJ	G MAJ	C MAJ	G MAJ	E MIN	A MIN	D MAJ
D MAJOR	D MAJ	A MAJ	D MAJ	G MAJ	D MAJ	B MIN	E MIN	A MAJ
A MAJOR	A MAJ	E MAJ	A MAJ	D MAJ	A MAJ	F♯ MIN	B MIN	E MAJ
E MAJOR	E MAJ	B MAJ	E MAJ	A MAJ	E MAJ	C♯ MIN	F♯ MIN	B MAJ
B MAJOR	B MAJ	F♯ MAJ	B MAJ	E MAJ	B MAJ	G♯ MIN	C♯ MIN	F♯ MAJ
F♯ MAJOR	F♯ MAJ	C♯ MAJ	F♯ MAJ	B MAJ	F♯ MAJ	D♯ MIN	G♯ MIN	C♯ MAJ
C MAJOR	C MAJ	G MAJ	C MAJ	F MAJ	C MAJ	A MIN	D MIN	G MAJ
F MAJOR	F MAJ	C MAJ	F MAJ	B♭ MAJ	F MAJ	D MIN	G MIN	C MAJ
B♭ MAJOR	B♭ MAJ	F MAJ	B♭ MAJ	E♭ MAJ	B♭ MAJ	G MIN	C MIN	F MAJ
E♭ MAJOR	E♭ MAJ	B♭ MAJ	E♭ MAJ	A♭ MAJ	E♭ MAJ	C MIN	F MIN	B♭ MAJ
A♭ MAJOR	A♭ MAJ	E♭ MAJ	A♭ MAJ	D♭ MAJ	A♭ MAJ	F MIN	B♭ MIN	E♭ MAJ
D♭ MAJOR	D♭ MAJ	A♭ MAJ	D♭ MAJ	G♭ MAJ	D♭ MAJ	B♭ MIN	E♭ MIN	A♭ MAJ
G♭ MAJOR	G♭ MAJ	D♭ MAJ	G♭ MAJ	C♭ MAJ	G♭ MAJ	E♭ MIN	A♭ MIN	D♭ MAJ

MOVING CHORDS

DEVELOPING MOBILITY WITH OPEN-STRING AND BARRE CHORDS

The primary chords
In the major keys, the primary major chords are those built on the tonic (**I**), subdominant (**IV**), and dominant (**V**). They are related to each other with a series of strong musical movements. When combined, these chords may be used to create music and melody of considerable variety.

Music is frequently built around a few closely related chords. G major, C major, and D major are the **I**, **IV**, and **V** chords from the key of G. They may be played easily by using open-string voicings and are commonly found in all styles of music. Combining open-string and fretted barre voicings creates many variations on these chords. Playing the three chord types through the variations below will help develop a basic understanding of primary chord movements.

Primary chord movements
A thorough understanding of the primary major chords in every key forms a secure foundation on which to build a comprehensive vocabulary for accompanying songs and improvisation. There are a number of positions for each chord, and these may be played in many different ways.

ROOTS ON THE 6TH AND 5TH STRINGS

With the exception of D major in the open-string voicing, the chords in this section are placed with their lowest root note on either the 6th or the 5th string. The numbers in circles show the fingers to be used; circles without numbers represent optional notes.

G MAJOR (OPEN-STRING)

C MAJOR (OPEN-STRING)

D MAJOR (OPEN-STRING)

G MAJOR (6TH-STRING ROOT)

C MAJOR (5TH-STRING ROOT, OPTIONAL 1ST STRING)

D MAJOR (5TH-STRING ROOT, OPTIONAL 1ST STRING)

G MAJOR (5TH-STRING ROOT)

C MAJOR (6TH-STRING ROOT)

D MAJOR (6TH-STRING ROOT)

VARIATIONS ON G-C-D

Play through the three chord variations using G, C, and D major. Use all of the different voicings shown above to create as many combinations as possible. The order of the three chords can also be altered to give D-G-C, D-C-G, and C-G-D. Practise all the combinations using minor and seventh chords. Playing each of these combinations will help you to develop chordal technique. One way to play through the three-chord examples is to use four downstroke beats on each of the first two chords and eight on the last chord. This extends the chords into a four-bar sequence of 4/4 time.

TRANSPOSING G, C, AND D

When similar types of standard voicing are used to play a three-chord sequence, the pattern of movements is very easy to remember visually on the fingerboard. A fixed series of the three chords – G, C, and D major – can be transposed to other keys by shifting the entire system of shapes to different fret positions. For example, G, C, and D major are raised a semitone to the key of A♭ by moving the entire progression up by one fret. Moving up the fingerboard one fret at a time transposes the sequence in ascending semitones. Moving down the fingerboard from the G position on the 3rd fret transposes the sequence in descending semitones to F♯/G♭, F, and finally E on the open-string position.

ROCK CHORDS

The movement of chords using **I-IV-V** in a blues twelve-bar format is one of the most widely used basic structures in rock music. The three chords can be played as a series of sustained open-string chords or fretted shapes. Major chords are often reduced from a triad with a third to a chord that consists of just roots and fifths – the third is not played. The chords, in a **I-IV-V** sequence in G, are sometimes written as G5, C5, and D5. The root and the fifth for each major chord can be played on the 5th and 6th strings. An additional octave root can be included on the 4th or the 3rd string. Other voicings can be constructed with roots and fifths.

G MAJOR

C MAJOR

D MAJOR

A♭ MAJOR

D♭ MAJOR

E♭ MAJOR

F MAJOR

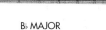

B♭ MAJOR

C MAJOR

G-C-D ON THE 6TH STRING

The sequence of chords G-C-D can be played by moving a single chord shape up and down the fingerboard. Starting with the G major chord on the 3rd fret, the shape can be moved up to the 8th fret to a C major chord, and then on to the 10th fret to give a D major chord.

G MAJOR
(3RD FRET)

C MAJOR
(8TH FRET)

D MAJOR
(10TH FRET)

G-C-D ON THE 5TH STRING

The sequence G-C-D can also be played using one shape based on a 5th-string root, moving up and down the fingerboard. Starting with the G major chord on the 10th fret, the shape can be moved down to the 3rd fret where it becomes C major, and back up to the 5th fret to D major.

C MAJOR
(3RD FRET)

D MAJOR
(5TH FRET)

G MAJOR
(10TH FRET)

PLAYING 5TH-STRING SEVENTHS

The chord sequence **II-V-I** in C major can be played using seventh shapes along the 5th string. Beginning with D minor 7 (**II**) on the 5th fret, the barre shape is moved up to the 10th fret and modified to a G dominant seventh (**V**). On the 3rd fret the chord is modified to C major 7 (**I**).

C MAJOR 7
(3RD FRET)

D MINOR 7
(5TH FRET)

G7
(10TH FRET)

THE MODAL SYSTEM

Modal degrees
The pattern of modes on each degree of the major scale is repeated in all twelve major keys. In G major the modes are G Ionian, A Dorian, B Phrygian, C Lydian, D Mixolydian, E Aeolian, and F♯ Locrian. The pattern of intervals is the same as in C major. For example, the Dorian modes on the second degrees of C major and G major have the same form.

Each of the seven degrees of the major scale can be treated as the starting point for a scale. These scales are known as *modes*, and are assigned classical Greek names. This way of classifying scales is an ancient system; it was developed by the church in the Middle Ages. The major scale is simply an *Ionian* mode: the modern key signature and harmonic system have evolved from it. The modes consist of notes played from different points of the scale. Every mode has a distinct series of fixed intervals, with the first note of the scale acting as a *principal note* for both melody and harmony. Each of the seven modal scales has its own recognizable sound and character.

The use of modes
Modes break the major system down into seven scales which can be used for composition and improvisation. Because of the precise order of tones and semitones, each mode has its own melodic flavour. Modes occur widely in folk and ethnic music, and form a basis for distinctive melodic shapes and patterns. They are also used in fully developed diatonic systems.

C Ionian scale
This is commonly referred to as the major scale. The Ionian scale has an order of intervals, from the root, composed of major and perfect intervals. Standard major harmony is based on this scale.

D Dorian
The Dorian mode is a minor scale. It has a similar structure to the Aeolian natural minor scale, except for the sixth, which is a major sixth from the root. This is one of the most widely used melodic modes.

E Phrygian scale
This minor scale has a distinctive sound arising from the minor and perfect intervals in relation to the root. The guitar has two octaves of the Phrygian mode in C, running between the bottom and top open strings.

F Lydian scale
This major scale has an augmented fourth in relation to the root, creating an unusual melodic flavour. F Lydian can be converted to the scale of F major (Ionian) by lowering the fourth by a semitone.

G Mixolydian scale
This major scale has a minor seventh in relation to its root. This mode is frequently used in all types of music. G Mixolydian can be converted to the scale of G major by raising the seventh by a semitone.

A Aeolian scale
This scale is usually referred to as the minor scale. It is used as a relative minor scale to the major, and as a primary scale for building chordal harmony, with harmonic and melodic variations.

B Locrian scale
This minor mode has a perfect fourth, a diminished fifth, and minor intervals in relation to the root. This is an interesting melodic pattern of notes which produces a highly unusual sound and effect.

PLAYING AND HEARING MODES

One of the most effective ways to hear and understand the different modes is to play the whole scale against the principal note, which should be placed in a low register on the guitar. The first note of a mode can be played against each of the scale notes and left to resonate under modal scale patterns. This sustained note is known as a *pedal note*; it underpins the other notes, and sets up a harmonic relationship which enables the musician to hear the sound and melodic characteristics in context. A pedal note is a note that is heard continuously through a section of music, as a note that is either repeated or sustained, at one pitch level. In the examples below, it is played below the notes of each mode by striking one of the lower strings and letting the note ring under the mode. The two lowest strings of the guitar – the 6th (E) and 5th (A) – can both be used as open strings under the E Phrygian and A Aeolian modes.

RE-TUNING

To play the low notes under the remaining five modes, the 6th and 5th strings must be tuned to the notes C, D, F, G, or B. To tune an open string to the required pitch, a higher-octave note is played on a fretted or open position, and one of the open lower strings is tuned to this note an octave below. For example, the note D is played on the 6th string by taking the open E string down by a tone. The open 4th string, D, is used as a reference point for the note D, and the open E is adjusted in pitch by releasing the tension on the string until the note drops down to the point where it resonates an octave below the higher D. The strings are tuned to the other principal modal notes by playing an open string or holding a fretted note as an upper-octave note and tuning the string up or down to a point an octave below.

USING PEDAL NOTES

The sustained low note – the pedal note – which is played with passages of moving notes under scales, melodies, and chords is similar to the *drone* note used in many areas of folk music. It is ideal for musical applications on the guitar, providing a foundation and a sense of continuity.

Playing the Ionian scale in C
Hold the note C on the 3rd fret of the 5th string, and tune the 6th string down to a C note an octave below. Play the re-tuned 6th string as a low C and play the Ionian/major scale ascending from the 5th string.

Playing the Dorian scale in D
Play the note D on the open 4th string, and tune the 6th string down to a D an octave below. Then, using the re-tuned 6th string as a low D, play the Dorian scale ascending from the 4th string.

Playing the Phrygian scale in E
The Phrygian mode ascends naturally using the notes of the C major scale. Play the open 6th string, and play the Phrygian mode ascending from E on the octave above, starting on the 2nd fret of the 4th string.

Playing the Lydian scale in F
Hold the note F on the 3rd fret of the 4th string, and tune the 6th string up to the note F an octave below Using the 6th string as a low F, play the Lydian mode ascending from the 4th string.

Playing the Mixolydian scale in G
Play the note G on the open 3rd string, and tune the 5th string down to the note G an octave below. Using the re-tuned 5th string as a low G, play the Mixolydian mode ascending from the 3rd string.

Playing the Aeolian scale in A
The open 5th string of the guitar is tuned to the note A. The Aeolian mode ascends from this note using the notes of the C major scale. Using the 5th string as a low A, play the Aeolian ascending from the 3rd string.

Playing the Locrian scale in B
Play B on the open 2nd string, and tune the 5th string to B an octave below. With the 5th string as a low B, play the Locrian ascending from the 2nd string. Finally, compare all the modal fingering positions with the scales on p.86.

Modal root note positions

In the key of C major, play a low E on the open 6th string, and ascend to the E two octaves above on the open 1st string. In the key of C this is a Phrygian mode, with the notes ranging across the fingerboard. This is often extended by two notes to form a playing position using the first three frets. The other six modes are picked out by playing the modal scale from the principal note. There are either two or three points where this pivotal note occurs using the notes up to the 3rd fret. Using all the notes on this full scalar position, play every mode, ascending and descending, from the modal root note, and compare the position of each to those of the others.

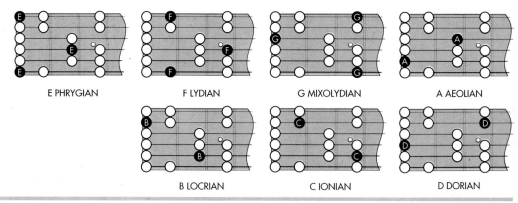

E PHRYGIAN   F LYDIAN   G MIXOLYDIAN   A AEOLIAN

B LOCRIAN   C IONIAN   D DORIAN

Fretted modal positions

The modes should be played as both an ascending and a descending series of one-octave, eight-note scales, starting with C major. These scales can be played using either open string or fretted positions. Play each of the modes beginning with the C Ionian (the major mode) which starts on the 3rd fret of the 5th string. Play D Dorian starting on the second note of the C major scale position, and finishing with an added top D. The successive modes are played by moving across the fingerboard. Using a fretted position also enables you to move the modes along the fingerboard to other keys. By moving the C major modes up one fret, the system will be transposed to a position based around the key of Db.

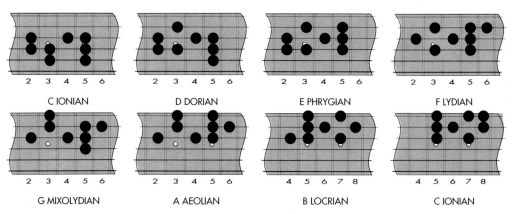

C IONIAN   D DORIAN   E PHRYGIAN   F LYDIAN

G MIXOLYDIAN   A AEOLIAN   B LOCRIAN   C IONIAN

MODES IN C AND G

Each of the seven modes can be played as an ascending series of one-octave scales, starting with the note E on the open 6th string. Compare the structure of the modes and their fingering in the context of the overall position. The shape and sequence of tones and semitones in each mode should be memorized as a fixed shape in this basic open-string position. After thoroughly learning the modes based on the notes of the C major scale, play the scale of G major from the 3rd fret of the 6th string. The Mixolydian scale from G on the 3rd fret ascends with the notes G-A-B-C-D-E-F. When this pattern is changed to the Ionian (major) scale from G, it uses the notes G-A-B-C-D-E-F♯. The introduction of F♯ changes each of the C major related modes to a G major mode. Play each of the modes from E Phrygian, starting from the open 6th string. Now play them one at a time, raising the F natural note in each scale to F♯. The modes from E, converted to the key of G, become E Aeolian, F♯ Locrian, G Ionian, A Dorian, B Phrygian, C Lydian, and D Mixolydian.

E PHRYGIAN   B LOCRIAN

F LYDIAN   C IONIAN

G MIXOLYDIAN   D DORIAN

A AEOLIAN

EXTENDING CHORDS

CHORD ADDITIONS USING MODES

Upper notes
When a modal scale is written over two octaves, the primary method for building chords can be shown in thirds. Chords use every other note of the scale until the root note is repeated two octaves higher, on the fifteenth note of the scale. This gives every note of the scale as a chord addition. In practice, notes of the scale are not always added in this way. The thirteenth often functions as a sixth and is a common addition to triad harmony built from the root third and fifth. It is referred to as the sixth unless it is combined with other chord additions in certain voicings.

By taking the scale tone seventh chords occurring in the key of C and extending their structure over two octaves, it is possible to form a full vocabulary of modal chords from every degree of the major scale. Modal chords can be built up in thirds until the root note, two octaves above, is reached. Some additions beyond the seventh are dissonant, and rarely occur in most types of guitar music. Additions frequently have two designations, depending on their octave position. With chord symbols these are used to suggest the position for the note in relation to the root. In practice most additions are interchangeable and their designation depends on the type of voicing. For example, in practice the eleventh is frequently placed as a fourth above the root, but if the chord is voiced with a seventh or a further extension, the addition may be positioned and labelled as an eleventh.

Hearing extended chords
Some scale notes have an unusual effect when added to basic chord forms. When a full modal scale is played over the related chord, unusual or dissonant notes stand out. For example, with the chord of C major 7 the fourth (eleventh) changes the harmonic quality of the chord, making it sound unmusical. Adding extra notes depends on the context, the type of music, and the particular chord voicing. The effect can be heard by playing chords as triads on each modal degree, then individually adding the four remaining notes of the related scale.

Ionian major I
The C major chord uses all the scale additions of the major scale/Ionian mode except the note F. They are the sixth/thirteenth (A), the seventh (B), and the ninth (D). The fourth/eleventh (F) of the scale is dissonant and alters the character of the chord.

Dorian minor II
The D minor chord uses all of the scale additions of the Dorian mode: the sixth/thirteenth (B), the seventh (C), the ninth (E), and the fourth/eleventh (G). Minor chords built on the Dorian mode can be extended to include all the related scale notes without sounding dissonant. This is one of the most common minor chords, and is used as the basis for standard extensions.

Phrygian minor III
E minor is not often extended beyond the seventh (D) in the Phrygian mode. The ninth (F) sounds dissonant above the root; it can only be used with certain types of voicing. The note A occurs as a fourth/eleventh. The sixth/thirteenth (C) is a minor sixth interval. This can sound unusual with certain applications.

Lydian major IV
*The F major chord uses all the scale additions of the Lydian mode: the sixth/thirteenth (D), the seventh (E), and the ninth (G). The fourth/eleventh (B) is added as a sharp eleventh, but is often represented as a flat fifth in chord symbols. The **IV** chord is used as a standard major with a sixth, seventh, or ninth, or as a Lydian ♭5/♯11 chord with additions. A normal fifth can be combined with the ♭5/♯11 chord.*

Mixolydian major V

The G major dominant chord uses all of the scalar additions of the Mixolydian mode. The seventh (F), ninth (A), and fourth/eleventh (C) are all additions to the dominant chord. The note C acts as a suspended fourth when the third is left out. The note E is referred to as a thirteenth when the chord contains either a seventh or added scale notes. When E is added to the basic triad it is referred to as a sixth.

Aeolian minor VI

The A minor chord uses all of the scalar additions of the minor scale/Aeolian mode. It can be extended using the seventh (G), the ninth (B), and the eleventh (D) notes. The sixth, or thirteenth, is the note F – when used with certain voicings this addition can produce a dissonant sound. It is most commonly used as a flat sixth addition to the chord.

Locrian diminished VII

The B diminished chord can be extended to a minor seventh flat five with the addition of the seventh (A). The fourth/eleventh (E) is often added, but the ninth (C) sounds dissonant above the root. The note G is the sixth/thirteenth. It is often treated as the root note of a related G dominant inversion.

PLAYING MODAL ARPEGGIOS

Play the seven modal arpeggios from the root note of each degree of the major scale. The C modal arpeggios below are placed at their lowest pitch on the guitar, using the 1st string for higher notes. Starting with C on the 3rd fret of the 5th string, play the arpeggio as a series of ascending thirds, with E on the 4th string, G on the open 3rd string, B and D on the 2nd string, and F, A, and C on the 1st string. Listen to each note and pick out weak or dissonant-sounding scale notes in each arpeggio. Play all the arpeggios and compare them with the modal scales in the key of C major. The D arpeggio starts from the 4th string, and the arpeggios from E, F, G, A, and B have been moved down to start on the 6th and 5th strings. When a series of thirds is played over two octaves with every element of the modal scale, the sound and character of the notes can be heard in relation to the root as a series of harmonies.

MAJOR KEY CHORD CHART

The chords on the major scale are shown below with their constituent notes. On each degree of the scale there are various types of extended chord in frequent use. Abbreviations are used for writing chord types down as symbols: **M** or **MAJ** can be used to represent *major*, and **m** or **MIN** – *minor*. The letter name, triad abbreviation, or other term also has a number for the chord addition. For example, **GM7** indicates a G major triad with the addition of a seventh. The notes that make up the chord between the root and the upper extension are put together to give the chord the structure it requires. Different voicings can be used. A particular chord voicing does not always contain all of the elements that make up the full structure: when it is extended to ninths, elevenths, and thirteenths, elements of the chord are often left out. For example, the full extension of a G dominant thirteenth chord contains the seven notes G, B, D, F, A, C, and E. With only six strings on the guitar, one or more notes have to be omitted in order to play a practical voicing.

Reference chart

The seven chord notes, running from the root to the thirteenth/sixth in each chord, are written from left to right. The seven chord roots built on each of the modal degrees are shown in the first column, and their structure as a series of thirds is written alongside on each line.

		1	3	5	7	9/2	11/4	13/6
I	MAJOR/IONIAN	C	E	G	B	D	F	A
II	DORIAN	D	F	A	C	E	G	B
III	PHRYGIAN	E	G	B	D	F	A	C
IV	LYDIAN	F	A	C	E	G	B	D
V	MIXOLYDIAN	G	B	D	F	A	C	E
VI	MINOR/AEOLIAN	A	C	E	G	B	D	F
VII	LOCRIAN	B	D	F	A	C	E	G

Chords in C major

The main chord types in frequent use are shown in the chart on the right. Sixths, sevenths, ninths, elevenths, and thirteenths, and combinations of sixths and ninths, occur as the main chord types in a major key. There are a large number of further combinations of intervals used in jazz, classical composition, and some types of ethnic folk music.

		4TH	6TH	7TH	9TH	11TH	13TH	6/9	FURTHER TYPES
C	MAJOR	C SUS4	C 6	C M7	C M9			C 6/9	C 6/7 C ADD F C 6/9M7
D	MINOR		D m6	D m7	D m9	D m11	D m13	D m6/9	
E	MINOR			E m7		E m11			E PHRYGIAN CHORDS
F	MAJOR		F 6	F M7	F M9	F M7♯11		F 6/9	F 6/7 F M9♯11 F 6/9M7
G	MAJOR	G SUS4	G 6	G 7	G 9	G 11	G 13	G 6/9	
A	MINOR			A m7	A m9	A m11			A AEOLIAN CHORDS
B	DIMINISHED			B m7♭5		B m11♭5			B LOCRIAN CHORDS

Transposing modal chords

The major system of modal chords is built in each major key with the same type of structure and additions. For example, in the key of G major the scale G-A-B-C-D-E-F♯ is used as the basis for the I-VII series of chords. All the chord types are built from these root notes and are developed with the same rules as the C major scale.

		4TH	6TH	7TH	9TH	11TH	13TH	6/9	FURTHER TYPES
G	MAJOR	G SUS4	G 6	G M7	G M9			G 6/9	G 6/7 G ADD C G 6/9M7
A	MINOR		A m6	A m7	A m9	A m11	A m13	A m6/9	
B	MINOR			B m7		B m11			B PHRYGIAN CHORDS
C	MAJOR		C 6	C M7	C M9	C M7♯11		C 6/9	C 6/7 C M9♯11 C 6/9M7
D	MAJOR	D SUS4	D 6	D 7	D 9	D 11	D 13	D 6/9	
E	MINOR			E m7	E m9	E m11			E AEOLIAN CHORDS
F♯	DIMINISHED			F♯ m7♭5		F♯m11♭5			F♯ LOCRIAN CHORDS

CHORD CONSTRUCTION

ALTERED DOMINANT AND SEVENTH CHORDS

Dominant extensions
The diagram below shows a series of notes in relation to the note G, on the fifth degree (V) of the C major scale. The notes beneath the stave are from the scale of C major. Those above the stave are other notes that may also be used in combination with the dominant chord.

Dominant chords may be used in many different ways: they act as the **V** chord in major and minor harmony, and as an altered form to replace basic chords in blues, jazz, and many other types of music. The flexibility of the dominant chord can lead to a wide range of additions that use all the notes available from the root, with the exception of the major seventh. This type of harmonic structure has a great number of possibilities for voicing; many of the most unusual chord types are dominant sevenths with added notes.

Additions
In the C major scale, the notes added to the G major triad are the seventh, ninth, eleventh, and thirteenth notes of the G Mixolydian mode (see p. 88). The other notes are approached as fifths, ninths, elevenths, and thirteenths, with adjustments made using flats and sharps.

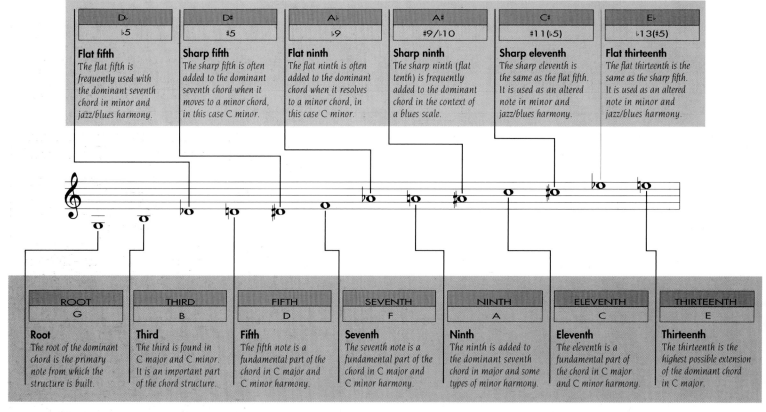

Db	D#	Ab	A#	C#	Eb
b5	#5	b9	#9/b10	#11 (b5)	b13(#5)

Flat fifth
The flat fifth is frequently used with the dominant seventh chord in minor and jazz/blues harmony.

Sharp fifth
The sharp fifth is often added to the dominant seventh chord when it moves to a minor chord, in this case C minor.

Flat ninth
The flat ninth is often added to the dominant chord when it resolves to a minor chord, in this case C minor.

Sharp ninth
The sharp ninth (flat tenth) is frequently added to the dominant chord in the context of a blues scale.

Sharp eleventh
The sharp eleventh is the same as the flat fifth. It is used as an altered note in minor and jazz/blues harmony.

Flat thirteenth
The flat thirteenth is the same as the sharp fifth. It is used as an altered note in minor and jazz/blues harmony.

ROOT	THIRD	FIFTH	SEVENTH	NINTH	ELEVENTH	THIRTEENTH
G	B	D	F	A	C	E

Root
The root of the dominant chord is the primary note from which the structure is built.

Third
The third is found in C major and C minor. It is an important part of the chord structure.

Fifth
The fifth note is a fundamental part of the chord in C major and C minor harmony.

Seventh
The seventh note is a fundamental part of the chord in C major and C minor harmony.

Ninth
The ninth is added to the dominant seventh chord in major and some types of minor harmony.

Eleventh
The eleventh is a fundamental part of the chord in C major and C minor harmony.

Thirteenth
The thirteenth is the highest possible extension of the dominant chord in C major.

Chord tone scale
All the notes can be placed in a one octave chromatic scale. Only F# is missing. Compare the altered notes: they have different names according to position.

G	G#	Ab	A	A#	Bb	B	C	C#	Db	D	D#	Eb	E	F	G
ROOT	b9	b9	9	#9	b10	3	4/11	#4/#11	b5	5	#5	b13	13	7	OCTAVE

ARPEGGIO EXERCISE

Play the ascending thirds from the root note (G), using the chord additions in C major: G-B-D-F-A-C-E. Add the altered tones by playing the arpeggio slowly and hearing them in relation to the standard fifth, ninth, eleventh, and thirteenth. Dominant chords often consist of standard and altered notes.

SEVENTHS

Ten different seventh chords can be built from any root, by using three superimposed notes. Most chords are based on thirds over a root note; in seventh chords, the first third to be placed over the root is either a minor third or a major third. This note can be combined with additional thirds, or major seconds, to form triads. In relation to the root, the perfect fifth is raised by a semitone to form an augmented fifth (*sharp five*), or lowered by a semitone to form a diminished fifth (*flat five*). These combinations can form one major triad, one augmented triad, one major triad with a diminished fifth, one

minor triad, or one diminished triad. A third is added above the fifth, to create three different types of seventh interval from the root: minor seventh, major seventh, and diminished seventh. The addition of the seventh results in a total of ten different types of seventh chord (including unusual variations). When different chord types are built from one root note, for example C, their combinations of intervals can be compared. Only one chord in the C series is built exclusively using the notes of C major – the other chords are related to various different keys and scales. Build up the chords in stages from the C root on the 3rd fret of the 5th string. Each seventh

chord can be viewed as a series of building blocks, from the root to the third, third to fifth, and fifth to seventh. The sound and structure of each chord varies. Although they are named as a series of thirds with altered notes from the root, the gaps between the four notes in a seventh chord, in each stage from the root to the seventh, sometimes use other intervals in addition to the standard major and minor thirds. The possible intervals are shown below by a series of colour-coded squares: red indicates a major second interval; blue, a minor third; yellow, a major third; and white, a perfect fourth.

Major triads
The major triad is a minor third above a major third. The chord is altered by adjusting the fifth up or down a semitone. The sharp fifth creates an augmented chord with an upper major third above the lower major third. The diminished fifth creates a major chord type with a flat fifth. This is a major second above a major third.

MAJOR 2ND
MINOR 3RD
MAJOR 3RD
PERFECT 4TH

Minor variations
The minor triad is a major third above a minor third. It is altered by moving the fifth down by a semitone. The flat fifth creates a diminished chord with an upper minor third above the lower minor third. The fifth on the minor is not raised by a sharp – if it is moved up a semitone, it becomes the root of a major chord.

MAJOR 3RD · MINOR 3RD

C MAJOR · C AUGMENTED · C MAJOR ♭5 · C MINOR · C DIMINISHED

Major and dominant seventh
The major seventh has a major third interval between the fifth and the seventh. The dominant seventh has a minor third interval between the fifth and the seventh.

Major and dominant seventh sharp fifth
The major seventh sharp fifth has a minor third interval between the fifth and the seventh. The dominant sharp fifth has a major second.

Major and dominant seventh flat fifth
Both the major seventh flat fifth and the dominant seventh flat fifth have an interval of a major second between the third and the fifth.

Minor seventh and minor/major seventh
The minor seventh has a minor third interval between the fifth and the seventh. The minor/major seventh has a major third interval between the fifth and the seventh.

Minor seventh flat fifth and diminished seventh
The minor seventh flat fifth has a major third interval between the fifth and the seventh. The diminished seventh has an interval of a minor third.

C MAJOR 7 · C MAJOR 7♭5 · C MAJOR 7♭5 · C MINOR 7 · C MINOR 7♭5

C DOMINANT 7 · C 7♯5 · C 7♭5 · C MINOR/MAJOR 7 · C DIMINISHED 7

CHORD FINDER

Fingerboard symbols
On the fingerboard diagrams throughout the chord finder, numbers inside circles show which left-hand fingers are used. Circles over the nut indicate that open strings should be played. A circle on the fretboard, with no number, shows that the note is optional. A white bar connecting strings represents a barre or a half-barre. The **X** symbol shows that a string is not played.

Over the following eight pages is an extensive range of chords built from fifth-, sixth-, and fourth-string roots. Altogether, there are 89 chord shapes with roots placed on the 3rd fret. Each shape may be moved up or down the fingerboard to any of the twelve fret positions, providing over a thousand different chords. It is important to practise chords so that adjacent strings that are *not* part of the harmony are not accidentally played. To begin with, accuracy may be difficult to achieve on some of the shapes. However, a controlled technique for playing chords will become second nature with constant practice.

Finding a chord
To find a chord type, first select a string position. For example, in order to play a B7♭9, go to the 5th-string chords based on C roots. Look through the chords until you come to C7♭9 on page 96. If this shape is then moved down one fret to the B root on the 2nd fret, B7♭9 is formed. Some chord types are voiced more easily using certain strings.

ROOTS ON THE 5TH STRING

Using chords with the roots based on the 3rd fret of the 5th string gives all the chord types a C root. From this point, they can be compared harmonically, and the constituent notes can be memorized in relation to a C root. The chords that are rooted on the 5th string work well for sequences, and are particularly effective when combined with those that are based on a 6th-string root. Chords with a 5th-string root often have adjacent outer or inner strings that are not played. The player should prevent these unused strings from ringing by letting the sides of the fingers rest naturally against them. This type of chord is generally played without a full barre.

Chord notes
The intervals shown on the fingerboard are named from the root (in this case, C). The same pattern can run from any fret position on the 5th string. The twelve chromatic semitones can be used as a root for any chord.

C MAJOR 7TH (CΔ7) This uses C (root), G (perfect fifth), B (major seventh), and E (major third). Play the 5th, 4th, 3rd, and 2nd strings.

C DOMINANT 7TH (C7) This uses C (root), G (perfect fifth), B♭ (minor seventh), and E (major third). The strings used are the 5th to the 2nd.

C MINOR 7TH (C-7) Play C (root), G (perfect fifth), B♭ (minor seventh), and E♭ (minor third) on the 5th, 4th, 3rd, and 2nd strings.

C MINOR 7TH FLAT 5TH (C-7♭5) The notes played are C (root), G♭ (diminished fifth), B♭ (minor seventh), and E♭ (minor third).

C DIMINISHED 7TH (C°7) The notes used are C (root), G♭ (diminished fifth), B♭♭/A (diminished seventh/major sixth), and E♭ (minor third).

C DOMINANT 7TH FLAT 5TH (C7♭5) The notes used are C (root), G♭ (diminished fifth), B♭ (minor seventh), and E (major third).

C DOMINANT 7TH SHARP 5TH (C7♯5) This chord uses C (root), G♯ (augmented fifth), B♭ (minor seventh), and E (major third).

C MAJOR 7TH SHARP 11TH (CΔ♯11) The chord uses the notes C (root), F♯ (augmented 4th/11th), B (major seventh), and E (major third).

C MINOR/MAJOR 7TH (C-Δ7) Play C (root), G (perfect fifth), B (major seventh), and E♭ (minor third) using the 5th to the 2nd strings.

C MAJOR 6TH (C6) This chord uses C (root), E (major third), A (major sixth), and C (octave root). Play all the strings from the 5th to the 2nd.

C MINOR 6TH (C-6) The notes are C (root), A (major sixth), E♭ (minor third), and G (perfect fifth). Play the 5th, 3rd, 2nd, and 1st strings.

C MAJOR 9TH (CΔ9) Play the notes C (root), E (major third), B (major seventh), and D (major ninth). The 5th to the 2nd strings are used.

C DOMINANT 9TH (C9) Play C (root), E (major third), B♭ (minor seventh), and D (major ninth) using the 5th to the 2nd strings.

C MINOR 9TH (C-9) The chord is formed using the notes C (root), E♭ (minor third), B♭ (minor seventh), and D (major ninth).

C dominant 11th (C11) This chord uses C (root), F (perfect fourth/eleventh), B♭ (minor seventh), D (major ninth), and G (perfect fifth).

C minor 11th (C-11) The notes are C (root), F (perfect fourth/eleventh), B♭ (minor seventh), E♭ (minor third), and G (perfect fifth).

C dominant 13th (C13) Play C (root), E (major third), B♭ (minor seventh), D (major ninth), and A (thirteenth) on the top five strings.

C dominant 7th flat 9th (C7♭9) For this chord the notes are C (root), E (major third), B♭ (minor seventh), and D♭ (minor ninth).

C dominant 7th sharp 9th (C7♯9) The chord notes are C (root), E (major third), B♭ (minor seventh), and D♯ (augmented ninth).

C suspended 4th (C sus 4) This chord consists of C (root), G (perfect fifth), C (octave root), and F (perfect fourth/eleventh).

Additional 5th-string chords

There are a great many other chords that can be voiced with their roots on the 5th string. Twenty additional chord shapes are shown below. These consist of both alternative voicings for widely used chord types, and a number of extended and altered-note chords. These developed chords are part of the extended vocabulary for compositional structure in most types of music, from popular styles through to classical music.

C major 7th (C△7) C, B, E, and G form this chord. The 4th and 6th strings are not played.

C dominant 7th (C7) Here the notes are C, B♭, E, and G. The 4th and 6th strings are not played.

C minor 7th (C-7) This chord is formed from C, B♭, E♭, and G. The 4th and 6th strings are not used.

C minor 7th flat 5th (C-7♭5) C, B♭, E♭, and G♭ are played in this chord. The 4th and 6th strings are not used.

C diminished 7th (C°7) The notes are C, B♭♭ (A), E♭, and G♭. The 4th and 6th strings are not played.

C major 6th (C6) The notes are C, E, A, and E. The 1st and 6th strings are not played.

C MAJOR 7TH (CΔ7)
To form this chord, C, E, G, B, and E are used. The 6th string is not played.

C DOMINANT 7TH (C7)
C, E, B♭, C, and E are used to play this chord. The 6th string is not played.

C MINOR 11TH (C-11)
The chord notes are C, B♭, E♭, and F. The 4th and 6th strings are not used.

C MINOR 13TH (C-13)
The notes are C, B♭, E♭, and A. The 4th and 6th strings are not played.

C MAJOR 6/9 (C6/9)
In this chord the notes are C, E, A, and D. The 1st and 6th strings are not used.

C MAJOR 6/9 SHARP 11TH (C6/9♯11)
C, E, A, D, and F♯ are used here. The 6th string is not played.

C MINOR 6/9 (C-6/9)
This chord consists of C, E♭, A, and D. The 1st and 6th strings are not played.

C MIN/MAJ 9TH (C-Δ9)
The chord is formed from C, E♭, B, and D. The 1st and 6th strings are not used.

C MAJOR 7TH SHARP 5TH (CΔ7♯5)
Here the notes played are C, G♯, B, and E, between the 3rd and 6th frets.

C AUGMENTED (C+)
C, E, G♯, and C make up this chord. The 1st and 6th strings are not played.

C DOMINANT 7 SHARP 5TH SHARP 9TH (C7♯5♯9)
C, E, B♭, D♯, and G♯ are played here. The 6th string is not used.

C DOMINANT 9 FLAT 5TH (C9♭5)
The chord uses C, E, B♭, D, and G♭. The 6th string is not played.

C MINOR FLAT 6TH (C-♭6)
The notes are C, A♭, E♭, and G. The 4th and 6th strings are not played.

C MAJOR ADDED 9TH (Cadd9)
C, E, G, D, and E are played in this chord. The 6th string is not played.

ROOT CHORDS ON THE 6TH STRING

Building chords from a root on the 6th string enables the guitarist to play low-register chords as well as full-sounding five- and six-note voicings. Many of the most complex and attractive harmonies are played using all six strings. Five- and six-note chords are often reduced by not playing the 5th string. This gives a more balanced sound. In these instances, the doubled thirds or fifths are left out. Altering voicings in this way also enables chords to be moved around with more flexibility. Many of the standard added-note voicings have a rather bottom-heavy and muddy texture when the four lower strings are sounded together.

Chord notes
The intervals shown on the fingerboard are named from the root (in this case, G). The same pattern can run from any fret position on the 6th string. Any of the twelve chromatic semitones can be used as a root for any chord.

G MAJOR 7TH (GΔ7) G (root), F♯ (major 7th), B (major 3rd), and D (perfect 5th) are played on the 6th, 4th, 3rd, and 2nd strings.

G DOMINANT 7TH (G7) This chord is formed from G (root), F (minor 7th), B (major 3rd), and D (perfect 5th).

G MINOR 7TH (G-7) This chord uses the notes G (root), F (minor 7th), B♭ (minor 3rd), and D (perfect 5th).

G MINOR 7TH FLAT 5TH (G-7♭5) The notes are G (root), F (minor 7th), B♭ (minor 3rd), and D♭ (diminished 5th).

G DIMINISHED 7TH (G°7) Play G (root), F♭/E (diminished 7th/ major 6th), B♭ (minor 3rd), and D♭ (diminished 5th).

G DOMINANT 7TH FLAT 5TH (G7♭5) This chord consists of the notes G (root), F (minor 7th), B (major 3rd), and D♭ (diminished 5th).

G DOMINANT 7TH SHARP 5TH (G7♯5) Play the notes G (root), F (minor 7th), B (major 3rd), and D♯ (augmented 5th).

G MAJOR 7TH SHARP 11TH (GΔ7♯11) Play G (root), F♯ (major 7th), B (major 3rd), and C♯ (augmented 4th/11th).

G MINOR/MAJOR 7TH (G-Δ7) For this chord the notes played are G (root), F♯ (major 7th), B♭ (minor 3rd), and D (perfect 5th).

G MAJOR 6TH (G6) This chord consists of the notes G (root), E (major 6th), B (major 3rd), and D (perfect 5th).

G MINOR 6TH (G-6) This chord consists of the notes G (root), E (major 6th), B♭ (minor 3rd), and D (perfect 5th).

G MAJOR 9TH (G△9) Play this chord using the notes G (root), F♯ (major 7th), A (major 9th), and D (perfect 5th).

G DOMINANT 9TH (G9) Play G (root), B (major 3rd), F (minor 7th), A (major 9th), and D (perfect 5th) on the bottom five strings.

G MINOR 9TH (G-9) The notes used are G (root), F (minor 7th), B♭ (minor 3rd), D (perfect 5th), and A (major 9th).

G SUSPENDED 4TH (G SUS 4) G (root), D (perfect 5th), G (root), C (perfect 4th/11th), D perfect 5th), and G (root) are used.

G DOMINANT 11TH (G11) Play G (root), F (minor 7th), A (major 9th), and C (11th) on the 6th, 4th, 3rd, and 2nd strings.

FURTHER 6TH-STRING CHORDS

Chords played with 6th-string roots have a different balance from those with roots on the 5th string. Other types of voicing are often used for easily playable and balanced added-note chords. This is partly due to the order of intervals running across the fingerboard from a bottom-string root. Some chord voicings that are moved across from the 5th string are impossible to play, or sound indistinct, in a low register. Positioning the root on the 6th string enables the guitarist to play a wide range of close harmonies and altered dominant chords.

G MAJOR 6/9 (G 6/9) For this chord, play G, B, E, A, and D. The G on the 1st string is optional.

G 6/9 MAJOR 7 (G6/9△7) To play this chord, sound G, B, E, A, D, and F♯. All strings are used.

G MINOR 11TH (G-11) Play the notes G, F, B♭, and C. The 1st and 5th strings are not used.

G DOMINANT 13 (G13) In this chord the notes are G, F, B, and E. The A on the 1st string is optional.

G MINOR 13TH (G-13) The chord uses the notes G, F, B♭, and E. The A on the 1st string is optional.

G DOMINANT 7TH SHARP 9TH (G7♯9) The notes are G, B, F, A♯, and D. The 1st string is not played.

G MINOR 6/9 (G-6/9) This chord is played with the notes G, E, B♭, D, and A. The 5th string is not used.

G MAJOR 7TH SHARP 5TH (GΔ7♯5) Sound the notes G, F♯, B, and D♯. The 1st and 5th strings are not used.

G MINOR FLAT 6TH (G-♭6) G, E♭, B♭, and D are played here. The G on the 1st string is optional.

G MINOR/MAJOR 9TH (G-Δ9) The chord is formed from G, F♯, B♭, D, and A. The 5th string is not played.

G DOMINANT 7 SHARP 5TH SHARP 9TH (G7♯5♯9) Sound G, F, B, D♯, and A♯. Use all the strings except for the 5th.

G DOMINANT 7 SHARP 5TH FLAT 9TH (G7♯5♭9) Play G, F, B, D♯, and A♭. The 5th string is not used in this chord.

G DOMINANT 13TH FLAT 9TH (G13♭9) This chord uses G, F, B, E, and A♭. The 5th string is not played.

G DOMINANT 7TH FLAT 9TH (G7♭9) To form the chord play G, F, A♭, and D. The 1st and 5th strings are not used.

G DOMINANT 9TH FLAT 5TH (G9♭5) The chord notes are G, F, A, and D♭. The 1st and 5th strings are not played.

G DOMINANT 13TH SHARP 9TH (G13♯9) The notes are G, B, F, A♯, and E. A on the 1st string is optional.

FOURTH-STRING ROOTS

On the four upper strings of the guitar the range of chordal possibilities is more limited. Eleventh and thirteenth chords can be constructed, but with only four voices; they lack some of the important notes that give certain chords their harmonic character. The upper-string chords are ideal for supporting melody. Their bright clear sound, good separation, and high register also make them useful for chord fills in group playing.

UNDERSTANDING CHORD SHAPES

To develop an understanding of chord types and voicings, it is useful to play all of the shapes on a C fret. With 4th-string root chords added, each shape and voicing on the 6th, 5th, and 4th strings should be compared by moving the 4th-string shapes up to C on the 10th fret, and the 6th-string shapes up to C on the 8th fret. You will notice that although a number of chords

Chord notes
The intervals shown on the fingerboard are named from the root (in this case, F). The same pattern can run from any fret position on the 4th string. Any of the twelve chromatic semitones can be used as a root for any chord.

contain the same order of notes, because of the string-tuning intervals across the fretboard they have very different shapes. Moving a voicing across the fingerboard on

the same fret is also a useful exercise; for example, try moving G on the 3rd fret of the 6th string to C on the 5th string, and then to F on the 4th string.

F MAJOR 7TH (FΔ) In this chord the notes are F, C, E, and A. The voicing order is root, perfect 5th, major 7th, and major 3rd.

F DOMINANT 7TH (F7) The chord is formed from F (root), C (perfect 5th), E♭ (minor 7th), and A (major 3rd).

F MINOR 7TH (F-7) This chord uses the notes F (root), C (perfect 5th), E♭ (minor 7th), and A♭ (minor 3rd).

F MINOR 7TH FLAT 5TH (F-7♭5) This chord consists of the notes F (root), C♭/B (dim. 5th), E♭ (minor 7th), and A♭ (minor 3rd).

F DIMINISHED 7TH (F°7) F (root), C♭/B (diminished 5th), E♭♭/D (diminished 7th/major 6th), and A♭ (minor 3rd). are used.

F SUSPENDED 4TH (F SUS 4) Sound C, C, F, and B♭. The 5th and 6th strings are not played.

F DOMINANT 7TH FLAT 5TH (F7♭5) Play F, B, E♭, and A. All strings from the 4th to the 1st are used.

F DOMINANT 7TH SHARP 5TH (F7♯5) The chord notes are F, C♯, E♭, and A. The 5th and 6th strings are not used.

F MAJOR 7TH SHARP 11TH (F∆7♯11) The chord contains F, B, E, and A. Use the 4th to the 1st strings.

F MIN/MAJ 7TH (F-∆7) The components are F, C, E, and A♭. The bottom two strings are not played.

F MAJOR 6TH (F6) For this chord use F, C, D, and A. The bottom two strings are not played.

F MINOR 6TH (F-6) To sound F-6, play F, C, D, and A♭. The bottom two strings are not used.

F MAJOR 9TH (F∆9) The chord consists of the notes F, A, E, and G. Use only the 1st to 4th strings.

F DOMINANT 9TH (F9) The chord notes are F, A, E♭, and G. Use all strings except the 5th and 6th.

F MINOR 9TH (F-9) To form F-9, play F, A♭, E♭, and G. All except the 5th and 6th strings are used.

F DOMINANT 7TH SHARP 9TH (F7♯9) The chord is formed from F, A, E♭, and G♯. The 1st to 4th strings are used.

F DOMINANT 7TH FLAT 9TH (F7♭9) The notes are F, A, E♭, and G♭. 5th and 6th strings are not played.

PLAYING MAJOR SCALES

LEARNING TO PLAY THE MAJOR SCALE IN EVERY KEY

Keynotes
The position of each scale below is determined by the lowest **keynote** on the fingerboard. The keynotes run from the first note in E major on the open 6th string to the first note in E♭ major on the 1st fret of the 4th string. The keynotes for E major, F major, F♯/G♭ major, G major, and A♭ major start on the 6th string. A major, B♭ major, B major, C major, and D♭ major start on the 5th string, and D major and E♭ major start on the 4th string.

The capability of playing in all twelve major scales is vital to mastering the guitar. Music is very often transposed from one key to another, altering the pitch, or changing its mood and colour. The position and structure of different scales must be memorized in order to play them comfortably. Music also modulates between keys. This involves a movement away from the scale position in one key to another, often using the same area of the fingerboard. Mastering the major keys is a skill that can be easily developed. Start by taking the basic one-octave positions for each key, and compare them with their closely related scales. The range of each scale can gradually be extended to cover the entire fingerboard in stages.

Patterns
The pitch position of each scale in relation to the open strings creates a series of different **patterns**. C major consists of a particular pattern of open string and fretted notes. When G major is played, it starts a fourth below C major: the series of intervals is the same, but the pattern changes at the top of the scale because of the position of fretted and open-string notes.

C major
This position uses the open strings and the first three frets on the fingerboard. The C major scale starts on the note C on the 3rd fret of the 5th string. This is the lowest keynote for C. The scale ascends with D, E, and F on the 4th string; G and A on the 3rd string; and B and C on the 2nd string.

G major (1 sharp)
This position uses the open strings and the first four frets on the fingerboard. The G major scale starts on the note G on the 3rd fret of the 6th string. This is the lowest keynote for G. The scale ascends on the 5th string using A, B, and C; continues on the 4th string with D, E and F♯; and ends with the open G.

D major (2 sharps)
This position uses the open strings and the first four frets on the fingerboard. The D major scale starts on the note D on the open 4th string. This is the lowest keynote for D. The scale ascends on the 4th string with E and F♯; on the 3rd string with G and A; and on the 2nd string with, B, C♯, and D.

A major (3 sharps)
This position uses the open strings and the first four frets on the fingerboard. The A major scale starts on the open 5th string. This is the lowest keynote for A in standard tuning. The scale ascends with B and C♯ on the 5th string; D, E, and F♯ on the 4th string; and G♯ and A on the 3rd string.

E major (4 sharps)
This position uses the open strings and the first four frets on the fingerboard. The E major scale starts on the note E on the open 6th string. This is the lowest keynote for E. The scale ascends with F♯ and G♯ on the 6th string; A, B, and C♯ on the 5th string; and D♯ and E on the 4th string.

B major (5 sharps)
This position uses an open string and the first four frets on the fingerboard. The B major scale starts on the note B on the 2nd fret of the 5th string. This is the lowest keynote for B. The scale ascends with C♯ on the 5th string; D♯, E, and F♯ on the 4th string; G♯ and A♯ on the 3rd string; and open B.

ENHARMONIC SCALES

Three major scales consist of the same notes played at the same pitch, in the same sequence, but with a different set of note names. They are F♯/G♭, C♯/D♭, and B/C♭.

For example, the notes in the key of F♯ are F♯, G♯, A♯, B, C♯, D♯, E♯, and F♯. The notes in the key of G♭ are G♭, A♭, B♭, C♭, D♭, E♭, F, and G♭. In both series of major scales the notes are

identical. The term *enharmonic* is used to describe the same notes, scales, or chords with different names. In practice, however, the keys of C♭ and C♯ are rarely used.

F♯ major (6 sharps)

The F♯ major scale does not use open strings. It starts with the F♯ on the 2nd fret of the 6th string. This is the lowest keynote for F♯ in standard tuning. The scale ascends with G♯ on the 6th string; A♯, B, and C♯ on the 5th string; and D♯, E♯, and F♯ on the 4th string. E♯ is the same as F.

C♯ major (7 sharps)

This position uses the first four frets on the fingerboard. It does not use open strings. The C♯ major scale starts on the note C♯ on the 4th fret of the 5th string. This is the lowest keynote for C♯ in standard tuning. The scale ascends with D♯, E♯, and F♯ on the 4th string; G♯ and A♯ on the 3rd string; and B♯ and C♯ on the 2nd string.

G♭ major (6 flats)

This position uses the first four frets on the fingerboard. The G♭ major scale starts with the note G♭ on the 2nd fret of the 6th string. This is the lowest keynote for G♭ in standard tuning. The scale ascends with A♭ on the 6th string; B♭, C♭, and D♭ on the 5th string; and E♭, F, and G♭ on the 4th string. C♭ is the same as B.

D♭ major (5 flats)

This position uses the first four frets on the fingerboard. It does not use any open string notes. The D♭ major scale begins with the note D♭ played on the 4th fret of the 5th string. This is the lowest possible keynote for D♭ using standard tuning. The scale ascends from the 4th string with the notes E♭, F, and G♭. A♭ and B♭ are played on the 3rd string, and C and D♭ are played on the 2nd string.

A♭ major (4 flats)

This position uses the first four frets on the fingerboard, and one open string. The A♭ major scale starts with A♭ on the 4th fret of the 6th string. This is the lowest keynote for A♭ in standard tuning. The scale ascends with B♭, C, and D♭ on the 5th string; E♭ and F on the 4th string; and open G and A♭ on the 3rd string.

E♭ major (3 flats)

This position uses one open string and the first four frets on the fingerboard. The E♭ major scale starts on the note E♭ on the 1st fret of the 4th string. This is the lowest keynote for E♭ in standard tuning. The scale ascends with F on the 4th string; open G, A♭, and B♭ on the 3rd string; and C, D, and E♭ on the 2nd string.

B♭ major (2 flats)

This position uses open strings and the first three frets on the fingerboard. The B♭ major scale starts on the note B♭ on the 1st fret of the 5th string. This is the lowest keynote for B♭. The scale ascends with C on the 5th string; open D, E♭, and F on the 4th string; and open G, A, and B♭ on the 3rd string.

F major (1 flat)

This position uses the open strings and the first three frets on the fingerboard. The F major scale starts on the note F on the 1st fret of the 6th string. This is the lowest keynote for F. The scale ascends with G on the 6th string; open A, B♭, and C on the 5th string; and open D, E, and F on the 4th string.

MAJOR-SCALE FINGERING

MOVING SCALE PATTERNS AROUND THE FINGERBOARD

Major fingering
The patterns in the diagrams below are shown in every key. They can all be moved along the fingerboard. The black circles on the diagrams show the note positions, alongside the numbered frets.

When a scale pattern is played using fretted notes, the shape and the fingering can be moved up and down the fingerboard to other pitch levels using fret positions as the starting point for different keys.

This is useful for acquiring scale positions in different keys without having to learn the note names in each series. This is one advantage of the fretted guitar fingerboard, which can be used visually.

Key movement
When scales are played using the cycle of keys, jumps in fifths and fourths take the major scale up and down one string. When a scale pattern is moved between adjacent strings, large jumps are unnecessary.

MOVING A FINGERING PATTERN

The open-string C major scale pattern provides the shape for each key position. The scales derived from this pattern are composed of fretted notes which must be played with an altered fingering. In these cases the first finger plays the equivalent of the open-string note positions.

C MAJOR (OPEN-STRING FINGERING)

Db MAJOR (FRETTED FINGERING)

C MAJOR
1 2 3 4 5

G MAJOR
7 8 9 10 11 12

D MAJOR
1 2 3 4 5

A MAJOR
7 8 9 10 11 12

E MAJOR
4 5 6 7 8 9

B MAJOR
8 9 10 11 12 13 14

F#/Gb MAJOR
4 5 6 7 8 9

Db MAJOR
1 2 3 4 5

Ab MAJOR
7 8 9 10 11 12

Eb MAJOR
2 3 4 5 6

Bb MAJOR
8 9 10 11 12 13 14

F MAJOR
4 5 6 7 8 9

ALTERNATIVE FINGERING

The fretted fingering pattern shown here also starts with C major from the 3rd fret of the 5th string. The notes ascending from C move up and across the fingerboard, using four frets and three strings. This pattern can be moved up and down the 5th string to play the twelve major scale keynotes.

C MAJOR SCALE

Moving to a 6th-string keynote
This fingering pattern can also be played from a keynote position starting on the 6th string. By using the 5th and 6th strings, the cycle of keynote positions can be played between the 2nd and the 8th frets. Note that this fingering pattern starting from the 5th and 6th strings cannot be moved on to 4th-string keynotes: the interval between the 2nd and 3rd strings is a major third, and the 2nd string fingering has to be moved up a fret.

C MAJOR
1 2 3 4 5

G MAJOR
1 2 3 4 5

D MAJOR
4 5 6 7 8 9

A MAJOR
4 5 6 7 8 9

E MAJOR
4 5 6 7 8 9

B MAJOR
1 2 3 4 5

F#/Gb MAJOR
1 2 3 4 5

Db MAJOR
2 3 4 5 6

Ab MAJOR
2 3 4 5 6

Eb MAJOR
4 5 6 7 8 9

Bb MAJOR
4 5 6 7 8 9

F MAJOR
7 8 9 10 11 12

STRETCH FINGERING

The C major scale is played using stretch fingering; it covers five frets and three strings. The first three notes are played by moving up the 5th string, using a wider stretch between the fingers. This is also repeated on the 4th string.

6th-string keynote

This fingering pattern for the major scale can also be moved on to a 6th-string keynote. By using the 5th and 6th strings, the cycle of fingering positions can be played between the 1st and the 7th frets.

3 4 5 6 7

C MAJOR

3 4 5 6 7

G MAJOR

4 5 6 7 8 9

D MAJOR

4 5 6 7 8 9

A MAJOR

7 8 9 10 11 12

E MAJOR

2 3 4 5 6

B MAJOR

2 3 4 5 6

F♯/G♭ MAJOR

4 5 6 7 8 9

D♭ MAJOR

4 5 6 7 8 9

A♭ MAJOR

6 7 8 9 10 11

E♭ MAJOR

1 2 3 4 5

B♭ MAJOR

1 2 3 4 5

F MAJOR

TWO-OCTAVE FINGERING

There are a number of ways to play scales on the guitar. When a major scale is extended over two octaves, there are certain points on the fingerboard where it is necessary to shift the left-hand position. This is due simply to the tuning and construction of the instrument. If C major is played as an ascending scale from the lowest C keynote on the guitar, the scale can be played from two different starting positions on the fingerboard – the 3rd fret of the 5th string, and the 8th fret of the 6th string. The five patterns below start from the 5th string.

C major with 1st string shift
The first octave open-string position is extended to G on the 3rd fret of the 1st string without moving the overall left-hand position. To play the top three notes of the second octave, the left hand is moved up between the 5th and 8th frets.

C major with 3rd string shift
The first octave standard position is played up to the seventh note (B) without changing the overall left-hand position. To play the second octave of the major scale, the left hand is moved up between the 5th and 8th frets.

C major with 2nd string shift
The first octave open-string position is extended to F on the 6th fret of the 2nd string. To play the top four notes of the second octave, the left hand is moved up between the 5th and 8th frets, where the fourth finger is placed on the note G.

C major with 4th string shift
The first five notes of the standard major position are played without changing the left-hand position. To play the remaining notes of the first octave, and the second octave, the left hand is moved up between the 4th and 8th frets.

C major with stretch fingering
Both octaves in this exercise are played in one flowing movement without using a break in fingering or a marked shift in left-hand position. As the left hand moves upwards, the thumb can be kept in the same area

FINGERING ON THE 6TH STRING

C major standard position from the 6th string

Unlike the examples shown on the previous page, this two-octave C major scale pattern starts on the 8th fret of the 6th string. A standard one-octave position is extended across all six of the strings, forming two octaves. Play both octaves across the fingerboard, ensuring that you do not move the thumb position.

Second finger This C major scale starts with the second finger playing the 8th fret of the 6th string.

C major starting with the fourth finger

This two-octave pattern also starts on the 8th fret of the 6th string. However, in this example, the pattern should be played starting with the fourth finger. The scale is extended across all six of the strings using a block of five frets. This pattern should be played without moving the thumb position.

Fourth finger This C major scale starts with the fourth finger playing the 8th fret of the 6th string.

C major 6th-string pattern with stretch fingering

This pattern starts on the 8th fret of the 6th string. Both octaves are played with three notes on each string, using stretch fingering. As the left hand moves upwards, the thumb should be kept in approximately the same area. The first finger must be moved up accurately onto each consecutive string position.

First finger This C major scale starts with the first finger on the 8th fret of the 6th string.

C MAJOR FINGERING IN CONTEXT

The three main two-octave C major fingerings (black circles) are shown in the context of the surrounding C major notes (white circles). The patterns should be played, comparing the points at which they overlap or diverge. An extended fingering area combining all the patterns should be memorized.

C MAJOR SCALE NOTES

Further comparisons
The fourth-finger and stretch patterns are shown in relation to other C major scale notes. Try extending each double-octave pattern using the notes shown in white circles.

C MAJOR SCALE NOTES

C MAJOR SCALE NOTES

TRANSPOSING A TWO-OCTAVE PATTERN

The patterns shown above can all be shifted around the fingerboard, allowing the scales to be played in any key. Fixed shape transposition is easily achieved by moving the pattern to a fret, using any 6th or 5th string keynote. In this way, when a C major pattern starting on the 8th fret is moved down by one fret, to B on the 7th fret, all the notes drop by a semitone, and the new major scale of B runs across the fingerboard from the new keynote. If the C major pattern on the 8th fret is moved up by one fret, to D♭ on the 9th fret, all of the notes move up by a semitone, and the new major scale of D♭ runs across the fingerboard from the new keynote. Try moving the positions around the cycle of twelve keys.

Fingering block
The outlined area shows a standard two-octave major scale fingering pattern as a block that can be moved up and down the fingerboard to be played in any key. The F♯/G♭ major scale is shown starting from the 2nd fret, and the C major scale from the 8th fret.

| F | | F♯ | G♭ | G | | G♯ | A♭ | A | | A♯ | B♭ | B | | C | | C♯ | D♭ | D | | D♯ | E♭ | E |

FULL MAJOR SCALE

PLAYING THE FULL SCALE POSITIONS

nking patterns
ne pattern on the first twelve
ets in each key can be
nemorized visually by linking
locks of the major scale
ngering patterns. Learn the
nape and position of one
ey at a time, starting with
C major. Compare the
welve-fret pattern with the
osition of the two-octave
cales that have keynotes on
oth the 5th and 6th strings.

Each scale in every key is made up of seven notes. These notes are played on every string, forming a pattern along the fingerboard. Major scale patterns surround each keynote, and the order of intervals can be seen as a series connecting every octave scale. Mastering these scale positions is an important skill for musicians in all areas. It is essential for jazz soloing, and for developing the ability to improvise over chord changes and harmonies in other styles. The scales are shown in a sequence following the cycle of keys in fifths. The first scale is C major, which uses the notes C, D, E, F, G, A, and B. The keynotes – C, in the first instance – are indicated by black circles.

Above the 12th fret
Each open-string note is repeated, an octave higher, on the 12th fret. Therefore, the pattern of notes and chords for each key runs upwards from the 12th fret in the same sequence as the open-string position. The diagrams below show the fingerboard to the 15th fret. Some guitars have twenty-four frets, which allow the pattern to be repeated.

C MAJOR
The scale uses the notes C, D, E, F, G, A, and B. The pattern from the open string to the 11th fret repeats from the 12th fret. The keynotes (C) are all marked as black dots.

G MAJOR
The scale uses the notes G, A, B, C, D, E, and F♯. The pattern from the open string to the 11th fret repeats from the 12th fret. The keynotes (G) are marked as black dots.

D MAJOR
The scale uses the notes D, E, F♯, G, A, B, and C♯. The pattern from the open string to the 11th fret repeats from the 12th fret. The keynotes (D) are marked as black dots.

A MAJOR
The scale uses the notes A, B, C♯, D, E, F♯, and G♯. The pattern from the open string to the 11th fret repeats from the 12th fret. The keynotes (A) are marked as black dots.

E MAJOR
The scale uses the notes E, F♯, G♯, A, B, C♯, and D♯. The pattern from the open string to the 11th fret repeats from the 12th fret. The keynotes (E) are marked as black dots.

B MAJOR
The scale uses the notes B, C♯, D♯, E, F♯, G♯, and A♯. The pattern from the open string to the 11th fret repeats from the 12th fret. The keynotes (B) are marked as black dots.

F♯/G♭ MAJOR

This scale uses the notes F♯, G♯, A♯, B, C♯, D♯, and E♯ (G♭, A♭, B♭, C♭, D♭, E♭, and F). The pattern from the open string to the 11th fret repeats from the 12th fret.

D♭ MAJOR

The notes used in this scale are D♭, E♭, F, G♭, A♭, B♭, and C. They form a pattern from the open string to the 11th fret; this repeats from the 12th fret. The keynotes (D♭) are marked as black dots.

A♭ MAJOR

The components of this scale are A♭, B♭, C, D♭, E♭, F, and G. The pattern from the open string to the 11th fret repeats from the 12th fret. The keynotes (A♭) are represented by black dots.

E♭ MAJOR

The notes used here are E♭, F, G, A♭, B♭, C, and D. As in the scales above, the pattern from the open string to the 11th fret repeats from the 12th fret. The keynotes (E♭) are shown as black dots.

B♭ MAJOR

This scale consists of the notes B♭, C, D, E♭, F, G, and A. Again, the pattern from the open string to the 11th fret repeats from the 12th fret, and the keynotes (B♭) are marked as black dots.

F MAJOR

The scale uses the notes F, G, A, B♭, C, D, and E. The pattern from the open string to the 11th fret repeats from the 12th fret. The keynotes (F) are all represented as black dots.

REFERENCE POINTS

When a scale is played or written down, there are a number of positions from which it can be started on the fingerboard. For example, C at one pitch level is on the 8th fret of the 6th string and the 3rd fret of the 5th string. From either of these points it can move up through its major scale by one octave to the 5th fret of the 3rd string, the 1st fret of the 2nd string, the 10th fret of the 4th string, or the 15th fret of the 5th string. The major scale can also be played on one string from each keynote – C on the 3rd fret of the 5th string can ascend to C on the 15th fret. Eight one-octave major scales are shown. Play each scale using different positions and fingering patterns. The choice of position depends on the context and the type of music.

C major
The scale at this pitch can be played using a number of fingering patterns from the 3rd fret of the 5th string and the 8th fret of the 6th string.

G major
To play the scale at this pitch, patterns from the 10th fret of the 5th string, the 5th fret of the 4th string, and the open G string may be used.

D major
The D scale can be played at this pitch by using patterns from the 10th fret of the 6th string, the 5th fret of the 5th string, and the open D string.

A major
The A scale at this pitch can be played using a number of fingering patterns from the 5th fret of the 6th string and the open A string.

E major
At this pitch, E major can be played from the 12th fret of the 6th string, the 7th fret of the 5th string, and the 2nd fret of the 4th string.

F major
This scale, at this pitch, can be played from the 13th fret of the 6th string, the 8th fret of the 5th string, and the 3rd fret of the 4th string.

B♭ major
The scale at this pitch can be played using a number of fingering patterns from the 6th fret of the 6th string and the 1st fret of the 5th string.

E♭ major
The E♭ major scale, at this pitch, can be played from the 11th fret of the 6th string, the 6th fret of the 5th string, and the 1st fret of the 4th string.

RIGHT-HAND TECHNIQUE

When the same scale is played in different positions it affects both the left and right hands. Three of the most commonly used left-hand scale patterns for one octave of C major are shown below. The type of pattern, and the number of notes on each string, will determine how right-hand technique should be used. The first of the examples has one note on the 5th string, three on the 4th string, two on the 3rd string, and two on the 2nd string. The second example has two notes on the 5th string, three on the 4th string, and three on the 3rd string. The third example has three notes on the 5th string, three on the 4th string, and two on the 3rd string. Facility in starting a scale passage with either the **I** or the **M** finger, and control over the fingers for note patterns across the strings, both need attention. When using a plectrum, picking direction varies according to the number of notes per string. Control of picking direction is essential for effective movement between the strings, especially when playing fast passages. A suggested approach to plectrum direction is shown under each of the scales.

OPEN-STRING POSITION

STANDARD POSITION

STRETCH POSITION

DEVELOPING CO-ORDINATION

One of the most effective approaches to developing control and technique is to break scalar passages down into their most basic movements. This lets the player concentrate fully on the co-ordination between the hands. More extensive combinations of notes may be developed in stages. Separation between the notes fingered by the left hand, and precise timing with the fingers or a plectrum held by the right hand, are vitally important. Changes in position, and the sequence in which the right hand strikes the notes, vary according to the type of passage. Repeating patterns and short motifs based on specific numbers of notes will bring different fingers back to play the same note. This also affects plectrum technique, where the same note is played with an upstroke or downstroke according to context. Moving to other strings with a plectrum often involves crossing a note which has just been played in order to sound the next string. With practice this should become a natural movement. Work slowly through each of the exercises that are shown below; practise both the alternative fingerings given for starting the patterns with the **I** or **M** fingers, or the suggested plectrum strokes.

Exercise 1 (C-D)
*Start with either **I** or **M**; alternate between the two. For a plectrum, start with a downstroke.*

Exercise 2 (B-C-D)
*Alternate between **I** and **M**, starting with either. Play with alternating plectrum direction.*

Exercise 3 (B-C-D-C-B)
*Begin the exercise with **I** or **M**; practise starting with either finger. If using a plectrum, play with alternating picking direction.*

Exercise 4 (B-C-D-B-C-D)
*Practise starting with **I** and **M**. Play with alternating plectrum direction, starting with a downstroke on the first three notes and an upstroke on the second three.*

Exercise 5 (C-D-E-D-C)
When playing this exercise with a plectrum, note that after striking D, the plectrum must move over D to play E, and over E to return to D.

Exercise 6 (B-C-D-E)
*Practise with both **I** and **M**, leading with either. Alternating plectrum direction is used for B-C-D.*

Exercise 7 (B-C-D-E-D-C-B)
*Alternate the **I** and **M** fingers, starting with either. Use alternating plectrum direction, and note that it is necessary to move back over the note E in order to descend to D.*

SCALE-TONE CHORDS

STANDARD EXTENSIONS IN EACH KEY

Chord harmonies
The structure and shape of every major key is the same in relation to the note that is used as the keynote, i.e., the first degree of the scale. Each major scale has a fixed system of chord harmonies. In the chart below, the chord types on each degree line up vertically. Five chord extensions – sixths, sevenths, ninths, elevenths, and thirteenths – are highlighted across the page by different-coloured bands.

The twelve keys each contain an extensive series of chord types. The basic system of chords in a particular key is created using the notes of the scale. In all keys, the seven scale notes are used to form the roots of the chord types. The chords in each key are assigned Roman numerals: **I** is the first note of the scale, **II** the second, **III** the third, **IV** the fourth, **V** the fifth, **VI** the sixth, and **VII** is the seventh. This system is repeated at every level in lower and higher octaves. The triads on the root notes are all extended. Their use and level of development depend on the style and form of the music and on the requirement for certain types of harmonic colour.

Comparing keys
The system below has up to five different chord types on each degree. Compare chords and their relationships in one key by transposing them to all the other keys, and reduce chords to triads. One chord type on a root also occurs in different keys. For example, D minor 7 is a **II** chord in C, a **VI** chord in F, and a **III** chord in Bb.

C MAJOR The major scale notes C, D, E, F, G, A, B, and C are written as the roots for each group of **I** to **VII** chords.

	I	II	III	IV	V	VI	VII	I
SIXTH	C MAJ 6	D MIN 6		F MAJ 6	G MAJ 6			C MAJ 6
SEVENTH	C MAJ 7	D MIN 7	E MIN 7	F MAJ 7	G 7	A MIN 7	B MIN 7b5	C MAJ 7
NINTH	C MAJ 9	D MIN 9		F MAJ 9	G9	A MIN 9		C MAJ 9
ELEVENTH		D MIN 11	E MIN 11	F MAJ 7#11	G11	A MIN 11	B MIN 11b5	
THIRTEENTH		D MIN 13			G13			

G MAJOR The major scale notes G, A, B, C, D, E, F#, and G are written as roots for each group of **I** to **VII** chords.

	I	II	III	IV	V	VI	VII	I
SIXTH	G MAJ 6	A MIN 6		C MAJ 6	D MAJ 6			G MAJ 6
SEVENTH	G MAJ 7	A MIN 7	B MIN 7	C MAJ 7	D 7	E MIN 7	F# MIN 7b5	G MAJ 7
NINTH	G MAJ 9	A MIN 9		C MAJ 9	D9	E MIN 9		G MAJ 9
ELEVENTH		A MIN 11	B MIN 11	C MAJ 7#11	D11	E MIN 11	F# MIN 11b5	
THIRTEENTH		A MIN 13			D13			

D MAJOR The major scale notes D, E, F#, G, A, B, C#, and D are written as roots for each group of **I** to **VII** chords.

	I	II	III	IV	V	VI	VII	I
SIXTH	D MAJ 6	E MIN 6		G MAJ 6	A MAJ 6			D MAJ 6
SEVENTH	D MAJ 7	E MIN 7	F# MIN 7	G MAJ 7	A 7	B MIN 7	C# MIN 7b5	D MAJ 7
NINTH	D MAJ 9	E MIN 9		G MAJ 9	A9	B MIN 9		D MAJ 9
ELEVENTH		E MIN 11	F# MIN 11	G MAJ 7#11	A11	B MIN 11	C# MIN 11b5	
THIRTEENTH		E MIN 13			A13			

A MAJOR The major scale notes A, B, C#, D, E, F#, G#, and A are written as roots for each group of **I** to **VII** chords.

	I	II	III	IV	V	VI	VII	I
SIXTH	A MAJ 6	B MIN 6		D MAJ 6	E MAJ 6			A MAJ 6
SEVENTH	A MAJ 7	B MIN 7	C# MIN 7	D MAJ 7	E 7	F# MIN 7	G# MIN 7b5	A MAJ 7
NINTH	A MAJ 9	B MIN 9		D MAJ 9	E9	F# MIN 9		A MAJ 9
ELEVENTH		B MIN 11	C# MIN 11	D MAJ 7#11	E11	F# MIN 11	G# MIN 11b5	
THIRTEENTH		B MIN 13			E13			

E MAJOR The major scale notes E, F#, G#, A, B, C#, D#, and E are written as roots for each group of **I** to **VII** chords.

	I	II	III	IV	V	VI	VII	I
SIXTH	E MAJ 6	F# MIN 6		A MAJ 6	B MAJ 6			E MAJ 6
SEVENTH	E MAJ 7	F# MIN 7	G# MIN 7	A MAJ 7	B 7	C# MIN 7	D# MIN 7b5	E MAJ 7
NINTH	E MAJ 9	F# MIN 9		A MAJ 9	B9	C# MIN 9		E MAJ 9
ELEVENTH		F# MIN 11	G# MIN 11	A MAJ 7#11	B11	C# MIN 11	D# MIN 11b5	
THIRTEENTH		F# MIN 13			B13			

B MAJOR The major scale notes B, C#, D#, E, F#, G#, A#, and B are written as roots for each group of **I** to **VII** chords.

	I	II	III	IV	V	VI	VII	I
SIXTH	B MAJ 6	C# MIN 6		E MAJ 6	F# MAJ 6			B MAJ 6
SEVENTH	B MAJ 7	C# MIN 7	D# MIN 7	E MAJ 7	F# 7	G# MIN 7	A# MIN 7b5	B MAJ 7
NINTH	B MAJ 9	C# MIN 9		E MAJ 9	F#9	G# MIN 9		B MAJ 9
ELEVENTH		C# MIN 11	D# MIN 11	E MAJ 7#11	F#11	G# MIN 11	A# MIN 11b5	
THIRTEENTH		C# MIN 13			F#13			

ENHARMONIC CHORDS

Chords are generally written down with a root letter relating to a key. The overlap of the F♯ and G♭ major scales results in the same chords given different letter designations. For example, F♯ major 7 is identical to G♭ major 7. The way the chord is named is largely dependent on context. In a harmonic modulation from a flat key, G♭ would be the more appropriate chord name. If a piece of music using this chord is related to a sharp key, F♯ would be used. The labelling of *enharmonically* identical chords can depend on the role of the guitar with other instruments. In music with frequent modulations, different letter names for chords are often written in a manner that can appear arbitrary. For example, G♯ minor 7 may be written as A♭ minor 7. Music in chord symbol form can, therefore, be written in two ways. For example, A minor 7, A♭ minor 7, G minor 7, G♭ 7, and F major 7 can also be written as A minor 7, G♯ minor 7, G minor 7, F♯7, and F major 7 respectively. The ability to understand this ambiguous labelling is very important in reading music.

F♯ major
The major scale notes F♯, G♯, A♯, B, C♯, D♯, E♯, and F♯ are written for the roots in each group of the chords I to VII. E♯ is the same as F.

	I	II	III	IV	V	VI	VII	I
SIXTH	F♯ MAJ 6	G♯ MIN 6		B MAJ 6	C♯ MAJ 6			F♯ MAJ 6
SEVENTH	F♯ MAJ 7	G♯ MIN 7	A♯ MIN 7	B MAJ 7	C♯ 7	D♯ MIN 7	E♯ MIN 7♭5	F♯ MAJ 7
NINTH	F♯ MAJ 9	G♯ MIN 9		B MAJ 9	C♯ 9	D♯ MIN 9		F♯ MAJ 9
ELEVENTH		G♯ MIN 11	A♯ MIN 11	B MAJ 7♯11	C♯ 11	D♯ MIN 11	E♯ MIN 11♭5	
THIRTEENTH		G♯ MIN 13			C♯ 13			

G♭ major
The major scale notes G♭, A♭, B♭, C♭, D♭, E♭, F, and G♭ are written for the roots in each group of the chords I to VII. C♭ is the same as B.

	I	II	III	IV	V	VI	VII	I
SIXTH	G♭ MAJ 6	A♭ MIN 6		C♭ MAJ 6	D♭ MAJ 6			G♭ MAJ 6
SEVENTH	G♭ MAJ 7	A♭ MIN 7	B♭ MIN 7	C♭ MAJ 7	D♭ 7	E♭ MIN 7	F MIN 7♭5	G♭ MAJ 7
NINTH	G♭ MAJ 9	A♭ MIN 9		C♭ MAJ 9	D♭ 9	E♭ MIN 9		G♭ MAJ 9
ELEVENTH		A♭ MIN 11	B♭ MIN 11	C♭ MAJ 7♯11	D♭ 11	E♭ MIN 11	F MIN 11♭5	
THIRTEENTH		A♭ MIN 13			D♭ 13			

D♭ MAJOR The major scale notes D♭, E♭, F, G♭, A♭, B♭, C, and D♭ are written as roots for each group of I to VII chords.

	I	II	III	IV	V	VI	VII	I
SIXTH	D♭ MAJ 6	E♭ MIN 6		G♭ MAJ 6	A♭ MAJ 6			D♭ MAJ 6
SEVENTH	D♭ MAJ 7	E♭ MIN 7	F MIN 7	G♭ MAJ 7	A♭ 7	B♭ MIN 7	C MIN 7♭5	D♭ MAJ 7
NINTH	D♭ MAJ 9	E♭ MIN 9		G♭ MAJ 9	A♭ 9	B♭ MIN 9		D♭ MAJ 9
ELEVENTH		E♭ MIN 11	F MIN 11	G♭ MAJ 7♯11	A♭ 11	B♭ MIN 11	C MIN 11♭5	
THIRTEENTH		E♭ MIN 13			A♭ 13			

A♭ MAJOR The major scale notes A♭, B♭, C, D♭, E♭, F, G, and A♭ are written as roots for each group of I to VII chords.

	I	II	III	IV	V	VI	VII	I
SIXTH	A♭ MAJ 6	B♭ MIN 6		D♭ MAJ 6	E♭ MAJ 6			A♭ MAJ 6
SEVENTH	A♭ MAJ 7	B♭ MIN 7	C MIN 7	D♭ MAJ 7	E♭ 7	F MIN 7	G MIN 7♭5	A♭ MAJ 7
NINTH	A♭ MAJ 9	B♭ MIN 9		D♭ MAJ 9	E♭ 9	F MIN 9		A♭ MAJ 9
ELEVENTH		B♭ MIN 11	C MIN 11	D♭ MAJ 7♯11	E♭ 11	F MIN 11	G MIN 11♭5	
THIRTEENTH		B♭ MIN 13			E♭ 13			

E♭ MAJOR The major scale notes E♭, F, G♭, A♭, B♭, C, D, and E♭ are written as roots for each group of I to VII chords.

	I	II	III	IV	V	VI	VII	I
SIXTH	E♭ MAJ 6	F MIN 6		A♭ MAJ 6	B♭ MAJ 6			E♭ MAJ 6
SEVENTH	E♭ MAJ 7	F MIN 7	G MIN 7	A♭ MAJ 7	B♭ 7	C MIN 7	D MIN 7♭5	E♭ MAJ 7
NINTH	E♭ MAJ 9	F MIN 9		A♭ MAJ 9	B♭ 9	C MIN 9		E♭ MAJ 9
ELEVENTH		F MIN 11	G MIN 11	A♭ MAJ 7♯11	B♭ 11	C MIN 11	D MIN 11♭5	
THIRTEENTH		F MIN 13			B♭ 13			

B♭ MAJOR The major scale notes B♭, C, D, E♭, F, G, A, and B♭ are written as roots for each group of I to VII chords.

	I	II	III	IV	V	VI	VII	I
SIXTH	B♭ MAJ 6	C MIN 6		E♭ MAJ 6	F MAJ 6			B♭ MAJ 6
SEVENTH	B♭ MAJ 7	C MIN 7	D MIN 7	E♭ MAJ 7	F 7	G MIN 7	A MIN 7♭5	B♭ MAJ 7
NINTH	B♭ MAJ 9	C MIN 9		E♭ MAJ 9	F 9	G MIN 9		B♭ MAJ 9
ELEVENTH		C MIN 11	D MIN 11	E♭ MAJ 7♯11	F 11	G MIN 11	A MIN 11♭5	
THIRTEENTH		C MIN 13			F 13			

F MAJOR The major scale notes F, G, A, B♭, C, D, E, and F are written as roots for each group of I to VII chords.

	I	II	III	IV	V	VI	VII	I
SIXTH	F MAJ 6	G MIN 6		B♭ MAJ 6	C MAJ 6			F MAJ 6
SEVENTH	F MAJ 7	G MIN 7	A MIN 7	B♭ MAJ 7	C 7	D MIN 7	E MIN 7♭5	F MAJ 7
NINTH	F MAJ 9	G MIN 9		B♭ MAJ 9	C 9	D MIN 9		F MAJ 9
ELEVENTH		G MIN 11	A MIN 11	B♭ MAJ 7♯11	C 11	D MIN 11	E MIN 11♭5	
THIRTEENTH		G MIN 13			C 13			

HARMONIC RESOLUTION

THE V–I MOVEMENT AND ITS VARIATIONS

Transposition
The resolutions in this section should be played in every key. Take any I chord and count five steps up the scale to the V chord, and play it as a dominant seventh.

The movement from a dominant (**V**) to a tonic (**I**) chord is an important part of chordal harmony. It is a central mechanism in jazz music. Although **V-I** is a resolution

with a full close sound used for endings, it is also treated as part of a flowing movement of chordal harmony. It is frequently preceded by a **II** chord of the related key.

Using the cycle of fourths
From a dominant chord, resolve to a I chord using the cycle of fourths. Convert this I chord to a dominant seventh, and resolve this to the next chord a fourth away

---

THE LEADING NOTE

The seventh note of the C major scale, the *leading note* B, tends to resolve naturally to C (the tonic). B is the third of the dominant (**V**) chord, and the movement from B to C can be heard in the **V-I** resolution, when the third of the dominant chord of G major resolves to the root note of the tonic, C major. The fourth (F) has a strong tendency to resolve harmonically. When included as a seventh within the dominant chord, it moves to E, the third of the scale and the tonic chord.

Leading note (B)
The movement B to C can be heard using a two-note **V** chord. With G and B this resolves C major. The bass moves up a fourth – G to C.

Fourth note (F)
F, the fourth note, often falls to E. Play C major with F, and move F down to E. As the seventh in the G dominant seventh chord, it falls in **V-I**.

Tritone
The combination of F and B sets up a strong tension which needs to resolve. The notes have three tones between them, referred to as a "tritone".

Resolutions
The tritone interval is the same when F is placed above B. Each note must still move by a semitone for resolution.

Intervals
F above B has a tritone interval of a diminished fifth. F below B is an augmented fourth tritone.

Resolving both tritones
When F is below B, the two notes resolve to a C major chord. With F above B, the same movement can lead to a Gb/F# chord. The resolution to this chord can be used with F below B, and the movement is similar with F over B, resolving to C.

Tritone resolving to Gb/F#
The tritone, as two notes resolving in different directions, can lead to a movement to either C or Gb/F#. Compare these movements to the major chords above.

DOMINANT SEVENTH RESOLUTIONS

The tritone is now played in a number of different settings, where it is used within dominant chords as an important part of the structural resolution. The notes B and F are the third and the seventh of the G dominant seventh chord. As a tritone, these notes can be used to resolve the G dominant seventh chord to a C or a Gb (F#) chord, a semitone below. Gb major is normally preceded by a **V** dominant in its own key. The **V** chord in Gb major is Db major, or Db dominant seventh. The Db dominant seventh contains the notes F and B (Cb) as a third and seventh. Therefore, the Db dominant seventh chord resolves to Gb. With this tritone, it can also resolve down a semitone to a C chord. In everyday use, this overlap of dominant chordal harmony is used to vary the approach to a tonic I chord.

Note names Cb has been written as B natural for convenience.

Flat five harmony
When G is replaced by Db, the roots are a flattened fifth apart. Compare the movements of G7 to C or Gb major, and Db7 to C or Gb major.

Full voicings
With full voicings, movements from altered flat five chords must be made carefully. Play the **V-I** resolutions above. Compare Db7 to C major, and G7 to Gb major.

THE FLAT FIVE CHORD

The dominant seventh chord can be modified by moving the fifth note down a semitone. The chord G 7♭5 (G *dominant seventh flat five*) consists of G (root), B (third), D♭ (flat five), and an F (seventh). D♭ 7♭5 consists of D♭, F, G, and B(C♭). Both chords share these four notes and, under certain conditions, are interchangeable. The flat five is also written as a *sharp eleven* (G7#11).

G7 This root voicing is G-F-B-D.

G7♭5 This root voicing is G-F-B-D♭.

D♭7/A♭ This inversion is A♭-F-B-D♭.

D♭7♭5 This inversion is G-F-B-D♭. This chord shares the same notes as G7♭5.

THE II-V-I MOVEMENT

The movement from **V** to **I** is preceded by the **II** chord creating an extended approach with many variations. In C major this basic chord movement is D minor, G major, and C major. The **II** chord is sometimes an inversion of **IV** or **V** before it moves towards C. The **V-I** movement is developed using all of the scale note extensions of the **V** chord, and all those of the **I** chord except F. The added **II** chord uses all of its extensions.

II-♭V-I

A **II-V-I** movement is often played with a flat five (♭**V**). The root drops in semitones from D to D♭ to C. This creates a chromatic effect. These chord voicings sometimes descend against fixed upper notes.

INVERSIONS

Any chord can be inverted by taking the constituent notes and using an alternative voice for a bass note. If C major has the third (E) in the bass, and the other notes above, the voicing is termed a *first inversion* (shown as C/E). If the voicing has G in the bass, it is a *second inversion* (C/G).

First inversion | Second inversion

G dominant 7 This chord can be voiced as a root, first, second, and third inversion.

INVERSIONS IN RESOLUTIONS

Inversions are often used on the guitar for chord movements. They often use shared pivotal notes. Play G to C in the first example as a chord change over the same bass note. The second example uses a first inversion of G. The third example uses a second inversion. The fourth example uses a second inversion to resolve G to a first inversion of C.

THE MINOR SYSTEM

UNDERSTANDING MINOR SCALES

Intervals
The natural Aeolian minor scale has the following intervals from the root: major second, minor third, perfect fourth, perfect fifth, minor sixth, and minor seventh. The harmonic minor has a major seventh from the root which acts as the leading note in the scale. In comparison with the major scale, the harmonic minor has a minor 3rd and a minor 6th.

After the major scale, the most important scale system is the minor scale. This is based on the Aeolian minor mode on the sixth degree of the major scale. On every major scale, a minor scale may be played from the sixth note. In the key of C major, the scale begins on A. The resulting minor scale, which uses the notes A-B-C-D-E-F-G, is known as the *natural minor*. A sharp may be added to this scale, to raise the seventh degree by a semitone: the series of notes becomes A-B-C-D-E-F-G♯. This closely related scale is referred to as the *harmonic minor*. The addition of G♯ allows the minor scale to be used with harmonic resolutions that move to the tonic on the first note, A.

The relative minor
All major scales have a relative minor key with a scale and group of chords based around a minor keynote. The notes and chords are assigned Roman numerals (I–VII) in relation to the minor keynote. There are three different types of relative minor scale: they are the natural Aeolian minor, the harmonic minor, and the melodic minor.

A minor Aeolian scale
This is the natural minor scale. It starts on A and uses the notes of the C major scale starting from the sixth degree.

A minor harmonic scale
This scale starts on A and uses the notes of the C major scale except G natural, which is raised a semitone to G♯.

A NATURAL MINOR (AEOLIAN)

A HARMONIC MINOR

MINOR TRIADS
Natural minor triads from A are the same as those in C major, but they start from a different point. The *harmonic* minor triads are altered by the inclusion of G♯.

Harmonic minor arpeggios
Play through the triads of the harmonic minor system, noting the G sharps, and compare with the natural minor system.

Natural minor triads
The series of C triads on the left starts on the note A, which is a sixth above, or a third below, C.

Harmonic minor triads
By repeating the series with the addition of G♯, the third, fifth, and seventh triads are altered.

Hearing the change
Play through the series of arpeggios, paying special attention to the sound of G♯ on the third, fifth, and seventh arpeggios.

Adding a seventh
The harmonic minor series of triads can be extended with the addition of a seventh to each triad. This process is similar to the addition of sevenths to the major scale triads. The extra note is an interval of a third above the fifth on each triad. Adding a G♯ generates unusual harmonies on the I, III, and VII degrees.

Diminished chords
The diminished seventh chord on the seventh note of the scale has minor third intervals between the root, third, fifth, seventh, and octave root. Using this structure, any note can be used as the root of a chord. Diminished sevenths with roots of B, D, F, and G♯ (shown on the bottom line) all have the same notes, and are inversions of each other.

HARMONIC MINOR CHORDS

The harmonic minor system of chords can be extended to a series of sixths, sevenths, diminished sevenths, ninths, and further types. Some of these minor chords sound unusual, and have limited applications. They appear in sections of minor harmony, and are used for contrasting major and minor chordal movements.

	SIXTH	SEVENTH	DIMINISHED	NINTH	OTHER TYPES	
A		A MIN/MAJ7		A MIN/MAJ9	A MIN/MAJ11	
B		B MIN7♭5	B DIM7		B MIN11♭5	
C		C MAJ7♯5			C MAJ9♯5	C6♯5
D	D MIN6	D MIN7	D DIM7	D MIN9	D MIN7♭5	D MIN11♭5
E		E7		E7♭9	E7♯5	E7♯5♭9 · E7
F	F6	F MAJ7	F DIM7		F MIN/MAJ7	F MAJ7♯11
G♯		G♯ DIM7	G♯ DIM7		G♯DIM7 ADD E	

NATURAL AND HARMONIC MINORS

As an exercise in understanding the differences between natural and harmonic minor chords, play the series of seventh chords shown on the right. Compare the sound and structure of the chords when they are played as a sequence. The first chord is a minor chord with a major seventh. This is used in combination with a standard minor seventh in some progressions. The third chord sounds unusual and consequently is often avoided. The fifth chord is a dominant seventh. It acts as a **V** chord, and resolves to A minor 7 as a **V-I**. The minor **I** chord needs to use G♯ for resolution. The B minor 7♭5 is used in the scale as a **II** chord. This chord precedes **V** in a minor **II-V-I** sequence.

THE MELODIC MINOR SCALE

The melodic minor is the natural minor with the sixth and seventh notes raised a semitone. The diagrams below show three scales with an A keynote. The A harmonic minor scale has a distinctive sound, with a minor third interval between the sixth note (F) and the seventh note (G♯). This is very effective for certain types of music, and can impart an ethnic folk sound to minor passages. The melodic minor is a harmonic minor scale with a raised sixth degree, F♯, restoring a smooth movement of tone and semitone intervals. In short passages or in certain other contexts, the melodic minor can sound too close to the A major scale.

To keep a minor effect, the melodic minor is often played as a natural minor when descending. Compare the scales below. The melodic minor can be played in association with the harmonic minor and the ascending natural minor. The ascending melodic minor shares six notes with A major, but they are not closely related harmonically.

MELODIC AND FIXED MELODIC SCALES

The melodic minor scale has a different series of notes depending on the direction in which it is being played. In the key of A minor, the notes A, B, C, D, E, F♯, G♯, and A are played when ascending, and A, G, F, E, D, C, B, and A are played when descending. A fixed melodic minor scale, retaining the F♯ and G♯ in its descending form, is often used. The fixed melodic minor in A uses these raised notes for all types of movement. It has the character of an altered scale and, with its subsidiary modal scales from each point, is frequently used in ethnic folk, jazz, and classical music.

Melodic minor (up)
The melodic minor scale in the key of A incorporates the notes F♯ and G♯ as it moves up the scale.

Melodic minor (down)
The melodic minor scale in A uses the notes F and G with different fingering as it moves downwards.

Fixed melodic minor
The fixed melodic scale in the key of A uses the notes F♯ and G♯ as it moves in either direction.

MELODIC MINOR CHORDS

When the melodic minor is used for building harmony, the addition of F♯ creates a new series of chords. The triads and sevenths from the note A should be compared with the harmonic minor chords. There are three new triads and four new melodic minor seventh types. The melodic minor chords, with the inclusion of F♯, are further removed from C major harmony.

MAJOR/RELATIVE MINOR SCALE CHART

The major scale is the starting point for the minor system: each of the major scales has its own relative minor scale. The movement from major to minor is a shift in tonal centre. For example, in the second column below, the G major scale is played from E to E. The note E acts as the new tonal centre for the key of E minor. The minor key has a scale that is modified with the addition of a raised seventh to create harmonic sequences with resolutions to a tonal centre. The melodic

minor has a raised sixth as well as a seventh for ascending melodic movement, and the natural (Aeolian) scale for descending movement. The major/relative minor keys shown across the chart below are C major/A minor, G major/E minor, D major/B minor, A major/F♯ minor, E major/C♯ minor, B major/G♯ minor, G♭ major/E♭ minor, D♭ major/B♭ minor, A♭ major/F minor, E♭ major/C minor, B♭ major/G minor, and F major/D minor. The enharmonic equivalents for G♭ are not shown on the chart.

The major scale (below, first row)
The major scale has the following series of intervals: tone (major 2nd), tone, semitone (minor 2nd), tone, tone, tone, and semitone. There are seven modes in each major scale: Ionian, Dorian, Phrygian, Lydian, Mixolydian, Aeolian, and Locrian. The Ionian scale is the major scale – its first note is the major keynote. The Aeolian scale is the natural minor – its first note is the minor keynote. The major scales below follow the cycle of fifths in the keys of C, G, D, A, E, B, G♭ (F♯), D♭, A♭, E♭, B♭, and F.

MELODIC MINOR CHORDS

The melodic system can be extended. It is often used for minor harmony and altered modal scales in jazz, and for compositional structures in other areas of music. Certain chords are used in substitution: they are replaced by a voicing using another root note. For example, D7#11 and G#7#11 may sometimes be interchangeable.

	TRIAD	SIXTH	SEVENTH	NINTH	ELEVENTH	OTHER TYPES	
A	A MIN	A MIN6	A MIN/MAJ7	A MIN/MAJ9	A MIN/MAJ11		
B	B MIN	B MIN6	B MIN7		B MIN11		
C	C AUG		C MAJ7#5	C MAJ9#5	C MAJ7#5#11		
D	D MAJ	D6	D7	D9	D7#11	D13#11	
E	E MAJ		E7	E9	E11	E7#5	E9#5
F#	F# DIM		F# MIN7♭5	F# MIN9♭5	F# MIN11♭5		
G#	G# DIM		G# MIN7♭5		G#7#11	G#7#5	

COMPARING MINOR SCALES

The various forms of the minor scale as a relative system to the major scale are compared on the right. The chart shows the fingerboard from the nut up to the 7th fret. The circles mark the position of the notes in the A minor natural scale, running from open E on the 6th string to B on the 1st string. These are the same as the notes of the C major scale. The shifted circles shown with an arrow indicate that the notes G and F are raised by a semitone to G# and F#. The exercises should be played through the position in C major/A minor, A harmonic minor, A melodic minor, and A fixed melodic minor.

HARMONIC MINOR

MELODIC MINOR

The natural minor scale (below, second row)
This is the Aeolian mode of the major scale, which starts on the sixth (submediant) degree. The natural minor scale has the following series of intervals: tone (major 2nd), semitone (minor 2nd), tone, tone, semitone, tone, and tone. The minor scales shown start a minor third below the major scale. Following each major scale, find the relative minor keynote by counting three notes down, or six notes up, from the keynote of the major scale. For example, F major to D minor is F-E-D descending, or F-G-A-B♭-C-D ascending.

The harmonic minor scale (below, third row)
This is an altered Aeolian mode of the major scale, starting on the sixth (submediant) degree. It differs from the natural minor in that it has a raised seventh. To raise natural notes, a sharp is used; with flats, a natural is used. The harmonic minor scale has the following series of intervals: tone (major 2nd), semitone (minor 2nd), tone, tone, semitone, tone+semitone (minor third), and semitone. The minor scales follow a cycle of fifths from left to right. The harmonic minor scale begins on the same note as the natural Aeolian minor.

The melodic minor (below, fourth row)
This is based on the Aeolian mode of the major scale, starting on the sixth degree. It has sixths and sevenths raised by sharps. Flats are raised by naturals. The melodic minor scale has the following series of intervals: tone (major 2nd), semitone (minor 2nd), tone, tone, tone, tone, and semitone. In its descending form, the intervals from the keynote are: tone, tone, semitone, tone, tone, semitone, and tone. The fixed melodic keeps the ascending series of notes in the descending scale.

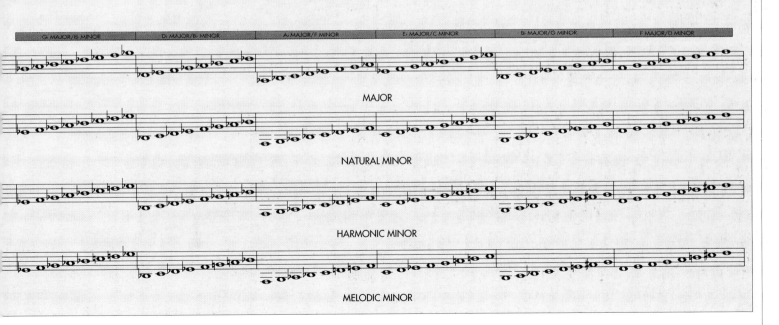

MAJOR

NATURAL MINOR

HARMONIC MINOR

MELODIC MINOR

THE HARMONIC MINOR SCALE

A two-octave A minor harmonic scale can be played from either the open 5th string or the 5th fret of the 6th string. It normally ascends through two octaves to A on the 5th fret of the 1st string. There are a number of fingering positions for the minor harmonic scale. Three of them are shown below with a fingerboard diagram and tablature, and with the two-octave scale on the stave.

THE MELODIC MINOR SCALE

A two-octave A minor melodic scale is also played from either the open 5th string or the 5th fret of the 6th string. It normally ascends through two octaves to A on the 5th fret of the 1st string Fingering for the minor melodic scale can be approached as altered harmonic minor fingerings, or as altered major fingerings. Two positions are shown with fingerboard diagrams and tablature.

Open-string position

This position, starting on open A, ascends using all the open strings apart from G: this is raised to G#. The three-fret jump on the 1st string may be difficult to accomplish at first.

Open-string position

This fingering pattern starts on the open A strin It ascends smoothly, with F# and G#, in tone and semitone steps, and uses all of the open strings apart from G.

5th-fret position

Starting on the 5th fret of the 6th string, play across the fretboard, shifting down to the 4th fret of the 3rd string. This fingering should be played without moving the thumb position.

5th-fret stretch positic

The minor melodic scale in A can be played from the 5th fret. Play C on the 5th string with the first finger This position requires a wide stretch between the first and second fingers.

5th-fret stretch position

Play this scale from the 5th fret. The notes C and F are played by the first finger. This position requires a wide stretch between the first and second, and the first and third fingers.

Major to melodic

The pattern above can be compared to the fingering patterns for major scales. Play C♮, with the first finger on the 5th string and the second finger on the 3rd string.

TRANSPOSING MINOR SCALES

The harmonic and melodic minor scales can be played from all keynotes by moving a position along the fingerboard as a block. If the A minor positions are moved up by four frets, the first note of the scale becomes C#. The harmonic and melodic fingering positions in C# minor are played using the same shape as the scale starting on A. Try transposing the scale patterns; start from the 5th string.

G HARMONIC   C# HARMONIC

G MELODIC   C# MELODIC

Transposing the harmonic minor scale

This fingering position can be moved along the 6th string using each fret as a keynote. The lined blocks show the positions for harmonic minor scales in the keys of G and C#.

Transposing the melodic minor scale

Any fingering position can be moved along the 6th string using each fret as a keynote. The lined areas show the positions for melodic minor scales in the keys of G and C#.

SINGLE-NOTE EXERCISES

DEVELOPING SCALE AND INTERVAL TECHNIQUE

Transposition
Most exercises in this section are based on a one-octave C major pattern. When the patterns become familiar, they can be played in other keys by moving the block up and down the fingerboard. Try extending the patterns to more than one octave, and converting them to modal and minor scales.

Major scales are simply orders of successive tones in a series of seconds. To vary scales, intervals greater than a second need to be introduced. Using different intervals results in countless variations on the scale pattern. Simple patterns are ideal for developing fingering technique and the facility to play a wide range of melodies. Exercises such as the ones shown on the next three pages are often used as a basis for improvisational technique. Practise them slowly at first, taking care over each element. Speed should be built up gradually.

Visual guide
Fingerboard diagrams of the exercises have been included to help familiarize the player with note positions and their overall pattern. C major scale notes are marked with white circles. The elements of each exercise are indicated by black circles: their note names are marked beneath each fingerboard diagram.

Three-note exercise
Move up and down the scale in groups of three notes. Play C-D-E, move back down to D, and then play D-E-F. Ascend using this pattern. The descending pattern moves down in a similar fashion, using three-note groups.

Four-note exercises
Move up and down the scale in groups of four notes. Play C-D-E-F, move back down by an interval of a third to the note D, and play D-E-F-G. The descending pattern moves down in a similar fashion, using four-note groups.

Exercise in thirds
This exercise shows major and minor thirds. Play C to E, then move back down to D, followed by F. When the top C has been reached, begin to descend by playing C to A, move up to B and play B to G, and continue.

Exercise in fourths

A pattern of ascending and descending fourths is difficult to play at first. Play C to F, move down a third to D, and play D to G. When top C is reached, descend by playing C to G, move back to B, and play B to F.

Ascending fourths

Five movements in intervals of fourths are used to reach C in one octave. To show the principles of this and similar exercises, the first three of these movements are shown above as notes on a fingerboard.

Descending fourths The exercise should be repeated in reverse descending an octave from C.

Triad arpeggios

This exercise uses arpeggios based on triads of the major scale. Play C-E-G, move down a fourth to D, and play D-F-A. Four arpeggios are used to reach top C. Descend with C-A-F, move up a fourth to B, and play B-G-E.

Ascending arpeggios

Four three-note ascending arpeggios are used to reach top C. The first three elements are shown above.

Descending arpeggios The arpeggios shown in the exercise on the far left should now be played descending from C-A-F to G-E-C.

Triads and scales

Arpeggios and scales are combined in this exercise. Play C-E-G, descend using F and E to the note D, and play the arpeggio, D-F-A. Descend with C-A-F, move back up using G and A to B, and play the next arpeggio B-G-E.

Three-note exercise with fourths

An ascending three-note pattern with fourths is played by starting on E, the third note of the scale. Play E, D, and C, move up to F, and play F, E, and D. The descending pattern starts on A. Play A-B-C. Move down a fourth to G and play G-A-B.

Seventh arpeggios

This exercise extends the three-note arpeggio to sevenths based on the major scale. Play C-E-G-B, move down a sixth to D, and play D-F-A-C. Three arpeggios are played using the note D on the 2nd string. Descend with D-B-G-E, move up a sixth to C, and play C-A-F-D.

Ascending seventh arpeggios
Two four-note arpeggios, extended to include the seventh, can be used to reach the octave. The third arpeggio extends the exercise beyond one octave.

Descending seventh arpeggios Starting on the note D, four arpeggios are used to descend.

Exercise in seconds and thirds

This exercise moves up and down the scale by playing three notes in a pattern of seconds and thirds. Play C-D-F, move down to D, and play D-E-G. In a descending form play C-A-G, move back up to B, and play B-G-F.

Variations on seconds and thirds

This exercise moves up and down the scale by playing three-note patterns of seconds and thirds. Play C-E-F, move down to D, and play D-F-G. In a descending form play C-B-G, move back up to B, and play B-A-F.

Intervals

Play the series of scale intervals from the bottom C to the top C. Start with C to D (second), C to E (third), and move from the smallest interval to the octave. Descend from the top C. Play C to B, followed by C to A.

Ascending scale intervals
Seven two-note movements, in increasing intervals, are used to ascend through one octave.

Fourth finger The descending movement from C to B can also be played with the fourth finger.

TECHNIQUES AND EFFECTS

PLAYING TECHNIQUES TO INCREASE THE RANGE OF SOUNDS AND TEXTURES

Hammering and pulling-off
The use of hammering and pulling off (see p. 56) is an extremely important technique in guitar playing. It allows music to be played with a flowing quality, and nuances in control and phrasing which cannot be achieved by picking every note out individually.

The guitar has a rich and varied range of tonal colours and sounds. These can be brought out by using a number of techniques involving alterations to notes, such as string bending and the use of tremolo arms, slides, hammering, and pull-offs. Trills, mordants, and other ornaments can also be used to embellish the sound of simple melodies. Play a scale, making use of all the textures: vibrato on each note, staccato, and varying degrees of muting and sustain.

Sliding
Practise sliding up and down the fingerboard as a way of moving from one position to another. Try to play a scale on one string with each finger in turn, sliding from note to note. This exercise will help to increase control and develop flexibility in left-hand movements.

THE SLIDE

To achieve this effect, one finger is used to slide notes in pitch up and down the fingerboard. Strike the note F, and then slide with the first finger up to the note G on the 3rd fret *without* releasing the pressure. This makes the note ascend in pitch. This process can also be used to descend from G to F by striking G and sliding down to F.

SLIDE WITH STRUCK NOTE

Strike the note F on the 1st fret of the 1st string. Slide the finger up to G on the 3rd fret, and strike the note. Reverse these movements to play a descending slide: play the note G, then slide the finger down to F and strike the note. Try another slide, ascending and descending over a single fret from F to F#. Extend it to a minor third, using G# on the 4th fret.

SLIDING UP TO A NOTE

This variation on the slide is produced by playing a note only after sliding the finger up from any fret position below it. Try sliding up to the note A on the 5th fret by placing the first finger on the 4th fret *without* playing the note, and sliding the finger up to the 5th fret where the note is then played. Repeat this exercise for all of the lower fret positions.

SLIDE WITH TRAIL-OFF

Strike a note and slide up or down three or four of frets, releasing the pressure at any time. This technique gives the effect of a note moving quickly up or down in pitch and then fading away. Extend the slide over a greater number of frets, and again release the pressure on the string at any point so that the sound dies away.

PORTAMENTO AND GLISSANDO

These techniques are based on the slide. *Glissando* is a type of movement that allows every note to be heard in an ascending or descending slide. This is often referred to as *portamento* on a guitar. The first and last notes are both struck. Passages of sliding notes may also be controlled in a way that emphasises certain points.

HAMMER-ON

The finger movements for this technique are the same as those for the *ligado* (see p. 56). Play F on the 1st fret with the first finger. While this note is ringing, place the third finger on the 3rd fret. As the third finger hits the 3rd fret, the *hammering* action causes G to sound. More than one note can be played by hammering.

PULL-OFF

This is a descending ligado. A note is struck and one or more subsequent lower notes are then sounded by pulling-off the fretted fingers. Place the first finger on the 1st fret, and the third finger on the 3rd fret. Play G on the 3rd fret, then take away the third finger, pulling the string downwards. This will sound F on the 1st fret.

HAMMERING A NOTE

Notes can be played on the guitar without strumming or plucking with the right hand. When any left-hand fingers are placed on a fret, the movement of the finger pressing the note against the fingerboard causes the note to ring. If this movement is made with more attack, notes can be sounded clearly. Try playing G and then pulling it off to sound open G.

THE TRILL

A trill is a very fast alternating movement between notes fretted by the fingers of the left hand. In essence it is a type of fast hammering technique combined with pull-offs. Play the note F then hammer G. Use a pull-off from G to sound F again. Play these notes as one rapid movement. Try playing a downward trill from G to E.

BENDING

Strike the note A, on the 5th fret of the 1st string, and bend the string upwards as it rings, to raise the pitch of the note. This technique is used to raise the pitch from microtonal nuances through to intervals as large as a third in blues playing. Try bending the note A one semitone to B♭.

PRE-BEND AND RELEASE

Hold down the note A on the 5th fret, then bend it up to a B♭ position *without* playing it. Hold it in position and strike the note. While it is ringing, pull the string back to its fret position, keeping the finger pressure on. This requires practice. It must be bent to positions where it is effective.

ACCIACCATURA AND APPOGGIATURA

The *acciaccatura* (or *crushed note*) is played very quickly just before a principal note. Play the note F *very* quickly just before playing G. The *appoggiatura* is also placed just before a principal note. It has half the time value of the note that it precedes.

MUTED NOTES

The letter **X** written at the end of a stem is a direction to play the strings percussively. Lay the left hand lightly across the strings in order to mute them, and play the notes; this produces a deadened sound. The palm of the right hand can also be used to muffle fretted notes to the point where they lose tonal quality.

TREMOLO PICKING

When a note is written with one or more small bars placed across the stem, the player is directed to repeat the note rapidly and continuously for the duration of its time value. Two bars indicate very fast movement. Try this technique, using either fast plectrum picking or right-hand **I** and **M** fingering.

MORDANTS

The two kinds of *mordant* are used as abbreviations for embellishments. The *upper mordant* represents an instruction to play the note itself, a note above it, and then the original note again as one single rapid movement. The *lower mordant* is a direction to play the note itself, a note below it, and then the original note again as one rapid movement.

VIBRATO TECHNIQUE

Hold E on the 5th fret of the 2nd string, rocking the tip of the finger rapidly from *side to side* within a small area behind the fret. This movement produces a minor pitch variation and causes the note to sustain longer. Thumb pressure must be released to allow the finger to move freely. Alternatively, move the finger *up and down* behind the fret. Both methods give a full and attractive tone to the notes on the fingerboard.

USING A TREMOLO ARM

Tremolo arm technique on the electric guitar is an important part of modern playing. A variety of effects can be created by pushing the arm down or pulling it up. Downward pressure lowers the pitch of single notes and chords, and pulling the arm upwards raises the pitch. Compare bending a note on a fret with the use of the tremolo arm. Hold E on the 12th fret of the 1st string, and bend it up to F natural. Now hold E without moving it, and with the second and third fingers pull the tremolo arm up to sound F. Move up to F, then let the arm down to lower the pitch to E. Further movement of the tremolo arm in either direction can be used to adjust the pitch range through a wide series of intervals. Play a phrase, and, on the last note, pull the tremolo arm up or push it down to sound a further note in the series. Try pulling the arm up very quickly to create textural variations with the note. Play a note with the tremolo arm pressed down, and let it return to a normal position. This gives a "scooped" effect to the note.

HARMONICS

Open-string *natural harmonics* occur over most frets. Three can be played by touching a string lightly over the 5th, 7th, and 12th frets (the 12th fret produces an octave harmonic). A note held on any fret has *artificial harmonics* between the fret and the bridge. Play F♯ on the 2nd fret and place the finger lightly over the 14th fret. This gives the octave harmonic. Play by touching the harmonic over the fret with the first finger and plucking the string with the thumb or the second or third finger. This can be played with a plectrum held between the thumb and the second finger.

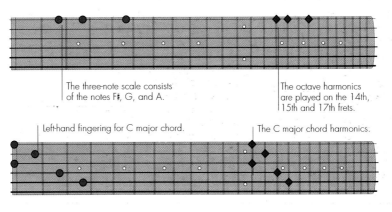

The three-note scale consists of the notes F♯, G, and A.

The octave harmonics are played on the 14th, 15th and 17th frets.

Left-hand fingering for C major chord.

The C major chord harmonics.

Variations
A diamond in place of a dot on a stave directs the player to use a harmonic. A series of variations on the different harmonics on a string are often played by brushing the side of the thumb and the plectrum across the strings, covering a wide string area from the fingerboard to the bridge. This is most effective on an electric guitar.

CHORD/SCALE RELATIONSHIPS

PLAYING ARPEGGIOS AND SCALES WITH CHORDS

Modulation

This system of modal seventh chords should be converted to all keys. Write out a major scale and the series of seventh chords, then play each chord with its arpeggios and scales.

In order to understand how scales and arpeggios relate to chords when soloing, it is important to look thoroughly at the major scale system. Chords must be extended beyond the triads to establish a harmonic framework as there is often a tendency to perceive minor blues scales against basic major, minor, and dominant chords.

Chord types

Five chord types from the major scale are represented below as a basis for chord improvisation. I, IV, and V a[re] major chords, II is a minor, and VII is a diminished chord.

SCALES, ARPEGGIOS, AND CHORDS IN C MAJOR

The chords in the C major scale are shown with added sevenths. There are two major sevenths, one dominant seventh, three minor sevenths, and one minor seventh with a flattened fifth. The complete series is C major 7, D minor 7, E minor 7, F major 7, G7, A minor 7, and B minor 7♭5. Play each chord followed by the full arpeggio. The upper extensions are further notes of the C major scale in thirds above the seventh of every chord. A strict application of C major extensions to each of the sevenths creates harmonic tension with certain chords.

CHORD SCALES

The full arpeggio on each chord uses all seven notes of the scale from the root. They can be played as a modal scale on each chord. By playing each mode against the chord, all the notes can be heard in context. Play each scale from the root over the seventh chords. Most of the notes work apart from the note F against C major 7, A minor 7, and E minor 7, and C over B minor 7♭5, and E minor 7.

Modal scales for chord types

There is one Mixolydian modal scale over the dominant seventh chord and one Locrian scale over the minor 7♭5 chord. There are three modal scales over a minor seventh. The Dorian over the II chord is the most practical. The two modal scales over a major seventh — the Major/Ionian and the Lydian scales — have a different character.

Chord arpeggios

Play a two-octave arpeggio using all the notes of the chord in one position. Compare the shape of each arpeggio when played in the sequence F-C-G-D-B.

C

D

F

G

B

Two-octave modal scales

Play a two-octave scale in the same position as the arpeggios. Emphasise the notes of the arpeggio. Compare the pattern with the two-octave scale.

C IONIAN/MAJOR

D DORIAN

F LYDIAN

G MIXOLYDIAN

B LOCRIAN

Chord/scale patterns

Play the chords (shown in black), which are derived from the scales. Each chord can be played in the same position as the scale and arpeggio on the fingerboard.

C MAJOR 7

D MINOR 7

F MAJOR 7

G7

B MINOR 7♭5

MODAL CHORDS

Play the modal scale against each of the seventh chords in C major. Look at the position of the chord and the mode in the two-octave C major scales shown on the right. Each principal note of a mode acts as a pivotal note and the root of the modal chord. Although each chord is composed of the first, third, fifth, and seventh degrees of each scale, adding further notes creates different harmonic effects. On the major seventh **I**, all the notes work in relation to the root, apart from the perfect fourth/eleventh. On the major chord **IV**, the augmented fourth – which is usually written as a flat five or sharp eleven – can be used with the chord. With the minor seventh chord **II**, all the notes work. In contrast, with the minor chord **III**, the minor second and minor sixth clash. The minor seventh chord **VI** has a major second in relation to the root which works with the chord, but also a minor sixth which tends to clash. All the intervals from the **V** chord work. In certain conditions, the fourth/eleventh clashes. The same goes for the **VII** chord, with the exception of the minor second, C♮. These *clash-tones* can be used as passing notes, but if they are stressed against the chord they sound weak or highly dissonant.

Major/Ionian
The major 7th **I** chord uses C, E, G, and B from this scale as the root, third, fifth, and seventh.

Dorian
The minor seventh **II** chord uses D, F, A, and C from this scale as the root, third, fifth, and seventh.

Phrygian
The minor seventh **III** chord uses E, G, B, and D from this scale as the root, third, fifth, and seventh.

Lydian
The major seventh **IV** chord uses F, A, C, and E from this scale as the root, third, fifth, and seventh.

Mixolydian
The dominant seventh **V** chord uses G, B, D, and F from this scale as the root, third, fifth, and seventh.

Aeolian
The minor seventh **VI** chord uses A, C, E, and G from this scale as the root, third, fifth, and seventh.

Locrian
The minor seventh flat five **VII** chord uses B, D, F, and A from this scale as the root, third, fifth, and seventh.

THE ROOT AND KEY CENTRE

When a succession of chords is written down as symbols in a chord sequence, it is important to be able to look at each chord type and relate it to a scale and key centre. Five of the chord structures that are found on the major modal system form the basis for most types of chord symbol. The major chord which has 6th, 7th, and 9th additions can be treated as either the **I** or the **IV** chord of a major key. As a major/Ionian **I** chord, the root is the keynote of the related major scale; thus C major 7 is found in C major. As a Lydian **IV** major chord with 6th, 7th, 9th, and ♯11 additions, the root is four notes away from the key centre – C major 7(♯11) is in G major. When a standard minor chord with 6th(13th), 7th, 9th, or 11th additions is played, it is usually treated as a **II** chord of the major key a tone below. This is because every note of the Dorian scale is effective as a minor chord extension. Therefore C minor 7 is found in B♭ major. The minor chord with 7th, 9th, and 11th additions also occurs as an Aeolian **VI** chord; C minor 7 can be approached as a chord in E♭ major. The major chord in the form of a Mixolydian dominant with 7th, 9th, 11th(4th), and 13th additions occurs as a **V** chord on the major scale. The root is five notes above the key centre; C7 is in F major. The Locrian minor seventh flat five chord with an eleventh addition only occurs as a **VII** on the major scale. C minor 7♭5 is in D♭ major. The root is a semitone below the key centre.

The major as a I chord The major **I** chord is built from the first degree of the major scale. When a major seventh occurs, or when it is extended using major/Ionian notes, it is on the major keynote of its own scale.

The minor as a II chord The minor **II** chord is built from the second degree of the major scale. When a minor seventh and its standard extensions occurs, it is one tone (major second) above or seven below a major keynote.

The major as a IV chord The major **IV** chord is built from the fourth degree of the major scale. When a major seventh or Lydian extension occurs, it is four notes (a fourth) above or five notes (a fifth) below a major keynote.

The major as a V chord The major **V** chord is built from the fifth degree of the major scale. When a dominant seventh or an extension occurs, it is five notes above or four notes below a major keynote.

The diminished as a VII chord The diminished **VII** chord is built from the seventh degree of the major scale. When a minor seventh flat five or an extension occurs, it is seven notes above or one semitone below a major keynote.

SCALES WITH SEVENTHS

It is important to compare the use of scales in the major system and the relative minor systems. When a series of seventh chords is written out on the major system and the relative harmonic and melodic minor scales, there are a number of points where materials can overlap. There is also a wide variation in the application of major and relative minor scales against chords. This is linked to their function and position within chord sequences. The major and minor scale systems provide a basis for melody and improvisation. Their modal scales cover most of the harmony written as chord symbols.

MAJOR SYSTEM

When each chord is played as a seventh it relates to other keys apart from C major. The **I** chord is also the **IV** chord of G major. **II** is the **VI** chord of F major. **III** is also the **II** chord of D major and the **VI** chord of G major. **IV** is the **I** chord in F. **VI** is the **II** chord of G major. **VII** is the **II** chord in A harmonic minor.

THE MINOR SYSTEM

I can be played with a melodic minor. **II** can be used with the Locrian mode. **III** can use the melodic minor. **IV** can use the Dorian mode. **V** can use either the Mixolydian or the melodic minor. **VI** can use the Lydian mode. **II**, **IV**, **VI**, and **VII** use the harmonic minor scale as diminished chords. With melodic minor chords, **II** can use the Dorian mode, **IV** can use the Mixolydian and as a 7♭5 the melodic minor. **V** can use the Mixolydian mode. **VI** can use the Locrian. **VII** as a 7♭5 can use the melodic minor.

MAJOR SYSTEM

Play the seventh chords as a sequence in C using the seven modes. Take each chord and play it on its own out of context. **I**, **III**, and **VI** suggest other modes. **II**, **III**, **IV**, and **VII** can use further modes in certain contexts.

HARMONIC MINOR

Play the seventh chords shown on the right as a sequence in the key of A minor using the harmonic minor modes. With each chord on its own, the related major and melodic minor modes can be used. The **II**, **IV**, **VI**, and **VII** chords can all be played as diminished inversions.

MELODIC MINOR

Play the seventh chords shown on the right as a sequence in the key of A minor using the melodic minor modes. With each chord on its own, other altered modes can be used. **IV** and **VII** as 7♭5 chords are inversions of each other. They use the melodic minor scales.

SEVENTH CHORDS ON A C ROOT

If seventh chord types are all written with their primary scale relationships based from a root of C, the scales and modes can be compared. The C chords use different scales in the major and minor key system. Six of the C chords are written with one alternative scale relationship. Some chords can be used with a large number of scales. The C major chord and the C minor/major chord are the only types that have the root on the keynote. The remaining chords all occur on other modal degrees of major and minor scale.

C major 7
*This is the **I** chord of the key of C major. C major 7 can also be treated as the **IV** chord when played in the key of G major.*

C dominant 7
*This is the **V** chord in the key of F major. C7 is shown above as the **V** chord of F harmonic minor. It can also be used as the **V** chord of F melodic minor.*

C minor 7
*This is the **II** chord of the key of B♭ major. The C minor 7 chord is shown above with the **VI** scale of E♭ major.*

C minor 7 flat 5
*This is the **VII** chord of D♭ major. It can also be used as the **II** chord when played in the key of B♭ harmonic minor.*

C diminished 7
*This can also be the **VII** chord of C♯ harmonic minor. With inversions using the notes F♯, A, and D♯, it can be related to G, B♭, and E harmonic minor.*

C minor/major 7
*As the **I** chord in the key of both C harmonic minor and C melodic minor, this chord can be used with either of the two scales.*

C7 flat 5
*This can be used as the **IV** chord of G melodic minor. It can also be used as the **VII** chord in the key of C♯ melodic minor.*

C7 sharp 5
*This can be used as the **V** chord of F harmonic and melodic minor. It can also be used as the **VII** chord in the key of C♯ melodic minor.*

C major 7♭5♯11
*When playing in the key of G major, C major 7♭5♯11 is used as the **IV** chord.*

Sequence of seventh chords
Using the C note as a reference point with chords and scale changes, play a sequence of seventh chords on the root C as a chord progression. Play four chords as one chord-type per bar over four bars at a slow tempo. Improvise through the chord changes, using the related scales, and compare chord types with keys and modes as they change from bar to bar. As an exercise, play all the seventh chords as each root letter name. Take each chord on a root, and play all the types with each scale and mode.

MODAL IMPROVISING

THE RELATIONSHIP BETWEEN CHORDS AND MODES

Chord sequences
The degrees of the major scale (**I–VII**) are shown below over eight bars containing chord symbols. A seventh chord has been used in each bar. The grey shading marks the chord type, which is then varied in a four-bar sequence. Play the chords and variations on each degree followed by the modal scale. To hear the harmonic effect of each note in context, it is helpful to record sequences on tape.

Harmonic effects are based on the use of chords, arpeggios, and counter-melodies. Single notes that are played with chords in composition or improvisation tend to function as extensions of the underlying harmonic structure: the sound and the melodic quality of a note played over a block chord depends on their relationship. Not all related modal scale notes work well with chordal harmony. For example, when an A minor seventh chord is played, all the notes of the Aeolian mode and the C major scale can be played over it except the note F, which clashes with the standard A minor root voicings. If F is included within a C chord voicing, it can sound dissonant. If an altered A chord voicing is built including F, it is possible to utilize the full scale, including the note F, for melody and improvisation.

Voicings and extensions
The series of melodic variations is played on each degree against both the related seventh chord and an extended harmonic structure. Modal chords have different voicings and structures that determine the sound of related modal notes. When C major is used over a standard C chord, the note F clashes when it is stressed. If the chord structure is modified using particular voicings including F, then F can be used as a melody note.

C MAJOR CHORDS (I)

Chords on the first degree of the C major scale are constructed from the notes C, D, E, G, A, and B. The major chord and its common extensions are C6, C major 7, C major 9, and C6/9. In the standard **I** chord form the note F is not used.

C IONIAN

Play the exercises against the standard chords. The seven-note arpeggio (in the fourth bar) includes the note F, which sounds dissonant when stressed against these chords.

D MINOR CHORDS (II)

Chords occurring on the second degree of the C major scale are constructed from the notes D, E, F, G, A, B, and C. Minor chords and their common extensions are used in all types of progressions. As a standard **II** chord, all the scale notes are used.

D DORIAN

Play the exercises over the standard chords. Try the full seven-note arpeggio against the D chord and its extensions. Dorian chords are important in melody and improvisation.

E MINOR CHORDS (III)

Chords on the third degree of the C major scale are built from the notes E, G, A, B, and D. The common extensions used are E minor 7, and E minor 11 without a ninth. As a standard **III** chord not all the scale notes are used. As an altered Phrygian chord the notes C and F can be included.

E PHRYGIAN

Play the exercises against the standard chords, and the full seven-note arpeggio with its extensions. Note that C and F are dissonant. Play the E Phrygian voicings; use the entire scale.

F MAJOR CHORDS (IV)

Chords on the fourth degree of the C major scale are constructed from the notes F, G, A, B, C, D, and E. The common extensions are F6, F major 7, F major 9, F6/9, and F major 7#11. They are used in all types of sequence and progression.

F LYDIAN

Play the exercises against the standard chords, and the full arpeggio against the F chord and its extensions. The Lydian scale creates an interesting sound with major chords.

G MAJOR CHORDS (V)

Chords on the fifth degree of the C major scale are built from the notes G, A, B, C, D, E, and F. The common extensions are G6, G7, G9, G11, and G13. They are used in all types of progressions. As a standard **V** chord all the notes of the scale are used.

G MIXOLYDIAN

Play the exercises against the standard chords, and the full seven-note arpeggio against the G chord and its extensions. Mixolydian chords are important for melody and improvisation.

A MINOR CHORDS (VI)

Chords on the sixth degree of C major use the notes A, B, C, D, E, and G. Common extensions are A minor 7, A minor 9, and A minor 11. They are used in many different types of progression. Altered Aeolian chords can also include the note F.

A AEOLIAN

Play the exercises against the standard chords, and the seven-note arpeggio against the A chord and its natural extensions. The F sounds dissonant when stressed on these chords.

B DIMINISHED CHORDS (VII)

Chords on the seventh degree of the C major scale are formed using the notes B, D, E, F, G, and A. Common extensions are B minor 7♭5, and B minor 11♭5 without a ninth. Altered Locrian voicings can also include the note C.

B LOCRIAN

Play the exercise against the standard chords, and the seven-note arpeggio against the B chord and its natural extensions. The note C sounds dissonant when stressed.

PLAYING MODAL SCALES AND CHORDS

Standard chords on each degree vary in their effect as a basis for improvising. For example, the C major **I** chords create a harmonic structure where the note F becomes dissonant. If each mode is played in the key of C, the F note must be avoided as an accented note over C chords in every position. Therefore, F Lydian as a mode is not practical because it is based around F as a principal note. In other modes F can be used as a passing note. The sound of each mode over a chord is defined by the shape and relation of the principal note to structures and voicings. For example, E Phrygian works well over a D minor 7 chord. The free use of all modes over one chord is best explored with the open-sounding tonal system based around the D minor **II** harmonies. This group of Dorian chords uses all of the notes of the scale within its chord voicings. There are no clashing notes, and each one of the modes can be used to improvise freely.

Chords on modal degrees

The fingerboard on the right shows seven positions for chords on each modal degree of the scale, running in the key of C major from F on the 1st fret to E on the 12th fret. F Major 7, using notes from the Lydian mode, is on the 1st fret. G7, using notes from the Mixolydian mode, is on the 3rd fret. A minor chords on the 5th fret must be voiced using the Aeolian mode. B minor 7 flat 5, using notes from the Locrian mode, is on the 7th fret. C major 7, using notes from the Ionian (major) mode, is on the 8th fret. D minor 7, using notes from the Dorian mode, is on the 10th fret. E minor chords on the 10th fret must be voiced using notes from the Phrygian mode.

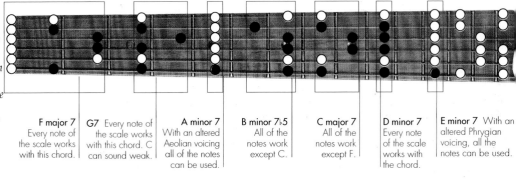

| F major 7 Every note of the scale works with this chord. | G7 Every note of the scale works with this chord. C can sound weak. | A minor 7 With an altered Aeolian voicing all of the notes can be used. | B minor 7♭5 All of the notes work except C. | C major 7 All of the notes work except F. | D minor 7 Every note of the scale works with the chord. | E minor 7 With an altered Phrygian voicing, all the notes can be used. |

MODAL POSITIONS ALONG THE 5TH STRING

Each mode in C should be played as a pattern with a standard fingering (see below, first column). Four of the modes in the second column can be played using stretch fingering, starting with the first finger. Practise the following modes: C Ionian (C major) on the 3rd fret, D Dorian on the 5th fret, E Phrygian on the 7th fret, F Lydian on the 8th fret, G Mixolydian on the 10th fret, and A Aeolian on the 12th fret. To begin with, this position may be rather difficult to play on a nylon-string acoustic guitar: instead, it can be played from the lower open-string position. Depending on the type of instrument used, B Locrian should be played on either the 2nd or the 14th fret. A series of modal positions can be played easily on most electric guitars from C on the 3rd fret up to an octave repeat of the C position on the 15th fret.

DOUBLE-OCTAVE MODAL POSITIONS

The modal scales can all be played over two octaves across the fingerboard starting on the 6th string. These scales are marked with black dots on the chart below. The modal scales ascending from the 5th string are marked in blue. When a mode is played from the 6th string, it can be fingered easily as a pattern without requiring a shift in position. Modes from the 5th string must be played with a shift in position or stretch fingering if they are to be extended over two octaves. The pattern starting from each string should be combined into one overall fingering position which covers a large area of the fingerboard. On the seven diagrams below, the notes in C which are not part of each fingering pattern are marked with white circles. The position of each mode in relation to the others should be memorized.

C IONIAN (SECOND FINGER)

C IONIAN (FIRST FINGER)

D DORIAN (FIRST FINGER)

D DORIAN (FIRST FINGER)

Stretch fingering

The stretch fingering positions played in this column all use the first, second, and fourth fingers to play three notes with two-fret gaps in a space of five frets.

E PHRYGIAN (FIRST FINGER)

F LYDIAN (SECOND FINGER)

F LYDIAN (FIRST FINGER)

G MIXOLYDIAN (SECOND FINGER)

G MIXOLYDIAN (FIRST FINGER)

Further stretch fingering

Using stretch fingering it is possible to play more than three notes on a string, although this can be very difficult in lower positions on the fingerboard where the fret spacing is wider. Some scale positions can be extended using four notes and four fingers per string. Try playing part of the A Aeolian scale from the 12th fret, using the first finger to play A, the second to play B, the third to play C, and the fourth to play D. Stretch fingering is used by jazz and rock guitarists.

A AEOLIAN (FIRST FINGER)

B LOCRIAN (FIRST FINGER)

C IONIAN (MAJOR)

D DORIAN

E PHRYGIAN

F LYDIAN

G MIXOLYDIAN

A AEOLIAN

B LOCRIAN

C MAJOR TO G MAJOR AND F MAJOR

There are several approaches to learning the full scale patterns in every key. With a thorough knowledge of the C major pattern over the entire fingerboard, a simple way of learning the patterns of the closely related G major and F major keys is to pick out the one note that differentiates them, and adjust the C pattern. The only difference between G major and C major is the note F♯, so every F note is simply moved up by one semitone. In a similar way, C major is converted to F major by picking out every B note and moving it down a semitone to B♭.

G MAJOR

F MAJOR

C MAJOR AND FURTHER KEYS

Every key can be cross-referred to C major and memorized as a pattern with a fixed number of variations. There are nine fingerboard diagrams below detailing the position of the C scale in relation to the remaining keys. They show clearly how two keys work as contrasting patterns on the fingerboard. The notes of the C major scale are marked as white circles, and the contrasting key is marked with black circles. Shared notes are black and white.

The relationship between the C major and D major scales can be used to explain the diagram. The two scales share the notes B, D, G, E, and A: the D major scale can be played in relation to C major by moving the notes F and C up a semitone. Study one area of the fingerboard – one octave of the open-string E Phrygian scale pattern in C major, starting on the 6th-string open E. E is shared with the key of D, F is in C only, G is in D and C, A is in C and D, B is in C and D, C is in C only, and D is in C and D. If the

E Phrygian modal scale is played with the notes C and F moved up by a semitone, the scale is converted to E, F♯, G, A, B, C♯, and D. This is a Dorian scale in D. The key centre of D is a tone above C, which moves all the modal patterns up by two frets. This can be extended along the fingerboard and repeated for all the other keys in relation to C major. Contrasting scales across the fingerboard is a useful exercise, providing the grounding for soloing and improvising through key changes.

C MAJOR/D MAJOR C MAJOR/B♭ MAJOR

C MAJOR/A MAJOR C MAJOR/E♭ MAJOR

C MAJOR/E MAJOR C MAJOR/A♭ MAJOR

C MAJOR/B MAJOR C MAJOR/D♭ MAJOR

C MAJOR/F♯/G♭ MAJOR

Key

○ C MAJOR
● CONTRASTING KEY
◐ SHARED NOTES

The C major notes are white. The contrasting key is black. Shared notes are black and white.

FINGERING POSITIONS

One of the simplest ways of learning a full scale position for each of the keys is to take one major scale pattern and memorize it as three modal fingering blocks. There are a number of ways of connecting all the modal patterns in one key across the fingerboard. Shown below is a system where extended double-octave major/Ionian, Phrygian, and Aeolian scales are played as three positions that cover the entire fingerboard. These positions cover every note and repeat in the higher octave positions above the 12th fret. As soon as the patterns have been mastered in C major, the next step is to move them as a visual block up and down the fingerboard. All the keys can be played by moving the extended patterns. For example, Db major is simply C moved up a semitone, and B major is C moved down a semitone.

Three blocks

The major scale fingering pattern is extended over two octaves. The Aeolian pattern is also extended and overlaps. The Phrygian pattern covers the scale notes above the major.

●	PHRYGIAN
◑	AEOLIAN
◐	OVERLAP
●	MAJOR

DUPLICATION

This is an example of a movement from one key to another. Notes are duplicated in other positions. C is played from the 3rd fret of the 5th string, ascending to G. It moves to the key of Ab major, starting on the 6th fret of the 4th string. The same series can be played starting with the note C on the 8th fret of the 6th string, moving to Ab on the 5th string. These two positions have the same set of notes.

C MAJOR

Db MAJOR

D MAJOR

Eb MAJOR

E MAJOR

F MAJOR

B MAJOR

Bb MAJOR

A MAJOR

Ab MAJOR

G MAJOR

Gb/F# MAJOR

THE PENTATONIC SCALE

LEARNING PENTATONIC SCALE TECHNIQUES AND POSITIONS

Extended patterns
The A pentatonic is shown in the box below from the open 5th string and, using the same notes, from the 6th string, where it can be extended more easily. These positions can be played in an upper octave from the 12th and 17th frets on an electric guitar.

The standard pentatonic scale consists of five notes within an octave. The minor pentatonic scale (see p. 74) occurs frequently as one of the primary scales in all types of music. Minor pentatonic scales are formed from major seconds and minor thirds. This type of scale is one of the most important series of notes after the major and minor scales. Mastering this form is vital in the development of skills in composition, improvisation, and playing melodies.

The full pattern
The two main pentatonic positions can cover notes outside a two-octave scale. In A minor, the open 5th-string pattern uses the two notes below on the 6th string; the other fingering has an extra top note. Additional notes can be played by stretching, shifting position, and sliding.

Two-octave pentatonic
This scale, running over two octaves, ascends in the sequence A-C-D-E-G-A-C-D-E-G-A.

FINGERING TWO-OCTAVE SCALES

The pentatonic scale from the lowest A note in standard tuning can be played from the open 5th string or, at the same pitch, on the 5th fret of the 6th string. The lower position from the open strings repeats as a pattern starting on the 12th fret, at a higher octave. These three positions must be memorized to cover the scale on the fingerboard. Play each position, and move between them by shifting the overall left-hand position. The patterns do not cover all the pentatonic notes on the fingerboard. The white circles show the notes of the pentatonic scale that are not covered by the notes on the stave.

Open position
Play from the open A to the G on the 3rd fret of the 1st string, using standard fingering. Try finishing the two-octave scale by playing G and A on the 1st string with the second and fourth fingers.

Fifth-fret position
Exactly the same notes can be played starting from the 5th fret of the 6th string. The top A on the two-octave scale can be played easily without either changing the fingering pattern or stretching.

Upper-octave position
The pentatonic scale in the upper octave is the same as the open-string pattern. It is played by using the first finger to play the octave equivalents of the open-string notes.

PENTATONIC MODES

The pentatonic scale can be played as a six-note pattern from any of its constituent notes. This creates five different scales, referred to as *modes* of the pentatonic scale. Each scale has its own sound, with the principal note acting as a pivot for the melodic shape and structure. The five scales can be viewed as pentatonic scales in their own right. They often occur as separate scales in folk and ethnic music. The relationship is similar to that between the major scale and modal degrees. The scales below should be played as six-note exercises within the standard pentatonic structure, and extended to two octaves. This will develop the flexibility needed for improvising with the standard pentatonic.

The five scales
Play these five pentatonic scales, based on a 5th-fret position, as a series of separate exercises. When these positions have been thoroughly memorized, move them to the second main pentatonic fingering pattern, which starts on the 5th string. When a pentatonic scale using the notes A-C-D-E-G has been mastered across the entire fingerboard, the five patterns can be played from any position of the scale in every register.

Starting on A Ascend with a minor third, major second, major second, minor third, and major second.

Starting on C Ascend with a major second, major second, minor third, major second, and a minor third.

Starting on D Ascend with a major second, minor third, major second, minor third, and a major second.

Starting on E Ascend with a minor third, major second, minor third, major second, and a major second.

Starting on G Ascend with a major second, minor third, major second, major second, and a minor third.

PENTATONIC VARIATION

There are several ways in which a scale can be played across the fingerboard. Standard fingerings using two notes on a string are often combined with stretch fingerings, which enable three notes to be played on a string. Pentatonic scales may be extended beyond two octaves by either stretching or shifting the overall left-hand position, from every note on each string in one position up to higher pentatonic positions and two-octave patterns. The minor pentatonic can be played with two 6th-string patterns beginning on the 1st and 2nd notes of the pentatonic. These start from the 5th and 8th frets. As a standard scale for soloing,

A minor pentatonic is often related to the Dorian mode, and the "major" pentatonic above it is Lydian. Therefore, both are related to G major. It is important to differentiate between the minor and major pentatonic scales in A, which are related to G, and the minor and major seven-note scales in the key of C major.

Minor pentatonic

The A minor pentatonic can be played starting with the 4th finger and running below the 5th-fret position. This overlaps with the 5th-string pentatonic. Practising this pattern increases familiarity with the pentatonic and extends fingerboard control.

Major pentatonic

This pattern is the second A minor pentatonic mode. It is often used as a "major" approach to its scale. In relation to the first note, it contains a major third and a major sixth. It is used in conjunction with the minor pentatonic to cover the fingerboard.

PENTATONIC EXERCISES

These exercises develop skill in playing the scale freely, and provide basic grounding and control for melody and improvisation. The first exercise is a series of ascending three-note patterns; this should be extended over two octaves. The second is an ascending four-note pattern. The third combines fourths and thirds, and the final exercise consists of intervals from the root. Move these exercises up to the higher-octave pentatonic, starting on the 12th fret. Try playing descending three- and four-note patterns.

THREE-NOTE

FOUR-NOTE

FOURTHS AND THIRDS

INTERVALS

Pentatonic to Dorian scale conversion

Five-note pentatonic scales can be converted to seven-note modal scales, related to a major key, by adding a second and a sixth. Natural extensions for the A minor pentatonic are B (the major second) and F♯ (the major sixth).

TRANSPOSING THE PENTATONIC

The first note of the minor pentatonic can be thought of as a type of keynote when used within a blues structure. The first chord normally starts on the same note as the minor pentatonic: this note is the key. Blues in the key of A normally uses major chords in conjunction with an adapted A minor pentatonic. A blues sequence starting on A using minor chords is referred to as Blues in A minor. The two main lower positions for pentatonic keynotes are based from the 6th or the 5th string. On the right, the C minor pentatonic on the 8th fret of the 6th string is transposed to F♯ on the 2nd fret. C minor pentatonic can also be played from the 3rd fret of the 5th string and moved up to a higher F♯ minor pentatonic on the 9th fret.

F♯ PENTATONIC

C PENTATONIC

C PENTATONIC

F♯ PENTATONIC

ROCK AND BLUES

TWELVE-BAR ROCK CHORDS AND SCALES FOR SOLOING

The key
Rock and blues music is often linked to a reference keynote, which is often the root of a primary chord, and the first note of the related scale.

Twelve-bar blues chords and rhythms are the starting point for most types of rock music. Pentatonic and extended blues scales are used with simple chord structures. The timing and feel for most twelve-bar rock music is derived from blues *boogie* rhythms.

Transposition
Keys based around open-string chords are commonly used in rock music. However it is important to be able to play in all keys.

THE PENTATONIC OVER CHORDS

In traditional rock and blues music, the pentatonic scale is the framework for playing over basic major and minor chords and some extended-note chords. The positions for these chords and pentatonic scales often overlap. A solo using the scale is often played across a chord position, and, as a guitarist changes from single notes to chords, the same area of the fingerboard may be used to play either scales over the chords or chords in scale positions. In the examples shown on the right, the circles in black are major thirds and the circles in half-tones indicate notes that are shared by both the chord and scale.

A major (5th fret)
Play A minor pentatonic across A major. The minor third note works perfectly well as a note for melodies or soloing.

A 7 (5th fret)
Play A minor pentatonic across the A7 chord. The minor third note in the scale is used as a note when playing melodies or solos.

A minor (5th fret)
Play A minor pentatonic over an A minor chord. All the notes in the A minor chord are also part of the A minor pentatonic scale.

A major (12th fret)
The A minor pentatonic scale should be played from the 12th fret using the minor third.

A 7 (12th fret)
Play A minor pentatonic across A7. The minor third note is used when playing melodies or solos.

A minor (12th fret)
Play A minor pentatonic over an A minor chord. All the notes in the chord are part of the scale.

Twelve-bar sequence
The pentatonic scale in all registers is used to play over the twelve-bar structure. Play a twelve-bar in A using major and dominant seventh chords for A, D, and E. The pentatonic scale fits over most chord types in each sequence. Play the A pentatonic over three octaves up to and beyond the 17th fret. An adapted minor chord sequence can also be used.

TWELVE-BAR IN ROCK

In many different types of rock and blues music, major chords are played with added notes and a *boogie* feel. The basic blues boogie rhythm is played over a twelve-bar sequence by taking each chord and using a dotted-quaver or a triplet feel. This is achieved by striking the chord on a down-beat and holding it over briefly before playing it again before the last element in a triplet quaver; alternatively, aim for a modified semiquaver feel.

A major with F#
Play open A, on the 5th string, and E, held with the first finger, on the 2nd fret of the 4th string. Add F# with the third finger. The note A on the 3rd string can be added to the A chord.

A major with F# and G
Extend the first pattern using the open A string with the note E on the 2nd fret of the 4th string. Add the note F# with the third finger, and, after playing F#, add the fourth finger to play G on the 5th fret.

TWELVE-BAR BLUES IN A

Using the chords A, D, and E, the pattern above is played through a twelve-bar sequence in A. Play the chords A-A-A-A-D-D-A-A-E-D-A-A. When playing the A and D chords, try not to strike the open lower strings below the root.

A MAJOR   D MAJOR   E MAJOR

Right-hand technique
Play the exercise with plectrum downstrokes as pairs of notes: root and fifth, root and sixth, and root and seventh. Each pair of notes is struck twice. The finger holding the fifth stays in position. The extra octave note can be played over the basic chords.

CHORDS ON FRETTED POSITIONS

These rock chords are also played on fretted positions. To play A, place the first finger on the 5th fret of the 6th string (A) and the second finger on the 7th fret of the 5th string (E). The fourth finger stretches to F♯ and G on the 5th string.

Optional notes
The third finger can be used to hold an optional upper-octave note on the 4th and 3rd strings.

A MAJOR   D MAJOR   E MAJOR

Fret positions
A major is on the 5th fret of the 6th string. The roots for D major and E major are on the 5th string. Play the D and E chords by moving the A shape up to the 10th and 12th frets on the 6th string.

SOLOING ON THE TWELVE-BAR

Playing over a twelve-bar sequence with a single pentatonic scale is the simplest approach to soloing. The next stage is to take each chord in the sequence and play the related minor pentatonic scale from its root, starting with the standard A minor pentatonic over A in the first four bars. On the fifth and sixth bars, when the sequence moves to the D chord, a D minor pentatonic scale using the notes D, F, G, A, and C should be played, returning to A minor pentatonic for bars seven and eight. When moving to E on the ninth bar, the pentatonic starts from E and uses the notes E, G, A, B, and D. In the tenth bar, the pentatonic moves down to D before returning to the A pentatonic for the final two bars. The E chord and the pentatonic E scale can be substituted for A in the twelfth bar. This acts as a **V** chord at the end of the sequence.

A MINOR PENTATONIC (OPEN STRING)   D MINOR PENTATONIC (OPEN STRING)   E MINOR PENTATONIC (OPEN STRING)

A MINOR PENTATONIC (6TH STRING)   D MINOR PENTATONIC (5TH STRING)   E MINOR PENTATONIC (5TH STRING)

A MINOR PENTATONIC (5TH STRING)   D MINOR PENTATONIC (6TH STRING)   E MINOR PENTATONIC (6TH STRING)

EXTENDING PENTATONIC SCALES

Three types of addition to the pentatonic scale are shown on the right. Added notes are shown in black. The first method adds a flattened fifth *blue note*. On A, E♭ is used for melodic phrases or as a passing note. The second extension adds a major third, played over major and dominant chords; on A, the note played is C♯. Finally, the pentatonic is converted to the Dorian mode by adding the major second and major sixth; on A, these are B and F♯. Additions are also shown over D and E. When improvising with the three pentatonics it is important to synchronize the scales with the chord changes.

A MINOR PENTATONIC (ADDED FLAT FIVE)   D MINOR PENTATONIC (FLAT FIVE)   E MINOR PENTATONIC (FLAT FIVE)

A MINOR PENTATONIC (MAJOR THIRD)   D MINOR PENTATONIC (MAJOR THIRD)   E MINOR PENTATONIC (MAJOR THIRD)

A MINOR PENTATONIC (DORIAN)   D MINOR PENTATONIC (DORIAN)   E MINOR PENTATONIC (DORIAN)

ADVANCED TECHNIQUES

EXTENDING SINGLE-NOTE CONTROL

Transposition
The techniques in this section must be played in all keys. Tapping should be tried along the fingerboard, and sweeping on every string. Stretch fingering can be difficult in the lower registers.

Virtuoso electric guitar playing has resulted in innovations and changes in technique. Fast playing, and flowing phrases with extended intervals, both demand skillful co-ordination. A modern guitarist will be able to play intervals across the fingerboard, use stretch fingering over all the strings, and fret tapping for higher elements.

String muting
When playing electric guitars at high volume, it is important to mute or damp open strings to stop them ringing. While using certain techniques, place the edge of the right hand on unused strings.

FRET TAPPING

The right hand can play notes by *tapping* the string. Tap G on the 1st string using the third finger of the *left* hand, then pull the finger off, sounding the open E string. Try doing this with the second finger of the *right* hand. Right-hand tapping, combined with left-hand fret positioning, makes it possible to play phrases with any intervals. A three-note movement can be played by tapping the 7th fret with the second finger of the right hand, pulling the note off to sound fretted G, and then pulling off with the left hand to sound the open E.

3RD FRET AND OPEN STRING (ABOVE)   TAPPING THE 7TH FRET (BELOW)

Hammer on G on the 3rd fret and pull off to the open E.

Tap B on the 7th fret, pull off to G on the 3rd fret, and pull off to the open E.

Tap C♯ on the 9th fret, and pull off to sound A on the 5th fret. Pull-off A to sound F♯.

Tap D on the 10th fret, and pull off to sound A on the 5th fret. Pull-off A to sound F♯.

Tap E on the 12th fret, and pull off to sound A on the 5th fret. Pull-off A to sound F♯.

TAPPING ACROSS THE FINGERBOARD

Play an E minor pentatonic scale across the fretboard, using open strings and the 2nd and 3rd frets. Extend the two notes on each string to a three-note motif by playing a high note with the second finger of the right hand. Tap across all the strings, playing (from top to bottom) the 10th, 10th, 9th, 9th, 9th, and 10th frets. Play repeating ascending and descending variations by pulling off to the open string with the left and right hands. Try cyclical phrases, starting with any note. Move up and down using tapping, hammering, and pull-offs.

1ST STRING   2ND STRING   3RD STRING   4TH STRING   5TH STRING   6TH STRING

The right hand
Some players tap with the first finger, while resting the thumb on the neck or the body to give stability. If the second finger is used, it is possible to hold the plectrum between the thumb and first finger and stabilize the tapping finger with the third and fourth fingers.

DIRECTIONAL CONTROL

Notes are played across the fingerboard with controlled directional picking (*sweep picking*), so that strings are played with economic movements. Scales are arranged in fingering patterns so that the plectrum is always on the correct side of the string it has just played for movement to the next string. Play an arpeggio using sweep picking. Release the pressure on the notes as they are played; they should ring as single notes without sustaining together.

Play D major 7th. Pick the notes as an arpeggiated chord, leaving each of the voices to ring for comparison.

Play D major 7th, picking single arpeggiated scale notes. Release the pressure after each note to stop it ringing.

Play a D major 7th arpeggio with descending scale notes. Start with C♯ on the 2nd string and pick upwards.

Play a D major extended arpeggio across five strings as a series of individual notes ascending and descending.

STRETCH FINGERING

Play a G major two-octave scale starting on the 10th fret of the 5th string. Divide the 15-note scale into five groups with three notes on each string. The first note in each group is played with a plectrum downstroke, and the two following notes are hammered. Practise the scale in this form, aiming to create a very even legato effect. Move the first finger quickly and accurately onto the fret positions for each of the strings. Play a descending scale by picking the first note in each group with an upstroke and sounding the two following notes with pull-offs. Play continuous ascending and descending patterns of notes on one string: stretch the fingers to reach extra notes above and below the positions, and move across to all the notes on adjacent strings. Try jumping across adjacent strings to all the other strings. Legato can be played without picking or pull-offs.

Double-octave position
After playing the double-octave position in G major, starting on the keynote, move to other modal positions using stretch fingering from each string. Memorize the fingering patterns as related blocks, and when they are familiar, transpose them to other keys.

Extending the position
Stretch to include notes outside the standard position. This will allow you to play larger intervals on one string.

Dorian with stretch fingering
This Dorian position can be used as a block and as an overlapping position with the the G major scale two frets below. The same notes in each scale are played from different positions. Develop further modal positions in G major.

Rhythmic control
Set a metronome to a slow tempo, and build up scale patterns and exercises over four bars using a diatonic turnaround pattern in C major with the roots C, A, D, and G. Build up from one note in the bar to sixteen. Develop speed on these exercises by increasing the tempo. Use standard picking techniques and make up new variations and combinations. Take the scales, pentatonic patterns, and arpeggios up to a higher octave that can be played without running out of upper-register notes on the fingerboard. Experiment with all types of fingerboard positions and left- and right-hand techniques.

SUBDIVISION OF THE BAR

The diagram on the right shows a 4/4 bar as a mathematical chart with all the notes in accurate time relationships. The left-hand side represents the first beat of the bar: each crotchet on the top row sustains for a quarter of the bar. The fifth crotchet represents the beginning of the next bar. Compare these with the crotchet triplets. The first of the triplet groups starts at the beginning of the bar, and the second starts at the same point as the third crotchet beat. The first note in each group of quaver triplets can be timed in relation to crotchet beats and quavers.

RHYTHM AND ACCENTS FOR SOLOING

Soloing over chords, in different styles of music, is influenced by the underlying rhythmic structure. Rock rhythms are often based around a 4/4 time signature with accents on the second and third beats of the bar, or quaver subdivisions as offbeats and onbeats. Rock, blues, and jazz rhythms all use quavers and triplets to create a floating rhythm. Rhythms based on triplets are played with a wide variety of feels; the last note in the group of tied triplets is placed according to convention or individual preferences. Compare the feels of rhythms using triplets and those using dotted quavers. Funk, Latin, and other styles ranging from Rap to Reggae often use rhythms with dotted quavers, semiquavers, and triplets. Combinations of ties and shifting accents create marked rhythms that derive their character from placing emphasis on certain parts of the bar. Play through all the rhythms shown on the right, using chords and single notes. Many of these are played in ensembles by drums or other instruments only. An awareness of the form and structure of rhythms and the position of accents and syncopated elements is important for playing in a group.

Accents and offbeats

On the top staves, play a four-beat rhythm as crotchets and quavers. Accent the second and fourth beats. Accent offbeat and downbeat quavers. Leave out beats and play syncopated offbeats.

12/8 and dotted quaver rhythms

Play 12/8 as four accented beats. Experiment with accents in different places. Play groups of tied beats in 12/8. Play dotted quavers in 4/4, and tie them across the main beats. Compare the difference between the 12/8 tied rhythm as four beats and the 4/4 rhythm with dotted quavers.

Subdivision

Break each beat in a bar of 4/4 into four semiquavers. Play all possible variations with semiquavers and ties, and add the accents and syncopated elements.

TIME SIGNATURE

The chart on the right has a central column showing time signatures from 2/4 to 6/4 as groups of crotchet beats within a single bar. The sign c is often used as an abbreviation for a time signature of 4/4, sometimes referred to as *common time*. The left-hand column shows time signatures with minims as the lower figure: 2/2 and 3/2 are the equivalent in time duration to 4/4 and 6/4. The right-hand column shows time signatures with quavers as the lower figure: 6/8 and 12/8 are equivalent in time duration to 3/4 and 6/4.

Main beats

Time signatures are often interpreted in terms of the relationship between individual notes and the overall position of main beats. For example, 6/4 is often written as two dotted minims, and 6/8 as two dotted crotchets. This separates the notes in each time signature into two main beats, and they are both referred to as duple time, grouped with 2/2 and 2/4, with two main beats in the bar. 9/8 is written as three dotted crotchet main beats and is referred to as "triple time", grouped with 3/2, 3/4, and 3/8. 12/8 is written as four dotted crotchet main beats in quadruple time and grouped with 4/4 and 4/2. Time signatures where these main beats can be split into even subdivisions are referred to as "simple time", and time signatures where the beats are split into three are referred to as "compound time". Uneven groups of notes over a bar, such as 5/4 or 7/8, can be treated as asymmetric time. These time signatures often have two or more main groups of beats in a bar in different places. For example, 5/4 can be played as one group of three crotchet beats followed by two beats, or two beats followed by three beats.

COMPARING STRUCTURES

DEVELOPING THE RELATIONSHIP BETWEEN CHORDS, ARPEGGIOS AND SCALES

Related scales
A chord is often related to more than one scale. The four notes of the diminished chord are part of four harmonic minor, and further diminished and synthetic scales. The four notes of a dominant chord with a sharp fifth occur in the melodic and harmonic minor, and whole-tone scales.

All chords, arpeggios, and scales should be compared with each other on one root. This is a very effective aid to learning the chord shapes and understanding how they relate to arpeggios and different scales. Try moving any type of C chord and related material to all the other C chords, arpeggios, and scales, and by changing the notes in stages. This exercise shows how the different chord types and arpeggios relate to scale patterns for soloing, and how minor structural changes can be related to modes and key centres.

Chord grouping
Take the major seventh and lower the fifth a semitone to form a major seventh sharpened eleventh (flat fifth) chord. Go back to the major seventh chord and lower the seventh to form the dominant seventh. Alter any voicing to other types on the same root, by moving notes in semitones.

C major 7
Play the chord of C major 7, the arpeggio, and the scale of C major from the root. Improvise with C major and G major, picking out the arpeggio notes in each key. Use the positions from the 3rd fret of the 5th string and the 8th fret of the 6th string. Move to all octave positions.

C major 7 ♯11(♭5)
Play the C major 7♯11 chord, the arpeggio, and the scale of G major as a Lydian mode from a C root. Improvise with G major and E minor harmonic, picking out the arpeggio notes in each key. Use the 5th- and 6th-string positions, and move to all octaves.

C dominant 7
Play the C dominant 7 chord, arpeggio, and the F major scale as a Mixolydian mode from a C root. Improvise with F major, F harmonic and melodic minor, and the C blues scale, picking out the arpeggio notes. Use 5th- and 6th-string positions, and move to all octave positions.

C7♯5
Play C dominant 7♯5, the arpeggio, and the C♯ melodic minor scale. The root is written as C, and A♯ is written as B♭. Play F harmonic and melodic minor, and the whole-tone scale. Pick out the arpeggio notes. Using 5th- and 6th-string positions, move to all octaves.

C7♭5
Play C dominant 7♭5 as a chord and arpeggio, and the G melodic minor scale from C. F♯ is written as G♭. Try C♯ melodic minor and whole-tone scales. Pick out arpeggio notes. Using 5th- and 6th-string positions, move chord and arpeggio patterns to all octaves.

C minor 7
Play a C minor 7 chord, and an arpeggio and scale of B♭ major as a Dorian mode from the C root. Improvise with B♭ major, E♭ major, and A♭ major, picking out the arpeggio notes in each key. Use 5th- and 6th-string roots, and move the chord and arpeggio patterns to all keys.

C minor 7♭5
Play a C minor 7♭5 chord, and an arpeggio and scale of D♭ major as a Locrian mode from the root. Improvise with B♭ minor with C♯ and D♯ melodic minor, picking out the arpeggio notes. Use the 5th- and 6th-string roots, and move them to all octaves.

C diminished 7
Play a C diminished 7 chord, arpeggio, and the diminished scale starting a tone or semitone from the root. Try the four harmonic minor scales starting on C♯, E, G, and B♭. Pick out the arpeggio notes in each scale and key. Use 5th and 6th roots, and move to all octaves.

C minor/major 7
Play a C minor/major 7 chord, the arpeggio, and the C melodic and harmonic scales from the root as one scale, including a major and minor sixth. Pick out the arpeggio notes in the scale. Use 5th and 6th roots, and then move the chord and arpeggio patterns to all octaves.

JAZZ PROGRESSIONS

A SERIES OF STANDARD JAZZ SEQUENCES AND BASS LINES

Chord transposition
Certain types of progression can be transposed by converting the main scale-tone chords on each tonal centre to Roman numerals.

Learning standard sequences is helpful for improvising within a structure. Standard blues and jazz forms can be memorized for use as structures on which to base further development. They provide ideal frameworks for chord substitution and creative chord thinking.

Blues variations
Play the variations, comparing each sequence with the basic jazz blues structure in the first example. All the sequences are in 4/4 time.

E7	A7	E7	E7	A7	A7	E7	C#7	F#m7	B7	E7	B7
E7	A7	E7	Bm7 E7	A7	A7	E7	C#7	F#m7	B7	E7 C#m7	F#m7 B7
E7	A7	E7	Bm7 Bb7	A7	A7	E7	G#m7 C#9	F#m7	F7	E7 C#7	F#7 B7
E7 Bb7	A7 Bb°7	E7/B	Bm7 Bb7	A7 Bb7	A7 F7	E7 Eb7	D7 C#7	F#m7	D7 Eb7	E7 G7	F#7 B7
E7	Ebm7 D7	Dbm7 C7	Bm7 Bb7	A7	Bb°7	E7/B C7	C#7	F#m7	B7	E7 G7	C7 F7

MINOR BLUES

Em7	Em7	Em7	Em7	Am7	Am7	Em7	Em7	F#m7b5	B7	Em7	Em7
Em7	F#m7	Em7	Em6	Am7 Bm7	Am7 Am6	Em7	Em7	F#m7b5	F7	Em7	B7#9

TRANSPOSITION: E TO C

E7	A7	E7	E7	A7	A7	E7	C#7	F#m7	B7	E7	B7
C7	F7	C7	C7	F7	F7	C7	A7	Dm7	G7	C7	G7

TURNAROUNDS

The term *turnaround* applies to chordal movements that start from one chord and turn around through a series of variations before returning to the beginning. These are normally based around the use of **V-I** movements at the end of a sequence. Develop a two-bar turnaround in stages. Play the chord sequence C major 7, A minor 7, D minor 7, G7, and C major 7. Convert all the chords to dominant sevenths or ninths. Now link the four chords with a series of bass notes. This creates a bass line with a note on every beat, running C-Bb-A-Db-D-Ab-G-B. The last note B leads back to C at the beginning of the two-bar sequence. Try flat fifth substitution on the turnaround. Move from C9 to Eb9 (the flat fifth of A7), and from D9 to Db9 (the flat fifth of G7).

STANDARD JAZZ SEQUENCE

This uses **II-V-I** movements with link chords. The first two bars are **II** and **V** chords, moving to **I** in the third bar and **V** in the fourth. The fifth bar is a **II** chord of the relative minor; the sixth is the relative minor **V**; the seventh is the relative minor **I**. The chord on the eighth bar acts as a dominant chord. Bars 17 to 24 are the major to minor **II-V-I** chords. Bars 25 to 32 form a cycle leading back to the beginning.

Dm7	G7	CM7	FM7	Bm7♭5	E7	Am7	A7
Dm7	G7	CM7	FM7	Bm7♭5	E7	Am7	Am7
Bm7♭5	E7	Am7	A7	Dm7	G7	CM7	FM7
Bm7♭5	E7	Am7 G♯7	Gm7 F♯7	FM7	Bm7♭5 E7	Am7	Am7

RHYTHM CHANGES

The sequence shown on the right follows a series of standard rhythm changes. The first four bars are a B♭ turnaround, followed by a **II-V-I** movement in E♭ with a link chord leading back to a turnaround. The middle eight section (bars 17 to 24) is a series of **II-V** movements in the cycle of keys running from G major, C major, F major, and B♭ major. The last section is a repeat of the first eight bars.

B♭7 G7	Cm7 F7	B♭7 G7	Cm7 F7	Fm7 B♭7	E♭ E♭m	B♭7 G7	Cm7 F7
B♭ B°7	Cm7 C♯°7	Dm7 G7	Cm7 F7	B♭ B♭/D	E♭ E°	B♭7 G7	Cm7 F7
Am7	D7	Dm7	G7	Gm7	C7	Cm7	F7
B♭ G7	Cm F7	B♭ G7	Cm7 F7	Fm7 B♭7	E♭ E°	B♭	B♭

SIXTEEN-BAR MINOR BLUES STRUCTURE

A minor 7 (**I**) is played for the first four bars. This is raised by a fourth (D minor 7) for two bars. A minor **II-V** chords take the sequence back to four bars of **I**. A movement to the **V** chord takes the sequence back to **I**.

| Am7 | Am7 | Am7 | Am7 | Dm7 | Dm7 | Bm7♭5 | E7 |
| Am7 | Am7 | Am7 | Am7 | CM7 Am7 | FM7 E7 | Am7 | Am7 |

BASS LINES

This is a bass line for the standard sequence shown at the top of the page. Try playing the notes with varying sequences, e.g., start with D and move to E above or drop to E below. After the root has been played at the beginning of the bar, the remaining notes are played as chord harmonies and link notes. Chord notes, the related scale, and notes to lead in from a semitone above or below a root are standard approaches.

D E F A	G A G B	C G C E	F E D C	B D F A	G♯ E D B	A B C E	C♯ B♭ A E
D E F A	G A G B	C G C E	F E D C	B D F A	G♯ E D B	A B C E	A E C A
F D B G♯	E F♯ G G♯	A B C E	B♭ G E C♯	D E F A	G F E D	C E A G	F E D C
B F D B	E D C B	A C G♯ F♯	G B♭ F♯ E	F A C B♭	B F E G♯	A B C E	A

CHROMATIC SEVENTHS

Jazz sequences can be filled by using chords chromatically as links. The examples shown on the right are based on a two-bar turnaround. On the last beat of the first bar, C7 is moved to B♭7 as a lead-in chord to A7. This chord movement acts like a bass line moving from B♭ to A. Similarly, A7 is played until the last beat of the bar when D♭7 leads back to D7. D7 is played until the final beat of the bar when A♭7 is used to lead to G7 which is used to return to a C chord.

CM7 / / /	Am7 / / /	Dm7 / / /	G7 / / /
C7 / / /	A7 / / /	D7 / / /	G7 / / /
C7 / / B♭7	A7 / / D♭7	D7 / / A♭7	G7 / / B7
C7 / / B♭13	A7 / / D♭7	D9 / / A♭13	G7 / / D♭7

SOLOING OVER CHORDS

IMPROVISING AND SOLOING OVER CHORD SEQUENCES

Modulation and extensions
The chord types below should be played with every root as a harmonic structure for improvising. Study each individual chord; play its modal scale, and memorize its key relationship. Sevenths can be voiced using standard upper chordal extensions relating to their scale. This does not affect scalar relationships if standard notes are used in the chordal structure. When playing over D minor 7 and using D Dorian in C major, the D minor seventh can be altered to a minor sixth, or extended to a ninth, eleventh, or a thirteenth, using notes from the Dorian mode.

Musical tastes affect the way we hear the relationship between chords and scales for the purpose of improvising. Preferences for different styles of music can lead to a divergence in the types of scales heard in relation to a chord and in the creative possibilities that are perceived. Many players prefer to play within a limited structure when soloing, using material taken from recordings and assembling a range of motifs (often known as *licks* or *cliches*) over chordal harmony. One of the best ways to develop the skills required to play over chords is constantly to work through chord sequences with a wide range of variations. These can then be analyzed and written down. Relationships can be memorized for playing with other musicians. Recording material on tape or using a sequencer allows musicians to work through chord changes, and to experiment with unfamiliar scales and new melodic or rhythmic ideas.

Chord symbols
It is important to understand the relationship between a chord symbol, mode, and key. Each chord type has at least one related scale. The position and harmonic function of a chord within a sequence will often suggest one particular scale, while the ear may suggest another. The majority of standard chords have clear ground rules for related scales, when they are taken out of context and played on their own as a short harmonic sequence. Lines and phrases that fit over chords often use notes that do not occur in the chord structure or the added harmonic extensions.

II and V chords
Play the D minor 7 on the second (**II**) degree, and G7 on the fifth (**V**) degree of C major. Use the D Dorian scale when playing D minor 7, and the G Mixolydian when playing G7. Play in C using every mode.

II chord
Play D minor 7 on the second (**II**) of C major, using D Dorian. When the sequence changes to A minor 7, play this as an A Dorian **II** chord in the key of G major. Play four bars in C major and four bars in G major.

V chord
Play the chord G7 on the fifth degree (**V**) of C major, using G Mixolydian. C7 is the **V** chord of F major. Play the C Mixolydian mode. Move from the key of C to the key of F major. Use each tonal centre fully.

The II-V movement
Play A minor 7 and D7 to form the **II-V** movement of G major, using A Dorian and D Mixolydian. D minor 7 to G7 is in the key of C, G minor 7 to C7 is in the key of F, and C minor 7 to F7 is in the key of B♭ major 7.

C scale chords
Play the seventh chords on each degree of the key of C as a chord sequence. Improvise on each chord, using its related mode. If the chord sequence is played quickly, clash tones, particularly on **III** and **VI**, can be used as passing notes. Play the **III** and **VI** chords using a Dorian scale, and the **I** chord using a Lydian scale.

C modal chords
Play the chords of the C scale, using modal additions on each degree. Play the mode on each chord. When the chords are adjusted to include modal tones, it is possible to play the first (**I**), third (**III**) and sixth (**VI**) degree chords without clash tones.

Pentatonic scales

In rock music, many chords are played based on three-note triads with doubled notes, or as "5" chords with roots and fifths. These chords have a pentatonic minor sound when used for soloing, and they can be related to the Dorian mode. Play a "5" chord, major, minor, minor seventh, and dominant seventh chords.

Minor chords

When a chord sequence in C major moves to its relative minor, major modes are used in conjunction with A minor scales. The major II-V-I is shown using modes and variations, moving to II-V-I on the relative minor using modes and minor scales. The relative minor I in the last two bars can use the Dorian mode from its root.

A Minor scale chords

Play the A harmonic minor scale sevenths and improvise over each chord. Harmonic and melodic minor scales can be used effectively on certain chords, particularly I and III. Major modes can be used with each chord shared with the major system.

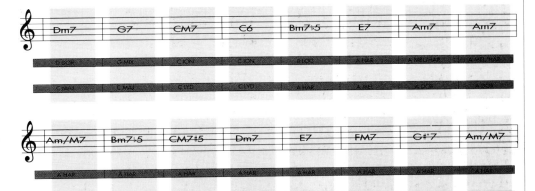

MAJOR AND MINOR II-V-I

The II-V-I movement may occur in a large range of variations. For example, a major II-V movement can be used to approach a major or minor I chord, and a minor II-V can be used to approach a minor or major I chord. Play the major II-V movement in C, using the Dorian and Mixolydian modes. Play the minor II-V in C; use modes and minor scales. When a II-V resolves to the C Minor I chord, play Aeolian or Dorian.

The II-♭V-I

The II-♭V-I movement occurs frequently in chord sequences. It may be approached in a number of different ways. On the ♭V play D melodic minor. Also try playing G♯ melodic minor as a variation from C♯ (D♭). When D♭13 is used as a full chord, play D♭ Mixolydian in G♭ major.

Modulations

Take one chord type and play a sequence based on a series of modulations on different roots. For example, play the minor seventh with a different chord root in each bar. Relate the chord to the mode from the first note and the primary tonal centre. Make up chord sequences of various lengths with different rhythms and time signatures.

Modulation with different chords

Write down sequences containing different chord types, using any root. Learn how to recognize a chord and how it relates to a mode and key centre. To begin with, work with different types of chords related to major modes and keys. As soon as this area is covered, introduce chords with minor scale relationships.

DEVELOPING VOICINGS

USING INVERSIONS AND FURTHER CHORD VOICINGS

Chord movements
In order to understand many of the more complex chord types, it is helpful to work within a single key. One approach is to take each of the seven major-scale triads and play through the chord changes using inversions. The next step is to add a seventh to every triad and experiment with the possible voicings. Using a full inverted seventh system, major and minor sixths can be seen as first inversions of minor sevenths and minor sevenths with a flat fifth.

The majority of chords are built by using combinations of thirds. For creating harmony, an approach in which triads are combined with added thirds, suspended fourths, and sixths covers a large part of the most commonly encountered guitar music. Chords may also be voiced with fourths and fifths. These types of harmony are very effective and are commonly found as two- and three-note structures in all types of music, and as extended forms in pop, jazz, and classical music. In addition, there are ways of forming chords and harmony that make use of other interval structures. For instance, when chords are made up from scale notes, each note can be placed in close proximity to the others to form intervals of seconds. Chords with voicings that include seconds, based on modes and scales, are used in folk and jazz.

Chordal transposition
Many of the effective chord voicings in one key cannot be transposed fully to another key. The guitar has a limited octave range, and the open strings are normally tuned to a standard pattern. For example, a piece of music in A major may use close harmony and open-string notes, with the low E string as a pedal note. If the music is transposed to another key, the same types of voicings using open strings may no longer be available.

TRIAD INVERSIONS

Play the seven C triads in root voicings. Take each of the chords and move the root to the top. This leaves the third in the bass, which is the lowest note: this is referred to as a first inversion. Take the third and put it at the top of the chord, leaving the fifth in the bass: this is known as a second inversion. Other positions can be used to place the remaining chord notes above the bass note.

INVERSIONS WITH SEVENTHS

It is possible, in theory, to play all of the seventh chords as inversions. By doing this the player can create a wide range of harmonic effects, which can be used to alter the function of the chords. There are practical limitations, though; the tuning of the guitar simply does not allow some inversions of sevenths to be played easily. Seventh chords have a third inversion where the seventh is placed in the bass. Play the series of seventh chords in C major in root voicings. Try playing all of the chords, first with the third in the bass as a first inversion, then with the fifth used in the bass as a second inversion, finally with the seventh in the bass as the third inversion. A large number of these chords are highly effective when used in chord sequences, particularly in some areas of modern jazz.

INVERSIONS IN A SEQUENCE

Each of the eight-bar chord sequences shown on the right should be played through as a repeating structure. Try transferring elements from one sequence to another. In the first eight bars, chords are used in root voicings. The second and third sequences have first, second, and third inversions replacing root inversions. All of these generate striking harmonic contrasts in comparison to root voicings. Inversions can be used in conjunction with root voicings to allow more than one version of a chord to be played in a bar.

TRIAD RELATIONSHIPS

Take the triads of the C major scale and play them in relation to all the other triads. A given triad can move to six other triads in the scale. In the exercise on the right, the triads on every scale degree have been placed in seven columns. Try all the movements, by taking the C major triad and moving it to all the others based on the major scale. This gives C major to D minor, C major to E minor, C major to F major, C major to G major, C major to A minor, and C major to B diminished. Repeat the exercise for the chords on each degree. The lines of chords on the stave across the scale show the chords moving by intervals. On the first line the chords move in scalar steps: C to D minor, D minor to E minor, E minor to F major, F major to G major, G major to A minor, A minor to B diminished, and B diminished to C major. On the second line the scale chords move in thirds. The third line covers fourths, and the fourth line covers fifths. Each movement can be inverted. A move from a triad to a chord a third above is harmonically similar to a move to a sixth below. On the fifth line, the movement to a chord a sixth above has been positioned a third below. The sixth line covers the move in sevenths, which is similar to a second below. Play all the chord movements with full voicings.

CHORDS IN FOURTHS AND FIFTHS

Chords can be constructed with superimposed fourths and fifths built from the root. In the first series of chords on the right, four-note fourth voicings move from C to B. The second series shows fourth chords with an extra note, a fourth above the top voice. The third set of chords has the root, an interval of a fifth, and two fourths. Try combining fourths and fifths to build further chord voicings.

CLOSE VOICINGS AND CLUSTERS

When chords are voiced with constituent notes in relationships using seconds, this produces *close voicings*. The first of the C major chords on the first stave is a C6/9 with an interval of a second between the ninth (D) and the third (E), forming a close voicing. The remaining chords work in a similar way. In the examples on the second stave, combinations of close voicings form *clusters*. The chords are shown as diatonic clusters, which create a particularly unusual harmonic effect.

CLOSE VOICING

CLUSTERS

CHORD SYNONYMS

Certain chord voicings can be labelled in various ways. Common overlaps include voicings and chords over different roots, inversions, or one triad positioned over another.

C/G	C/E	C/D	C/D	C/F	C/A	A MIN/C
G13 (SUS4/11)	C MAJ	D9 (SUS4/11)	D9 (SUS4/11)	F MAJ9	A MIN7	C6

E MIN/C	G/C	D MIN/C	A MIN7♭5/C	C7/G	C MAJ/D MIN	C MAJ/D MIN
C MAJ7	C MAJ9	F6	C MIN6	C7	D MIN11/A	F6/9 MAJ7

MELODY OVER CHORDS

SCALES AND MELODY USING MODAL CHORDS

Voicings
When all the notes on the scale are played with chord voicings over every root note, inversions are produced in some instances. Discordant harmonies occur when the top note clashes with the root or with another part of the chord structure. In the chart below, the major scale as a movement over modal chords is not a chord sequence.

Chords as blocks of vertical harmony can be used to play scales and melodies. Using this approach, an effective starting point is to experiment with a full system of harmonized notes in one key. Every major scale note can be placed over chords on each of the scale degrees, either by playing a scale note against all of the seven bass notes, or by playing all seven scale notes against one bass note. Several combinations, however, will give unusual chord voicings. Notes that are not part of the normal harmonic extensions must be voiced carefully so that chords do not sound weak or dissonant.

Two-note chords
Forming two-note chords by supporting a scale with an added interval is a simple way to harmonize notes. In the chart below, the C major scale is played with intervals **above** the scale notes. In addition, scale notes can be harmonized by playing them in pairs with intervals **below**. This technique is used to support melody and build chords with further voicings.

C MAJOR WITH MODAL CHORDS

C to C over C Ionian/major chords
The major scale ascends from C to an octave C, using different chord types in C major with a C root.

C to C over D Dorian chords
The major scale ascends from C to an octave C, using different chord types in C major with a D root.

C to C over E Phrygian chords
The major scale ascends from C to an octave C, using different chord types in C major with an E root.

C to C over F Lydian chords
The major scale ascends from C to an octave C, using different chord types in C major with an F root.

C to C over G Mixolydian chords
The major scale ascends from C to an octave C, using different chord types in C major with a G root.

C to C over A Aeolian chords
The major scale ascends from C to an octave C, using different chord types in C major with a A root.

C to C over B Locrian chords
The major scale ascends from C to an octave C, using different chord types in C major with a B root.

Thirds
Play E to E as thirds above the C major scale.

Fourths
Play F to F as fourths above the C major scale.

Fifths
Play G to G as fifths above the C major scale.

Sixths
Play A to A as sixths above the C major scale.

Sevenths
Play B to B as sevenths above the C major scale.

Octaves
Play C to C as octaves on the C major scale.

Ninths
Play D to D as ninths above the C major scale.

Tenths
Play E to E as tenths above the C major scale.

MELODY USING INTERVALS

The examples shown below are written in the key of C major, over a **II-V-I** movement based on D minor, G major, and C major chords. A melody played over chords often uses parts of the voicings. Melody over the chords is also played with scale notes. A combination of these two approaches is one of the simplest ways to play a single-note line over harmony. A scale or melody can also be supported with a series of lower intervals over chordal harmony. The single-note passages can be harmonized with intervals under each of the notes over block chords. Play the third example, which uses thirds: each note of the melody with the **II-V-I** chords is harmonized with thirds, and the entire passage can be played over the chord changes. The note B has been left as a single note. The fourth example uses fourths, and takes the same approach. The top two notes in each of the chords are fourths, and the single-note melody between the chords also uses fourths. In the fifth example, each note at the top of the **II-V** chords is shown supported by fifths. In the final example, each of the melody-notes is shown with sixths over the top of the **II** and **V** chords and supported by chord root notes.

1. CHORDS WITH MELODY

2. CHORDS WITH MELODY

3. CHORDS WITH MELODY SUPPORTED BY THIRDS

4. CHORDS WITH MELODY SUPPORTED BY FOURTHS

5. CHORDS WITH MELODY SUPPORTED BY FIFTHS

6. CHORDS WITH MELODY SUPPORTED BY SIXTHS

PEDAL NOTE

A pedal note under a series of chords or single notes creates a sense of flowing continuity and sets up a reference point for melodic and harmonic movement. Tune the 6th string down to a low D, and play the melody with block chords. Pick out the top note of each chord, and play the single line over the pedal note.

UPPER NOTE

An upper note is often played through a series of chord changes. The effect of the top note changes as the harmony moves underneath. In the example below, G is the eleventh of the first chord, an upper octave root of the second, the fifth of the third, and the ninth of the last. Play the upper note with the bass movement D-G-C-F.

PEDAL NOTE UNDER II-V-I

When a pedal note is played under a series of chords, the direction of the harmony can be retained but it changes its character. Play the **II-V-I** in C major with G under each chord. The G under the **II** changes it to an extended G dominant. The second chord is the G dominant with an altered voicing, and the last is the **I** with a fifth in the bass.

INTERNAL VOICES ON A MINOR

Chords often have movement on the middle voices while the top and bass notes are held in position. A scale or melody can be played on these internal voices. In the example below, A is held in the bass and C and E on the top two strings. B-A-G-F#-F-E are played as a descending scale.

C MAJOR ON THE 4TH STRING

Play C major 7, using the 4th string to play a scale or melody. With the little finger play D on the 12th fret, then C-B-A-G. To stretch to D and C you may need a barre for the chord positions. The scale changes the chord from C major 9 to C major, C major 7, C 6, and a variation of C major.

C MAJOR ON THE 3RD STRING

Play C major 7, using the 3rd string to play a scale or melody. With the little finger play F# on the 11th fret, then F#-E-D-C. To reach F# you may need a barre for the outer chord notes. The scale changes the chord from C major 7#11 to C major 7, C major 9, and C major 7 with an extra C.

BASS NOTE LINKS

Chords are often connected by playing changes while using a bass note to link movements. Below, descending diatonic notes are used with steps to fill the scale. Play the movement D minor 7-B minor 7♭5-E7#9-A minor 7. The bass note C links D minor 7 and B minor 7♭5, forming the line D-C-B. Play A minor 7, A minor 7 over G, F# minor 7♭5, F major 7, E7#5, and back to A minor 7. In the move from A minor 7 to F# the A root drops a tone to G, and this leads on to F# minor 7♭5. The bass root moves down a semitone to form F major 7. The bass drops by a semitone, and two middle notes by a tone and a semitone, to form E7#5. A series of chord movements using a descending bass line links two voicings of C major 7 with a cycle using modal chords to approach the **II-V-I**. Play C major 7, C major 7 over B, A minor 7, A minor 7 over G, F major 7, F major 7 over E, D minor 7, G7, and C major 7. This is a **I-VI-IV-II-V-I** with scale links.

SEQUENCE VARIATIONS

USING VOICINGS, SUBSTITUTIONS, AND INVERSIONS

Application
To control chord movements and compose or improvise creatively, it is important to be able to reduce a chord sequence to its basic movements. The sequences shown below move around a major and minor II-V-I. These mechanisms and voicings can be used in a standard jazz sequence. It is useful to write out the chords and locate all the V-I resolutions.

The potential of different chord voicings and movements can be explored by first becoming familiar with a framework of basic chords, and then using this structure as a guide in evaluating the sound and tonal quality of variations. If a chord sequence is played without regard to the melody, the movements of harmony and upper voices can be given free rein. When a piece is played solo the player can vary the bass line and make substitutions, so moving the sequence away from the original tonal centres. The **V-I** movements below, with approach chords and variations, form useful models for experimentation.

Transposition
Take the chord sequence below in its most basic form as a major II-V-I to a minor II-V-I and transpose it to every key. One of the simplest ways to do this is to locate the major I chord and treat this as a pivotal tonal centre for the whole sequence. The minor II-V-I chords can be found on the VII, III, and VI degrees of the major scale.

The major II-V
In this movement, the **II-V** approach to the major chord should be played using triads through to thirteenths with standard and close voicings.

The major I chord
Major **I** chords may be varied over one or two bars by revoicing them. One of the most common methods is to move a major seventh to a major sixth.

The minor II V
The minor **II-V** approach to the minor **I** chord should be voiced from triads through to extended chords. The **II** chord may be replaced by a diminished seventh.

The minor I chord
Minor **I** chords may be varied by moving minor sevenths to minor sixth chords. The minor seventh is converted at the end of the sequence below to a dominant seventh.

Major II-V variation
The **II** chord may be played as an inversion, and the **V** chord as a flat fifth.

Major I variation
A **IV** chord may follow a **I** chord. These chords may be connected with scalar steps.

Minor II-V variation
In this movement four diminished chords and a flat five are used.

Minor I variation
This moves in steps from the minor **I** to a diminished substitution for **V**.

Sequence 1
This is a major II-V-I to a relative minor II-V-I. The minor I is converted to a **V**7#5 chord, leading back to the beginning.

| Am7 | D9 | GM7 | G6 | F#m7♭5 | B7♭9 | Em7 | E7#5 |

Sequence 2
Here the major II-V-I supports a high B as the top note. The minor II-V-I has higher voicings, with a V7#5#9 at the end.

| Am9 | D13 | GM7 | G6 | F#m7♭5 | B7#5#9 | Em7 | E7#5#9 |

Sequence 3
The major II-V-I and the minor II-V-I are played with close voicings and open strings, with a V7#5♭9 at the end.

| Am9 | D9 | G6/9M7 | G6/9 | F#m11 | B13 | Em9 | E7#5♭9 |

Sequence 4
This is a major II-♭V-I to a minor II-♭V-I, with a V7#5 at the end. The bass line descends in semitones through both devices.

| Am7 | A♭7#5 | GM7 | G6 | F#m7♭5 | F7 | Em7 | E7#5 |

Sequence 5

Here the major II–♭V–I has close voicings. The minor II–V–I has a V9♭5 chord. The minor I chord uses a close voicing, and moves to a V13♭9 at the end.

Sequence 6

This major II–♭V–I uses close voicings and moves to a IV chord in the fourth bar. After the minor II–V–I the minor I moves to a V13 as a substitution.

Sequence 7

The major II and V chords use two voicings before moving to I and IV. The minor II ascends with inversions to the V, which uses two voicings.

Sequence 8

II moves to E♭ over D, which then resolves to I. The IV chord moves to an inversion of the minor II. The V leads to a series over a pedal note.

Sequence 9

Major II–♭V–I and minor II–♭V move to the minor I which ascends in steps up to a G♯ diminished seventh voicing, which leads back to the beginning.

Sequence 10

This major II–V uses inversions, and the I chord moves to IV in a step pattern. The minor II–V moves to a series of chords over a pedal note.

Sequence 11

A II chord here moves to a ♭V preceded by its own II chord, before resolving to I as an inversion. The ♭V and the related II are used for succeeding resolutions.

Sequence 12

Here a V moves to a series of I inversions by means of a diminished link chord. The minor II–V movement is played as a series of diminished chords.

Sequence 13

The major II–V–I moves to a minor II chord inversion. The V7♯5 moves to A♭ over B. The I is converted to an augmented chord, moving in whole-tone steps.

ADVANCED SCALES

FURTHER PENTATONIC SCALES AND SYNTHETIC FORMS

Pentatonic scales
Ethnic folk music often uses unusual types of pentatonic scale to provide melodic shape as well as form and structure. The principal notes from these scales sometimes provide both chordal harmony and a drone system, where pedal tones underpin the music. Try playing low pedal tones under the pentatonic scales by tuning the guitar to each of the notes in turn.

Chord progressions constructed with sophisticated harmonies may be used as a foundation for improvising with major and minor pentatonic scales, and with related modes. Each of these scales has its own distinctive tonal flavour. When ethnic or synthetic scales are built by altering the notes within the standard diatonic system, they frequently provide the material for extra colour in melodies and solos. Altered scales containing seven or more notes can be used to extend the diatonic system of soloing, and the chords that are created from such scales can be used to develop advanced harmonies.

Transposition
Transpose the pentatonic and chromatic scales, and all the related major key modes, in relation to the dominant chord to all root notes. The whole-tone and diminished scales are not transposable in the same way as other scale forms. As structures following a strict order of intervals, they occur on all chromatic roots as duplications of the five original scales.

PENTATONIC SCALES FROM C
Any two notes can be removed from a C major scale and its related modes in order to create a pentatonic scale. Notes may be taken out from different points, opening up steps of thirds or other intervals. Compare the scales on the right. The first is the major pentatonic without F and B. The second is a C pentatonic without E and B. The third is played without D and A, and the fourth without D and G.

PENTATONIC MODES
It is a useful exercise to compare the first two scales in relation to the standard minor pentatonic mode. The first pentatonic scale is the second mode of A minor pentatonic. The second scale is the fifth mode of D minor pentatonic. The third scale is C major without a second and sixth. The fourth scale is C major without a second and fifth. Try making up further pentatonic variations.

MAJOR AND MINOR PENTATONICS
In the key of C major there are three minor pentatonic scales, starting on D, E, and A, and three related major pentatonic scales, starting F, G, and C. The minor pentatonic starting on A has the major pentatonic starting as a mode on its second degree. The notes A-C-D-E-G-A run as a series C-D-E-G-A-C. The standard minor and major pentatonics shown on the right should be carefully compared.

C major/A minor
The C major and A minor pentatonic scales are modal versions of one another, both using the notes C-D-E-G-A-C.

F major/D minor
The F major and D minor pentatonic scales are modal versions of one another, both using the notes F-G-A-C-D-F.

G major/E minor
The G major and E minor pentatonic scales are modal versions of one another, both using the notes G-A-B-D-E-G.

Related scales
Play each pentatonic scale against the root chord, and the related major or minor chord. For example, A minor pentatonic over C major, and C major pentatonic over A minor.

PENTATONIC SCALE SYSTEM
This system is by Veryan Weston. A series of five pentatonic scales are made by raising each pitch one semitone in a sequence, termed "Interscalic Modulation". "Sequential Modulation" is achieved by raising pitches in another order. Using the common pentatonic, A is shifted up a semitone to A#, then D to D#, G to G#, C to C#, and finally F to F#. Two important pentatonic scales are anhemitonic (without semitones). The Common is built on a sequence of five ascending fourths, so A, D, G, C, F within an octave looks like the first example. The Overtone is built on the first five different pitches of the harmonic series D, E, F#, A, C.

Common pentatonic
This scale, found throughout the world, can be played from the D root. Try all the other notes as the root, giving five scales each with a totally different character.

Hirajoshi
This scale is related to the Japanese Hirajoshi scale. It is also an inversion of the previous Pelog scale.

Indian
Found in Rag Jog, the third is expressively flattened back to F when the scale descends. The Brindabani Sarang starts on G of this mode, with no type of 3rd.

Kumoi
This scale is related to the Japanese Kumoi scale and is an inversion of the previous Indian scale. All these scales are found within the Greek modal diatonic system.

Pelog
This is related to a version of the Balinese Pelog or Slendro scale. In this mode, it has a major 3rd, perfect 4th, perfect 5th, and major 7th.

Common pentatonic
After this sequence of modulations, it returns to the first type, but up one semitone. Try improvising with all these scales in the different modes and keys (transpositions).

THE WHOLE-TONE SCALE

The whole-tone scale is created from a series of major second (*whole-tone*) intervals. These intervals form a six-note scale within an octave, with an equal two-fret gap between each note – one note less than a diatonic scale. The scale starts at any point, and can use any note as a principal tone. There are two whole-tone scales: the second scale is built a semitone away from the first, and is composed of the other six chromatic notes.

Whole-tone harmony

Whole-tone scales can be used with certain chords. Play the augmented, the dominant flat and sharp five, and the dominant nine flat five and sharp five chords, from both whole-tone scales.

THE DIMINISHED SCALE

The diminished scale consists of a series of alternating major second and minor second intervals. A diminished scale from one note can start with either a tone leading on to a semitone, or a semitone leading on to a tone. There are three diminished scales altogether. The third scale is the same as the second scale, but moved up a semitone. This gives the possibility of alternating tone and semitone positions from every chromatic point. There are eight notes within the octave: with four semitones and four tones, this scale is extremely flexible.

Diminished harmony

Diminished scales can be used with diminished and altered dominant chords. Play a diminished chord on each scale note, and construct dominant chords with additions using the diminished scale.

THE CHROMATIC SCALE

The twelve notes of the chromatic scale cover every fret on the guitar. A good example of the use of chromaticism can be seen in the use of different elements over dominant chords. The dominant chord has a wide range of variations, using every note from the root except the major seventh. Certain notes played against a given chord are pleasing to the ear, and passages of chromatic harmony can be played between strong melodic points. Play a C dominant chord with altered upper note extensions and improvise freely, making use of the chromatic scale. Using the C dominant chord, play a series of modulating scales. Start with the Mixolydian scale from its root. Play the Dorian scale with E♭, using a pentatonic blues framework. Use further modulations from a C root playing the C Aeolian, C Phrygian, and C Locrian modes. This series of scales moves through the major key tonal centres F, B♭, E♭, A♭, and D♭. Modulate between two scales on the dominant chord. For example, try playing C Phrygian in A♭ to C Mixolydian in F. Adjust the C dominant altered chords to fit the scales.

FURTHER SCALES

A scale pattern using different intervals can be constructed within a single octave, extended beyond an octave, or formed between any points. The ten scales shown below are all octave scales. Some of these have been devised for use in classical composition, some are used as the basis for organizing systems of improvisation, and others are found in ethnic and non-Western music. Compare the scales by looking at their overall shape and order of intervals, and practise playing all of the subsidiary modes from each scale degree. Many of these scales are also modes of other scales: the Lydian augmented, C-D-E-F♯-G♯-A-B-C, is a *fixed melodic minor* (A-B-C-D-E-F♯-G♯) when it is played from A, an *overtone* scale (D-E-F♯-G♯-A-B-C) when it starts from D, and *super Locrian* (G♯-A-B-C-D-E-F♯) if it is played from G♯.

OVERTONE

LYDIAN MINOR

LYDIAN AUGMENTED

NEAPOLITAN MINOR

ENIGMATIC

DOUBLE HARMONIC

INDIAN-TYPE

ORIENTAL

MINOR 2ND AND MINOR 3RD

SUPER LOCRIAN

Synthetic scales

A wide range of scales can be constructed within a single octave. Many are modal inversions of major and minor scales.

Synthetic scales are often variations on these systems, using either a different number of notes within the octave or adjusted individual notes.

DEVELOPING CREATIVITY

CONTEMPORARY APPROACHES TO IMPROVISATION

The major modes
All the ideas on this page can be used for extending soloing capabilities. Experiment constantly with the diatonic scale system, using it as a framework for creativity. The major modes on their own can be used to provide an endless source of material for melody, composition, and improvisation. A wide range of musical possibilities can be explored and developed from working effectively within one small area and extending the horizon in stages.

Most areas of contemporary guitar playing can hardly be said to be innovative in any sense. Methods for improvisation are often based on stylistic imitation, which limits the imagination. The rules applied to the use of harmony and scales are either very limited or conservative. This tends to lock the player into an approach characterized by a narrow outlook.

Discipline and practice have often led to rigidity, and yet advanced approaches have been in existence for many years: there is simply no limit to the stylistic areas that can be explored. Elements from outside the standard frameworks are apparent in most types of music. Experimenting with tonality, and thinking analytically will extend a musician's vocabulary.

Application
Apply the ideas given on these pages to a chord sequence. For example, create a C major sequence consisting of chords with a structure using fourths and fifths. Solo freely using C major as a tonal centre using all types of intervals and motifs. Move towards chromaticism by using notes outside the scale. The position of the chromatic material in relation to the harmonic and rhythmic structure determines its effect.

CHROMATICISM AND SCALES

The major scale on the right can be viewed as a system of major second and minor second intervals. The gap between each can be filled with a chromatic step. Play every type of scale using chromaticism, with emphasis placed on the elements that make up the original scale. Improvise with C major using the five chromatic tones as passing notes, starting and ending phrases on a scale note. Try playing phrases starting on a chromatic note and ending on a scale note. An example of scale modification is shown below. Chromatic notes are added to the major scale. The adjacent scale notes above are then removed to form a synthetic scale.

CHROMATICISM WITH ONE NOTE

Play the C major scale, and improvise freely. There are five chromatic notes that can be added to the scale. Play five versions of the scale with the inclusion of a chromatic note. This note can be stressed within the scale or played as a passing note. Some chromatic notes work particularly well. The inclusion of G♯ is not uncommon: its use opens up a wider range of melodic and harmonic possibilities.

THE TWELVE-TONE SYSTEM

The twelve notes of the chromatic scale can be organized to form a structure of any type. This is a useful exercise for practising improvisation and developing technical control. Take the chromatic scale from C and move in any direction, using the remaining eleven notes without repeats.

Twelve-tone exercise
Make up a twelve-note phrase and move the series of notes down a semitone, retaining the overall shape and structure of the phrase. Move this phrase to the other ten chromatic roots.

IMPROVISING FROM PIVOTAL NOTES

Take the C major scale and improvise freely, using all the modal fingering patterns and positions. Move in any direction without any restrictions in length, phrasing, or rhythm. Pick out each note of the major scale, stressing it as a principal note. Build melodic phrases starting from and resolving to this note, using combinations of scalar and interval movements. This helps to develop directional control. Try playing passages of notes using a free approach and a major scale.

INTERVALS

The construction and tuning of the guitar, coupled with a limited technical approach, tends to condition the player, leading to improvisation with a predominantly scalar form. Passages of notes and melodies often to use seconds and thirds, with only occasional interval jumps. To open up a wider vocabulary of melodic material and increase technical facility, make up passages with combinations of intervals from fourths to octaves and beyond.

MOTIFS

Motifs often have the same shape, but start from different points on the scale. Play a three-note motif – starting with C-D-E – on every degree; the motif is taken through two further types of variation using minor seconds. Make up a phrase in C, repeating it from the other scale degrees. Now play the interval pattern as a structure that conforms to the combination of available intervals on other degrees. Play a three-note movement as a chromatic ascending structure. Take the motif C-D-E and move it up in semitones on the twelve notes before returning to C. Construct a motif with any form or shape, and move it to all the chromatic letter name roots.

Diatonic
Play the notes C, D, and E at the beginning of the C major scale. Play three-note ascending motifs with varying forms on each degree of the scale.

Transpositional
Shift the motif C, D, E by using a chromatic approach. Play the motif with the same shape in relation to C, D, and E on every chromatic point.

ATONAL HARMONY

When notes are combined in close voicings, or with non-standard scale tones, they often cease to function as diatonic chords relating to standard scales. Unusual or dissonant chords can be combined into sequences without clear tonal centres. Play through the four tonal centres, making up chord sequences and experimenting with additions to the chords. Obvious clash tones can be placed in the chords. Reconstruct all the voicings, and experiment with tonal relationships: include unusual non-scalar tones.

Clusters
Play the clusters above. You will notice that they sound highly dissonant.

Altered B chord
This chord is highly dissonant. It does not relate to standard scales.

Atonal sequence
This example can be interpreted as supporting a melody. As four individual chords they do not have straightforward tonal relationships.

Modifying a tonal centre
Take each tonal centre marked above and, with one or more of the chords in each key, form chord sequences. Experiment with linking chords by using all types of movement and resolution. Take the chords away from strict scale relationships with the use of chromaticism. Develop the harmony and improvise until the use of extra notes takes the music away from the tonal centre.

ALL THE THINGS YOU ARE

THE AUTHOR'S SPECIAL ARRANGEMENTS OF THIS STANDARD

Development
This was originally written by the American songwriter Jerome Kern (1885-1945) for the 1939 musical *Very Warm For May*.

This 36-bar song is an ideal vehicle to develop harmony. The series of modulating chords is also popular as a basis for linear improvisation. Below is the melody with standard jazz chords and three arrangements by author Richard Chapman.

Key comparison
Memorize the chord sequence as groups within each tonal centre. Play and learn the piece in other keys such as C major, too.

First eight bars
The first five bars have **VI-II-V-I-IV** in the key of A♭. This goes to **V-I** in the key of C over three bars. The melody is based on the third of each chord. It has words by Oscar Hammerstein, which have been left out here.

Second eight bars
The whole harmonic movement is repeated down a fourth with five bars following **VI-II-V-I-IV** in the key of E♭. This goes to **V-I** in the key of G.

Middle eight bars
The next section is a middle eight or bridge. It has a **II-V-I** in G major over four bars, a **II-V-I** in E major over three bars, and a linking C7#5 (**V**) chord in one bar, which leads back to F minor.

Last 12 bars
The opening melody returns. There are five bars with **VI-II-V-I-IV** in the key of A♭. A D♭ minor chord (**II** in C♭) steers the harmony to an extended ending. As the harmony approaches the final A♭, it runs through **III**, **♭III dim**, **II**, **V**, and **I**, which support the final phrases of the melody.

FIRST ARRANGEMENT

This arrangement is based entirely on close voicings: chord notes or additional notes from the related modal scale are placed so that they are a major second or minor second apart, adding an attractive impressionistic depth to the chords. Placing seconds on adjacent strings requires the guitarist to stretch the fingering shapes for chords. For example, an F minor 9 will have the G on the 3rd string held by the second finger and the A♭ on the 2nd string held by the first finger. This is a 4-fret stretch between the ninth of the chord and the third above it. Close voicings can be obtained by using open strings as well. Work out all the modal scale notes for every chord and try to find them throughout the fingerboard and open strings to create interesting voicings. These arrangements do not use the melody and have been kept rhythmically simple. They use two ♭5 substitutions in bars six and fourteen.

First eight bars
F minor 7 is converted to a close-voiced F minor 9. The order of notes is root, seventh, ninth, and third. This is moved as parallel harmony up to B♭ minor 9. This order of chord notes is retained and modified for each type of chord up to C major 9.

Second eight bars
A similar system of voicings and parallel movements is used for the next eight bars.

Middle eight bars
This approach continues with a rich six-note voicing on the E major 6/7. There is a wide stretch on the C7#5#9, where the first finger holds the D# and the G# on the top two strings.

Last 12 bars
The voicings from the first eight return before going to a D♭ minor 9 with a fretted E♭ and open E. The B diminished add G chord is turned into a Locrian-type close voicing, which moves to the final chords.

SECOND ARRANGEMENT

This developed arrangement turns the piece into interesting music with a number of harmonic devices and approaches. It moves further away from conventional jazz, using a compositional approach. The function of the chords is not as support for the melody or even as a framework for linear improvisation. There are more adventurous close voicings and flat five (♭V) substitutions and inversions. Step movements, where a chord can move up a related scale or mode, and bass links create variety and interest. Many of the chords are worked out as individual voicings first. Theory, involving systems of organizing chords, compositional thinking, improvisation, inspiration, and even fortuitous accidents, have contributed to playing and writing down this sequence. It stands on its own without the melody.

First eight bars

F minor 7 is converted to a close-voiced F minor 6/9 with the use of an open G string. A13♭5 substitutes E♭9. The series of chords from D♭ major 7#11 to C major 9 uses subtle common notes.

Second eight bars

C minor 7 has been converted to an inversion of C minor 11 with a G in the bass. This voicing has been moved as a parallel harmony to F minor 11/C. D9 has been converted to A♭7#9, which leads to E minor 9, a developed inversion of G major 7.

Middle eight bars

A minor 7 moves up to a first inversion C6, which pivots on the C to move to D7/C and then D7♭9. G major moves with a bass link through its related E minor chord to F# minor 7/C#. E major is turned into an ascending modal step movement.

First eight bars: F MIN6/9   B♭MIN9   A13♭5   A♭6/7/9   D♭MAJ7#11   D MIN11   D♭7#9#11   C MAJ9   C MAJ9

Second eight bars: C MIN11/G   F MIN11/C   B♭13   E♭MAJ6/7   A♭MAJ7   A MIN9   A♭7#9   E MIN9   E MIN9

Middle eight bars: A MIN7   C6   D7/C   D7♭9   G MAJ7   G MAJ7/F#   E MIN7   E MIN7/D   F#MIN7/C#   F#MIN7♭5/C   B7#5   B♭9   E MAJ6/7   F#MIN7/E   G#MIN7/E   A MAJ7/E   C7#5#9   C7#5#9

Last 12 bars

A high F minor 9 moves down using a standard B♭ minor 7 to an E♭13♭9. Here, the voice movement resolves the E natural (♭9th) up into an F (6th) in A♭ major 6/7. Five-note chords run from D♭6/7/9 to A♭ major 7, which rests with a four-note voicing.

Last 12 bars: F MIN9   B♭MIN7   E♭13♭9   A♭MAJ6/7   D♭6/7/9   D♭MIN13   C MIN11   B DIM ADD G AND C   B♭MIN9   A 13♭9   A♭MAJ7   A♭MAJ7

THIRD ARRANGEMENT

The final fully developed arrangement turns All The Things You Are into another harmonic composition, using similar approaches to the last version. This time there are more inversions, inner voice movements, and the use of a pedal tone G under a long section. Even when fully developing a jazz standard, the harmonic foundation must be accurate. It is still important to think in simple terms about the basic tonal centres or keys and the direction of the harmony. Throughout this arrangement melodic ideas have shaped many chord voicings and movements. Play the arrangements in time, but work on developing them in free time, without a fixed beat, as well. Compare chords in all the arrangements with the basic "jazz voicings" under the melody on the first page.

First eight bars
F minor 7 is converted to a close-voiced F minor 9 inversion with the fifth, C in the bass. This moves as a parallel voicing to Bb minor 9/F. Ab major 7 and Db major 7 become inversions with the fifth in the bass. The Ab is used to move into the Db minor 7b5/Ab.

Second eight bars
C minor 7 has been converted to a C minor 9 with the fifth, G in the bass. The G is retained in the bass as a pedal tone for the next chords all the way through until the tension is released on a simple G major 7.

Middle eight bars
The G pedal tone is retained for the A minor and D 11 chords, moving to G major 7. G continues under the F# diminished and F13 chord. The tension is released on the E major, which is played as a low close voicing. A G minor 13 chord and Gb9b5 (bV) lead back to F minor 7.

Last 12 bars
F minor/major 9 moves to F minor 9 with inner voice movement. Bb minor 9 to Bb minor 6/9 and Eb9 to Eb7b9 also use inner voice movement. Db minor 6/9 uses fretted and open B notes. B diminished add G uses two fretted D notes. Bb minor 6/7 uses an open G before going to the Eb13b9 and resolving to Ab major 9.

F MIN 9/C   Bb MIN9/F   Eb7b9   Ab MAJ 7/Eb

Db MAJ 7/Ab   D MIN7b5/Ab   G13b9   C MAJ6/7   C MAJ6/7/9

C MIN9/G   F MIN9/G   Bb13/G   Eb MAJ6/7/G

Ab MAJ7/G   D7b9/G   G MAJ7   G MAJ6

A MIN/G   D11/G   G MAJ7   G MAJ9

F# DIM/G   F13/G   E MAJ 9   G MIN13   Gb9b5

F MIN/MAJ9   F MIN9   Bb MIN9   Bb MIN6/9   Eb9   Eb7b9   Ab MAJ9

Db MAJ 9   Db MIN 6/9   C MIN9   B DIM ADD G

Bb MIN6/7   Eb9   Ab MAJ9   Ab MAJ9

SOUND AND AMPLIFICATION

For the modern guitarist, amplification, sound processing, and recording are important complementary skills. In fact, to many rock musicians, they are as central to their art as playing the guitar itself. With the myriad of valve and solid-state amplification, low-cost digital muliple-effects units, and reasonably priced home-recording equipment, the areas covered in this section of the book are now more accessible than ever before.

GUITAR AMPLIFICATION
AN INTRODUCTION TO AMPLIFYING THE ELECTRIC GUITAR

Choosing a guitar
Because guitars differ in their sonic characteristics, it is important to select a model which suits your musical purposes. If you are interested in only one type of sound, such as chunky rock textures, the task is relatively easy. Many players, though, want versatility. This can be achieved with certain guitars – the super-Strat, the coil-tapped Les Paul, the varitone-equipped Gibson semi, or the PRS. The other solution is to opt for two or more distinct instruments, and use each where appropriate.

The first electric guitars were produced with a single pickup. Height-adjustable polepieces were introduced in the 1940s, enabling players to balance the response for each string. Guitars with two or more pickups also began to appear around this time: the ability to switch between pickups, use combinations to produce different textures, and adjust the volume and tone controls for both lead and rhythm settings increased the versatility of the guitar. During the 1950s, the commercial success of solid-body guitars took place at the same time as the development of improved amplifiers, leading to new types of sound. The spectrum of colour produced by the electric guitar was fully utilized with the advent of guitar-based groups playing electric blues and rock music.

Creating a sound
Although there are hundreds of different amplifiers and effects on the market, certain approaches to enhancing guitar signals are used repeatedly. Distortion gives guitar a raunchy or sustaining edge. Reverb adds a subtle sense of space. Echo gives fast, rhythmic repeats or layer effects. Chorus, phasing, and flanging also provide interesting textures. A good amplifier will have powerful tone-shaping capabilities, either via its tone controls or thanks to electronics and speakers with a distinctive "voice".

GIBSON ES-175
This physically deep, hollow-bodied guitar with wooden bridge and humbucking pickups has a mellow, woody sound ideally suited to jazz styles. Over the years, it has become something of a standard choice in this application, with enthusiastic users ranging from Jim Hall and Joe Pass to Pat Metheny and Steve Howe. Yamaha and Ibanez also make fine jazz guitars.

Three-a-side, angled-back headstock
The headstock angle ensures that the open strings ring properly.

GIBSON ES-335
This famous "semi-solid" combines hollow-body and solid-body attributes. Acoustic cavities and "f"-holes give the sound a woody character, while the solid centre block provides much enhanced sustain. Famous 335 users include Alvin Lee, Chuck Berry, Larry Carlton, and B.B. King; this very versatile guitar also finds favour with pop and funk players.

Three-way toggle switch
This allows selection of the neck or the bridge pickup, or both together.

Body The hollow body gives good tone and sensitivity, but feedback problems may arise in a high-gain, high-volume rock situation.

Body The body depth, at around 5 cm (2 in), is modest compared with that of the 175. However the centre block and the overall size make this a relatively heavy instrument.

Humbucking pickups
These provide a mellow feel, although the bridge pickup will give a sharper sound than the neck pickup. These guitars were fitted with single-coil P 90's until 1957-8.

Pickups High-output, twin-coil humbuckers give a raunchy rock/blues sound with good touch-sensitivity.

Volume control

Tune-O-Matic Bridge

Tone control

Stud tailpiece

Wiring Each pickup has its own volume and tone control, so it is possible to switch between two sounds that differ not only in tone but in volume. This is useful for moving from ensemble to solo playing, or from chords to single-note passages.

Wiring The 335 has the standard Gibson layout of two volumes and two tone controls with three-way pickup selector, although some luxury versions (such as the 355 and Lucille) feature stereo wiring and the Varitone six-position tone selector.

A BRIEF HISTORY OF GUITAR AMPLIFIERS

Guitar amplification originally developed in the 1930s, and was based on the radio and hi-fi technology of the day. However, the first major advances were made in the 1950s and 1960s with the advent of Rock'n'Roll in the USA, and then the "Beat Boom" in the UK. Many Fender and Vox models from this era are now valuable vintage items, prized for their tone and quality of distortion, although any raunchy overdrive or biting "edge" was quite unintentional from a design point of view. With the UK heavy rock scene in the later 1960s came the development of the Marshall stack – a powerful amplifier with either one or two 4x12 in speaker cabinets – where distortion at high volume was purely intentional. The 1970s saw a craze for "hot-rodding", especially in the States, with amp-

techs squeezing more gain and greater distortion from classic Fender and Marshall designs. Randy Smith built "cascaded" gain-stages into his high-power 1x12 in Mesa/Boogie combo; the distorted output from one preamp stage was fed into the next, and so on, to give a very high sustaining, hi-gain distortion. By the end of the decade, all the major manufacturers offered "master volume" models that enabled distorted sounds to be obtained at any volume. Then came channel-switching, with three-channel designs such as the Boogie Mk III or Marshall Anniversary, allowing players to select clean, "crunch", or lead sounds via a footswitch. However big the venue or varied the set, it is now possible to take a small, versatile combo on stage, mike it up, and let the PA provide the "bulk" sound out front, with wedge monitors

filling in the on-stage sound. The latest developments include programmable pre-amps, digital effects, and MIDI control. Running parallel to this hi-tech "rack" approach is a renewed interest in the simple, high-quality combos and heads of the past, used with warm-sounding (if technically flawed) analogue effects such as tape echo. Similarly, solid-state technology – bi-polar transistors, FETs, ICs, MOSFETs, and so on – was meant to make "old-fashioned" valves redundant but has not succeeded, even after three decades of innovation. All-solid-state combos such as the Peavey Bandit are light and versatile. Hybrid designs are also enjoying a wave of popularity. However, the top end of the market is still dominated by all-valve designs, including vintage reissues.

GIBSON LES PAUL

This small but heavy, high-quality solid-body guitar is associated with rock playing and tremendous sustain. Though in 1952 Les Paul and Gibson were thinking of a clean, jazz sound rather than the fat, raunchy overload with which Eric Clapton, Jimmy Page, Keith Richards, and Mike Bloomfield made the model popular in the 1960s and 1970s. The first instruments had P90 single-coil pickups, but it is the Sunburst model with PAF Humbuckers from 1958–1960 that is the most coveted – and widely copied – variant.

Three-way toggle switch

Pickups These high-output Patent-Applied-For pickups (PAFs) will easily overload the input stages of a good amp. The dual-coil construction also keeps hum and buzz at bay.

Wiring This model has the standard two volumes and two tones. The neck pickup gives a rich sound, while the bridge pickup provides a fat sound with a biting edge. Selecting both with varied settings produces different types of sounds. Some players wire the pickups out of phase for a nasal mid-tone, associated with players such as Peter Green.

Volume control

Tone control

Six-in-line headstock As this is not angled back, a string-tree is used so that open treble strings ring properly.

FENDER STRATOCASTER

The Strat is probably the most familiar of all electric guitars, having been made popular by players from Buddy Holly and Hank Marvin to Jimi Hendrix and Eric Clapton. This solid-body instrument with three single-coil pickups gives a bright and clear sound with plenty of cut and "twang", while the controls are designed to offer plenty of subtle tonal variation. The combined tremolo unit/bridge is standard. It has a bolt-on neck that contributes to the characteristic resonance and tone.

Body The Strat is comfort-contoured and lightweight, with an ash or alder body.

Single-coil pickups The low output level makes the Strat sound cleaner than a humbucker-equipped guitar at a given amp setting.

Middle pickup

Tremolo arm

Wiring The standard instrument has a master volume and two tone controls. Many variations are possible with the use of the pickup selector.

FROM JAZZ TO ROCK

Distortion
If a very high-level signal is fed into an amplifier, for instance when playing a humbucker-equipped guitar, the early pre-amplifier stages distort to give the sound a fuzzy, sustaining edge. Using the amplifier on full volume pushes the power stage to the limit, producing a different kind of distortion and, in classic valve designs, a loose, warm sound. Overworked speaker cones also contribute to this effect.

Different styles of playing often make widely varying demands on amplifiers, particularly in terms of the distortion and volume level required. The Marshall stack, wah-wah pedal, fuzz-box, and tremolo-equipped Fender Stratocaster used by Jimi Hendrix and shown on the facing page are geared to produce extremely high levels of distortion and volume. This equipment would be unfamiliar territory, and perhaps an inappropriate set-up, for most jazz guitarists. These musicians would probably prefer the wide-band, distortion-free amplification given by the set-up shown below, which provides mellow acoustic tones and is also ideal for use in small, intimate settings.

Inside an amplifier
The principal sections inside an amplifier are the pre-amp, power-amp (output stage), and power supply. The pre-amp includes the input, tone circuitry, gain and volume controls, and effects loop. The signal then passes to the output stage, which provides the "magnification" needed to drive one or more speakers. The power supply converts AC mains power to DC, which is required to run the amplifier.

Gibson ES-175

The volume and tone controls can only subtract from the signals that come from the pickups; they cannot boost the volume, treble, or bass at all. The two tone controls (one for each pickup) work identically, either "rolling off" the treble or passing signals to the amp unhindered. The maple and plywood laminated body has tonal clarity and excellent acoustic resonance. This type of guitar is frequently used with the treble rolled off to give a warm "jazzy" sound. It is one of the few archtop jazz guitars to be used in rock music, in spite of feedback problems.

Selector switch This has a rubber mount, to prevent an amplified switching noise being heard from the soundboard when the guitar is used at high volume.

Pickups The ES-175 is fitted with two Gibson humbucking pickups.

Bridge Standard models are fitted with a metal "Tune-o-matic" bridge. This model has been fitted with a wooden bridge.

ARCHTOP AMPLIFICATION

Jazz guitarists often seek harmonic, melodic, and rhythmic inventiveness rather than layered sound-scapes or touch-sensitive distortion textures. This combination of a Gibson ES-175 guitar and Polytone amplifier is suited to jazz musicians, and has been used by Joe Pass and many other players. The single-channel combo has simple tone controls, with no overdrive or built-in effects. It does, however, feature solid-state amplification, driving a high-quality Eminence 12-inch speaker. The good bass extension and definition are ideal for the 175 with its humbucking pickups.

Polytone Mini-Brute I
The 90-watt model shown on the right dates from 1978. It features both high- and low-sensitivity input sockets, and treble and bass controls. A sliding tone filter switch is used for "bright", "middle", and "dark" tone selection. The Mini-Brute I has a single volume control: it is not possible to balance gain, channel volume, and master volume as you can with a modern channel-switching amplifier. A kick-proof grille protects the speaker cone.

Sliding tone switch

High- and low-sensitivity inputs

POLYTONE AMPLIFIERS

Polytone amplifiers were developed in the USA in the mid-1970s. During the design stage, several leading jazz guitarists were brought in as consultants. The small portable combo that was created had a clear, balanced solid-state sound; this proved ideal for the amplification of archtop guitars, which are frequently used by jazz players. The particular strengths of these amplifiers have also resulted in their use with the double bass and other acoustic instruments.

GUITAR EFFECTS

Foot-controlled effect units provide the player with sounds outside of the range of a normal guitar and amplifier combination. They put control of tone and distortion at the guitarist's feet so that the sound can be adjusted while both hands are kept on the guitar. Early units included: fuzz-boxes, which produce instant distortion; treble-boosters; volume and tone pedals, first designed for setting the volume or tone while playing but later used for "swell" and "wah-wah" effects; and tape-echo, creating single repeats or layered echo. Many floor units are battery-powered, but can also accept DC from mains adaptors; some are mains-powered. Units such as digital multi-FX may be mounted in a rack with a footswitch, or a MIDI controller may be used as an optional extra. Floor pedals are usually designed to receive guitar-level signals, whereas some rack units need line-level signals from, for example, a combo's FX loop or a stand-alone pre-amp.

THE MARSHALL STACK

The most effective way to use this Hendrix-style rig is to set all the controls to "10"; the guitarist can then control the distortion, tone, and loudness accurately by using the guitar's volume control and the effects pedals. Turning down the guitar reduces the level of the input signal, resulting in clean sounds. The wah-wah pedal may be used to boost the treble or bass, while the fuzz-box provides extra raunch and (by overloading the Marshall's input) helps create smooth lead-lines with extra-long sustain. Using the rig at full stretch gives grinding power-amp distortion and howling feedback; in experienced hands, though, the latter may be controlled to harmonize with the music.

Feedback and tremolo

The position of the guitar in relation to the speakers produces different levels of feedback. Tremolo control is also important. Jimi Hendrix was a master in this area, with an impressive repertoire of techniques. Modern tremolo systems such as the Kahler and the Floyd Rose are more acutely responsive than the older Fender unit, suiting fingerboard-tapping, rapid arpeggiating, and sweep-picking techniques.

Rosewood fingerboard

Pickguard This model features a discoloured early plastic pickguard.

Connections The guitar lead runs first into the wah-wah pedal, then into the Fuzz Face, which can be adjusted with the rotary controls. The output is finally plugged into the Marshall head.

Standby switch

Marshall head The output is nominally 100 watts, but with modification the head is capable of 150 watts. There is no reverb, channel switching, or master volume control.

Cabinet The top cabinet has a sloping front.

Arbiter Fuzz Face

Vox wah-wah pedal

Hendrix Stratocaster

This is the guitar used by Jimi Hendrix at the Woodstock festival. A stock 1968 model, this has neither special pickups nor customized wiring, but notice that it is reverse-strung, with the low E nearest to the volume control. This is because Hendrix played left-handed but (with Strats, at least) simply used right-handed guitars turned upside-down. Maple-fingerboard Strats like this one have a brighter sound than those for which rosewood is used, but the difference is subtle and Hendrix used both types widely. Some of his instruments were also re-wired and modified extensively.

Maple fingerboard

Strap button Hendrix moved the strap button to the body's lower horn for left-handed playing.

Laminated pickguard

Tremolo unit The arm has been removed from the tremolo unit.

HENDRIX AND EFFECTS

Jimi Hendrix enhanced his music with several different effects. At first he used a fuzz unit, then, when he moved to England, he switched to the Arbiter Fuzz Face, with a Vox wah-wah pedal. In the late 1960s Hendrix was joined by the engineer and inventor Roger Mayer, who built the Octavia. This unit is a frequency doubler which adds upper frequencies to the guitar signal. The Uni-Vibe is a filtering device that simulates a Leslie rotating speaker. It produces chorus and vibrato effects. One of the combinations used was the wah-wah with a fuzz unit, re-wired by Roger Mayer and fed through an Octavia to the Uni-Vibe.

Octavia The design ensures that the unit cannot be accidentally turned over on stage.

Uni-Vibe This unit has a separate floor switch to control the speed.

SPRING REVERB

THE IMPORTANCE OF REVERB TO THE GUITARIST

Small amplifiers

It is tempting to think that a large and heavy combo, or a powerful amp-top plus 4x12, must be better than a small, old-fashioned combo with a modest power rating. Many older models, though, are prized for their distinctive tone, classic good looks, fine build-up quality, and the fact that they can be wound up loud for natural valve distortion and compression at clubs or small gigs.

If electric guitars are played in a large acoustic space such as a hall or room, then the natural reverberation produced will add a satisfying "bloom" to the sound, smoothing out chord-work and helping individual lead-notes to die away gradually. This effect may be simulated within an amplifier by sending the guitar signal down long springs in the reverb section. "Spring reverb", as it was known, became a popular feature in the early 1960s. Fender, for instance, provided it first as a stand-alone unit (shown below), and then as a built-in effect in many of their medium-size and larger combos.

Speaker size

Although the 12-in speaker is now the standard choice for use with electric guitars, many famous combos have used other sizes. In general, bigger cones handle the bass-end easily, but are not so good at conveying detail and dynamic shading; thus the 4x10 in format may give a punchier sound than 4x12 in, and a 15-in speaker will set off the warmth and depth of a good six-string guitar.

Fender Telecaster

The Fender Telecaster is very much a "guitarists' guitar", chosen for the quality of its sound, a solid "feel", and overall simplicity. It is capable of producing a crisp, clean sound, or a raunchy thick-textured effect. Many of the finest players have favoured this solid-body instrument.

FENDER VIBROLUX

This 2x12 all-valve combo with brown Tolex covering dates from the early 1960s and has two channels – Normal and Bright – though players cannot change channels by footswitching as on a modern amplifier. The "Vibro" prefix indicates that it has built-in vibrato (hence the *speed* and *intensity* controls), but note that this is a rhythmic variation in volume rather than pitch, and gives a tremolo effect.

FENDER REVERB UNIT

In 1961, Fender offered spring reverb as a stand-alone unit with its own mains power-supply, before including the effect in many of its amplifiers the following year. The reverb unit was operated by plugging the guitar into the unit's single input and running a lead from the unit's output to the input on an ordinary amplifier. Signals arrived at the amplifier with reverb superimposed on them, and players were able to alter the proportion of affected to original signal, the depth of the effect, and its tone. The tone-shaping facility, and the sound from the all-valve circuitry, make this unit popular with many players.

Covering White or brown Tolex was used to cover Fender amplifiers in the early 1960s.

Circuitry The Fender reverb featured valve circuitry with its own power supply.

Screening-cans

REVERB TRAY

At the heart of this unit is the reverb tray or *pan*. This sturdy metal tray has a sprung subchassis which carries a delicate spring with a small transducer at each end. The electrical signal taken from the pre-amp is converted by the first transducer to a mechanical vibration, which is fed along the spring and changed back into an electrical signal at the other end. The *return* signal, with heavy reverb, is fed back to the pre-amp, where it is mixed with the *dry* signal sent by a direct route bypassing the reverb tray; *reverb level* alters the proportion. Usually, two or three springs run in parallel to cover bass, mid-range, and treble frequencies.

Swell control This feeds reverb by varying the amount of "swell".

Output

Tone control

Mix This control mixes the dry and reverb signals.

VALVE SOUNDS

THE VINTAGE VALVE SOUND OF THE FENDER BASSMAN

A combination of the clean, cutting edge and fine tone of the 4x10 Fender Bassman combo, produced in the late 1950s, make it both one of the most widely copied amplifiers of all time and a highly valued item of music memorabilia. The simple, all-valve circuit has no modern extras such as reverb or pull-boosts to dilute signal quality, while the *valve rectifiers* ensure that the amplifier gives rich-sounding compression and distortion when played at high volumes. Eddie Cochran, Buddy Guy, and Freddie King are among the many famous players who regularly used the Bassman.

Valve or solid-state?
Valves and transistors can both amplify guitar signals, the two technologies produce very different sounds. Solid-state models tend to be small and cheap to produce. They offer wide-band sound at low frequencies but may lack harmonic richness. Valve amps give interesting tones and tasteful overload, but are less effective for producing a hi-gain sound.

Hybrid amplifiers
There are two types of hybrid amplifier. The first has valves in the pre-amp, and a solid-state power-stage. The second combines a solid-state front-end with a valve power-stage. Modern rectifiers are usually solid-state. The valve rectifiers on early amplifiers were inefficient but had a distinct "feel". Valves are often included as an option on certain models.

Different materials
Fender Stratocasters with maple fingerboards have a slightly different sound and feel to those with rosewood fingerboards. The use of ash or maple for the body can also affect the resonance, tone, and body-weight. In addition, alterations in construction over the years can lead to wide variations between models.

Materials and finish This 1965 model has a rosewood neck with a three-tone sunburst finish. Rosewood was introduced in 1959. Around the same time, three-tone finishes started to replace the two-tone variety.

Pickups Modern Stratocasters are fitted with new pickups which alter the tone and output considerably.

Bridge cover Many players prefer to remove the "ash tray" bridge cover because it inhibits right-hand damping.

COMBINATIONS
Although the ubiquitous Stratocaster has partnered many amplifiers over the years, the original Fender company always presented certain combinations of guitar and amplifier as natural partners. Many famous recordings have been made with a combination of a 1950s Stratocaster with a Fender Bassman from the same period. This pairing was often used in conjunction with an Echoplex echo unit.

Presence

Volume 1

Volume 2

4X10 FENDER BASSMAN

This example is from 1956 or 1957 and has a standard Fender tweed finish. During this period, the models were fitted with bass and treble controls, but without "middle". They also had two valve rectifiers rather than one. The *presence* control, which was a major contributor to the amplifier's cutting tone, was part of the unit's power-amp circuitry: on many modern amplifiers presence is simply another pre-amp tone control. As a result of their enduring popularity, both the tweed Bassman and the brown Tolex Vibroverb, which was essentially the Vibrolux with built-in reverb, have been re-issued by Fender.

GETTING THE MOST FROM A VINTAGE AMPLIFIER

Vintage amplifiers can sometimes seem unyielding. They often have to be played at full volume to produce the right distortion and compression, while the dry sound and lack of reverb may be unattractive in a confined space. One solution involves using a speaker simulator. These soak up the excess power of the amplifier, turning it into heat, and leave a signal that may be sent directly to a speaker, mixing desk, or tape machine. The major drawback is that old style power-valves and output transformers are heavily stressed by regular use at full volume. Older speakers should last for a long time.

THE VOX AC30

A CLASSIC COMBO

Class "A"
The Vox AC30 differs from other guitar amplifiers in that it runs its power valves in the old-fashioned and inefficient Class "A" – a mode of operation which yields only 30 watts from the four EL84 valves. However, it produces sonic rewards, with satisfying sustain, dynamic "punch" even in overload, and overtones that enhance the sound of the guitar.

Early recordings by The Beatles, The Rolling Stones, The Shadows, and most of Queen or Rory Gallagher's music, are all enhanced by the sound of the Vox AC30 amplifier. Since its design in 1960, the AC30 has suited a wide range of musical styles, supplying a clean, punchy sound with harmonic richness even at relatively low volumes. As the decade passed by, these attractive qualities were complemented as the decades passed by increasing amounts of raunchy overdrive as the volume was wound up, especially on *Top Boost* models. The original combo was reissued in the early 1990s.

Controls
Combos designed up to the early 1960s almost always had top-mounted, rear-facing control panels. The idea was that the combo would sit at the front of the stage – often doubling as a PA system – and controls could be adjusted from behind. When the "backline" idea came in, control panels were moved to the front of the combos, some angled back for better legibility.

The Fender Stratocaster
One of the great strengths of the tried-and-trusted Fender Stratocaster is that it can serve so many styles superbly. When combined with an AC30 and an early tape echo unit such as a Watkins Copycat (below) or an Echoplex, it is possible to produce the sort of clean, rich, and powerful sound associated with music by many well-known musicians. By turning up the amplifier, hitting the strings harder, and adding a vintage fuzz-box such as the Tone-bender, players can produce a fine blues/rock sound in the style of Jeff Beck or Rory Gallagher.

AC30 SPECIFICATIONS
The all-valve, 30-watt, 2x12 AC30 has three channels – "brilliant", "normal", and "vib-trem" – each with high and low inputs, so a whole band (three guitars, bass, and two microphones) can plug in and play. The Bulldog speakers are famed for their tone, and pleasing "break-up" sound, but the earliest models could only just handle 15 watts each, so the coils sometimes burned out. The effects channel features both vibrato (pitch modulation) and tremolo (volume modulation).

Alternative combinations
Over the years, the Vox AC30 has been successfully used with many guitars. A combination of a Gretsch guitar and an AC30 can be heard extensively on early recordings by The Rolling Stones.

Handle The Vox AC30 has three carrying handles.

Covering Early Vox amplifiers had a beige cloth finish. Black plastic covering was introduced in the early 1960s.

Vox Teardrop Mk VI
This guitar was produced by Vox to complement their amplifier range. It has a Bigsby-type vibrato unit, three pickups, three controls, and a selector switch.

Level control

Attack control

Casing Die-cast aluminium is used for the unit's casing.

Tone-bender
Produced by Sola Sound at the beginning of the 1960s, the Tone-bender was one of the first commercially produced fuzz-boxes to appear in the UK. The attack control mixes the fuzz and normal signals, the level control adjusts the output volume, and an on-off footswitch can be used to bypass the effects circuit.

The Watkins Copycat
This echo unit was developed by Charlie Watkins. The guitar signal is recorded onto a continuous loop of tape; the echo is produced by a series of playing heads. Controls adjust the speed and depth of the echo. This unit went through a number of changes throughout the 1960s. Demand for tape-echo led to its reintroduction in the early 1990s.

RICKENBACKER 325

A Rickenbacker 325, finished in black, was used by John Lennon in his early Beatles days. Its construction and relatively low output single-coil pickups, gave the guitar a bright, "jangly" sound, with especially good mid-range definition and clear string separation. The Vox AC30 combo responds beautifully to these qualities, giving a crispness that can be heard on many recordings of the Beatles. This type of three-quarter-size Rickenbacker was first produced in 1958. This model has a small, semi-solid body made from pieces of routed maple, and a narrow, 21-fret unbound fingerboard made from African rosewood. The guitar has a short scale-length and a metal-plate vibrato. The three "toaster-top" pickups are controlled by a selector switch and two pairs of tone and volume controls with a mixer switch.

Neck The unusually small neck is made from maple and shedua laminates.

Control panel The controls are mounted on the top of a two-tier white, "plexiglass" pickguard.

Speakers Early Vox AC30s used Celestion G12 Bulldog speakers produced with a blue finish. The silver-grey finish, shown here, was introduced later.

Ventilation grills Heat is allowed to escape from the valves through a series of ventilation grills.

Input channels There are separate input channels for "vibrato" and "normal" channels.

Control panel The controls are segregated into three groups: vibrato, volume, and tone.

On-off switch

AC 30 HISTORY

The Vox AC30 grew from the diminutive but highly regarded AC15 combo used by groups such as The Shadows in the late 1950s. The drive for more power in live performances led Dick Denny to develop the AC30, which was effectively two AC15s driving a pair of Celestion 12-inch speakers specially made for Vox. The two-speaker format became very popular during the "beat boom" of the early 1960s, and was later applied to the AC15 and the less highly specified AC10.

Modifications

This classic combo has been widely used from the 1960s to the present day. During the 1970s, the design and construction of the AC30 was modified. Solid-state circuitry was used as a replacement for valves, changing the characteristic sound of the original amplifier. In 1990, Vox launched a reissue of the original combo from the 1960s. The AC30 has become a part of the standard equipment used by numerous pop musicians, ranging from bands with a single combo, to heavy rock guitarists using a large number for stadium performances.

EFFECTS OVER THE DECADES

Over the years, various effects set-ups have been *de rigueur* for the fashionable guitarist. The first popular effect was spring reverb, with or without tape-echo; later, fuzz-boxes, treble-boosters, and the wah-wah pedal became essential equipment for guitarists. By the 1970s companies such as MXR and Electro-Harmonix were offering vast ranges of battery pedals, including phasers and flangers. Morley produced expensive but sturdy steel-cased pedals. Later in the decade a large range of solid-state analogue effects, covering chorus, ADT, flanging, and echo became available. There were, however, compromises in frequency response. Stereo rack-mounted digital effects appeared in the 1980s, at first with studio price-tags, then in more affordable packages such as the Alesis Quadraverb. The late 1980s saw the widespread use of *multi-effects* units often used with a valve-based guitar pre-amp for authentic analogue distortion.

THE MODERN COMBO

THE VERSATILITY OF THE MESA/BOOGIE

Master volume
In the 1970s, the master volume became a standard feature. This allows distortion in the pre-amp when the power-amp is at a low volume. Early amplifiers had different channels for tonal emphasis and effects, but without a remote switching facility to obtain contrasting sounds. This flexibility is the main reason for multiple channels in modern amplifiers.

Gibson ES–335
The Gibson ES-335 remains one of the most popular designs because it can give good results with almost any amplifier. When used in conjunction with a Mesa/Boogie it can produce a lengthy sustain, and a smooth, bluesy overload. Combined with the Fender Twin reverb on the opposite page, the same guitar gives a rich, deep sound with good dynamics but no distortion on heavily played passages.

Body materials A solid centreblock running through the laminated maple body helps to give the guitar greater sustain.

When playing music that requires a mix of clean and distorted styles, combo amplifiers like the popular Mesa/Boogie are ideal. Three different sounds – "clean", "crunch", and "hi-gain lead" – can be set up and selected by a remote footswitching. When a five- or seven-band graphic equalizer is fitted, the tone can be radically altered without affecting the quality of the distortion. The Mesa/Boogie Mk III has a pair of footswitches controlling channel settings: the first can be used to switch from a rhythm to lead sound, the second gives a clean or distorted "crunch" sound used for rhythm playing.

MESA/BOOGIE SPECIFICATIONS
The model shown below is a Mk III combo finished in wicker and hardwood. It is an all-valve, "over-engineered" design which features spring reverb and three channels – "clean rhythm", "fat rhythm", and "high-gain lead" – each with some form of independent control. The single 12-in speaker is a Black Shadow. Some models also use a heavy-duty Electrovoice with a large magnet assembly, which provides great clarity. The combo's "Simul-Class" output stage allows a power choice of either 15 or 60 watts.

Five-band graphic equalizer

Hi-gain sounds
Over the past twenty years, rock players have sought more gain from amplifiers. Many now use hi-gain lead channels, providing smooth distortion, compression, and endless sustain; ideal for heavy rock playing. Recent technology makes this easy to provide, the major difficulty is preserving the full-bodied tone of the guitar whilst avoiding too much background noise.

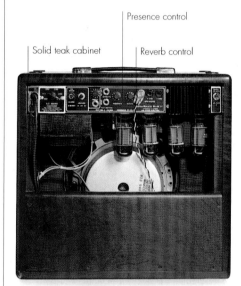

Solid teak cabinet

Presence control

Reverb control

MESA/BOOGIE SOUND

It was the compact (but very heavy and expensive), open-backed, Mesa/Boogie combo which made the 1x12 in format acceptable to blues and rock players. The design has not changed fundamentally since the 1970s. The five-band graphic equalizer on this model gives tonal versatility, allowing a reduction of the amplifier's inherent brightness. The sound can be further fine-tuned by swapping the 6L6 power valves for EL34s. A socket on the back panel also allows a line to be run out to a separate 1x12 in speaker cabinet.

FOOTSWITCHES AND EFFECTS

The majority of modern amplification systems are channel-assignable with the switching controlled either by dedicated, or MIDI-based footswitches. Some of the early amplifiers had built-in effects such as vibrato and tremolo. Since the 1970s, there has been a trend to provide effects loops – input and output points for external sound processing units – on amplifiers. Chorus and echo work well when linked up in this way, but effects that change signal-gain can be extremely noisy – these should be placed between the guitar and amplifier in the normal way. On some recent combos, channels with reverb and graphic equalization settings can also be controlled by footswitching. A very sophisticated switching system can be seen on page 170.

THE TWIN REVERB

AMPLIFICATION FOR PRODUCING A CLEAN SOUND

Some amplifiers are outstanding when it comes to producing clean sounds, but have little to offer when distortion or overdrive is required. The Fender Twin Reverb is one such combo: a 2x12 in valve amplifier that sounds superbly rich and deep with humbuckers, and very lively and detailed with single-coils, but even at high volumes will not produce a Marshall or Vox-style overloaded sound. The Roland JC 120 "Jazz Chorus" also excels at producing clean sounds. A high-specification all-transistor amplifier, it is one of the few Japanese combos to rank with the best British and American models.

Other factors affecting sound Two identical guitar and amplifier set-ups can sound very different. Factors affecting the final sound are: playing style; string gauge and condition; pickup height; quality of all leads and plugs; condition of pre-amp, effects, and batteries; and the quality and condition of valves – new valves are capable of transforming a dull sound.

lectro-acoustic guitars
relatively new breed of uitar, the electro-acoustic is deal for performing clean, neful material on stage. It usually of acoustic or semi-coustic construction, but ncludes a Piezo transducer nder the bridge saddle, and n on-board pre-amp. The enefits are acoustic sound nd good sustain without eedback. The disadvantage s a slightly artificial tone.

he changing face of the ES-335
he first Gibson ES-335s were launched in 958. They featured an unbound fingerboard vith dot inlays, PAF pickups, a long pickguard, nd clear-topped, gold-backed control-knobs. he strap buttons were made from cream lastic, and the metal parts nickel-plated. o begin with, the 335 was only available n a natural or sunburst finish. A very small umber of guitars were produced as a special rder with a red finish; this was introduced fully n 1960 as a replacement for the natural finish. By the middle of the 1960s, the accumulation f gradual changes had spoiled the original lesign. The guitar had block inlays on a ound fingerboard, patent number ickups, a trapeze tailpiece, a hort pickguard, metal-capped ontrol knobs, double-ring nachine-heads. The shape f the body and headstock ngle had also been slightly ltered. Some of these changes ffected the sound of the guitar.

Finish The laminated maple body of this model features a sunburst finish.

Twin Reverb specification
The Twin Reverb, originally produced with 80 watts driving two Jensen 12 in speakers, has a long history of modifications: Different types of speaker have been used, and the power output was increased to 100 or even 120 watts. These changes have led to combos from different periods producing very different sounds and tone.

Rear controls The back of the Twin Reverb houses standby and on/off switches, footswitch inputs, and a voltage selector switch for use in other countries.

FENDER TWIN REVERB
This powerful combo has become a standard choice for those seeking clean valve sounds. The Twin has two channels and high-quality, valve-driven reverb and vibrato effects.

Power output has varied over the years, but between 80 and 100 watts from the four 6L6GC valves is normal. The speakers used are frequently JBLs. From the middle of the 1960s, throughout the USA, the Twin was often bought by clubs and studios as the main high-quality amplifier for recording and performing. Many of the most famous musicians in all areas of popular music have performed using this classic amplifier.

EFFECTS FOR CLEAN PLAYING

Using a volume pedal or *violining* (rotating the volume control while playing), reverses a note's usual dynamic of a strong transient that dies away quickly; notes or chords seem to appear from nothing to full volume. A compressor provides clean sustain and will balance any differences in note volumes. This is useful for fast passages that mix single notes, string bends and two- or three-note chords, making compressors popular with country players. Chorus effects also help to give notes body and sustain without distortion. Chorus, compression and other effects can also be achieved with the use of individual floor units connected by a series of leads.

UPDATED CLASSICS

UPDATING THE ROCK SOUND OF THE MARSHALL STACK

Feedback
One way to alter the guitar's natural dynamic is by increasing gain and physical volume so that, when the guitar is in a certain position relative to the speakers, the notes begin "feeding back". Sustained notes are continually reproduced, and eventually grow in volume. Finger vibrato assists this process. Examples of Eric Clapton's skill in using this technique can be heard on the album "Bluesbreakers"

Over the years, certain set-ups have been considered by rock guitarists to be vital for producing particular sounds. The combination of a Marshall "stack" and a Gibson Les Paul guitar is a good example. The early set-up shown below, which is now extremely valuable, features the loud, and sweet-sounding, 45-watt JTM from the mid-1960s, teamed with a 1959 Sunburst Les Paul. The modern-day counterpart, shown opposite, combines a 100-watt, three channel, Marshall Thirtieth Anniversary head and speaker cabinet, with a 1990 Paul Reed Smith custom 10 Top guitar, a hybrid instrument that combines both Fender and Gibson attributes.

Vintage reissues
A number of early amplifiers, including Marshall, Fender, and Vox, are available as reissues. In most cases the circuitry is similar to the original except that printed circuit boards, rather than expensive, hand-wired tag-boards, are used. Famous speakers have also been reissued – some use modern materials, while others sacrifice hardiness and power for complete authenticity.

Gibson Les Paul Standard
Gibson first produced the Les Paul Standard, with a maple top and a sunburst finish, between 1958 and 1960. This superb example from 1959 has a 22-fret fingerboard with crown inlays, two PAF humbucker pickups, and a stud tailpiece with a height-adjustable Tune-o-matic bridge . The pickups are controlled by a three-way selector switch and two pairs of tone and volume controls. The small frets found on 1958 models were enlarged in 1959. In 1960, the depth of the neck was reduced. The specifications of the 1959 Les Paul have made it a much sought-after model.

Selector switch A feature of the Gibson Les Paul is that the pickup selector switch is mounted on the top half of the body away from the tone and volume controls.

Gibson PAF ("patent applied for") pickups

Serial number Found behind the headstock, this guitar is number 9 0403

MARSHALL JTM45
The first JTM45 amplifiers were produced in 1962. They were built by Jim Marshall and Ken Bran in their West London shop. The amplifier was influenced by the circuitry of the Fender Bassman. An unusual combination of components was assembled, producing a sound unlike any other amplifier. Marshall continued to modify and develop the JTM amplifier in stages before it was finally superseded in the late 1960s by the more powerful 100-watt head.

Cabinet This 4x12 slope-fronted speaker cabinet from the late 1960 houses four Celestion G12 speaker.

EFFECTS PEDALS

During the 1960s, rock players started to use effects pedals and high volume to produce a new type of electric sound. Some guitarists used a fuzz pedal with overdriven amplifier distortion and feedback, while others used an overdriven sound for sustain without effects. Wah-wah pedals were used at some time by most players. Eric Clapton's Cream recordings featured wah-wah blended with overdrive to produce a searing and expressive sound with a heavy texture. Individual approaches varied from using fuzz with overdrive, for increased sustain, to using a wah-wah pedal with a clean sound at high volumes.

Overdrive and wah-wah
The Colorsound Overdriver unit, produced by Sola Sound, features treble and bass controls as well as a drive control. The wah-wah unit manufactured by Jennings in the late 1960s was called the Cry Baby.

CHOOSING AN AMPLIFIER

Testing an amplifier before purchase is not an everyday occurrence; knowing what to look for makes the task less daunting. A methodical approach can pay dividends when comparing several models. First, if possible, the guitar for which the amplifier is being bought should be used, to ensure that the required sound can be obtained from that combination of equipment. The sound from the clean channel, with the channel volume low and master volume high, should be completely clean even when using humbucker pickups. Keeping the master volume low while turning the channel volume up full should give a "crunch" sound that adds edge to chord

work. Many players like the option of this sound. If the amplifier has a separate "crunch" channel, the sound should be compared with that of the overdriven clean channel. Easing the guitar's volume down or playing more gently should clean up the sound in both cases. With the lead channel set to a modest gain the guitar should retain good tone and dynamics; a high gain should produce a compressed and distorted sound with long sustain (possibly endless at full gain). At high levels background hum and hiss should not be too intrusive, and distortion should not have an overly harsh or "papery" edge. Tone controls should remain effective: it should still be possible to achieve a

traditional warm rock or a nasal heavy metal sound. At high volume the sounds should be powerful, while faithfully reproducing the frequency range of the guitar. Avoid amplifiers with clean channels that do not stay clean or that lose definition when used at high volume. On-board effects units, such as reverb, should not cloud the sound on lead settings. Vintage or reissue amplifiers should generate a distinctive sound without the use of full gain. When buying second-hand, amplifiers should be checked for all the above points, but also ensuring that the speakers are original, without misaligned coils, so that they work without buzzing on clean settings.

Paul Reed Smith custom 10 Top
This 1990 PRS guitar is built with a mahogany body and neck, with a two-piece flamed maple top. The 24-fret rosewood fingerboard has green pearloid inlays with an outline shape of birds in flight. Two humbucker pickups are governed by volume and tone controls, and a five-way selector switch. The PRS has clean sustain, excellent separation, and a wide range of colour. This makes it ideal for use with overdriven amplifiers.

Tremolo unit
The PRS features a "locking" tremolo system.

Dedicated footswitch Modern Marshall amplifiers feature a dedicated footswitch unit to change channels.

MARSHALL THIRTIETH ANNIVERSARY HEAD

This three-channel, 100-watt, all-valve head is a hybrid of new and old. The "crunch" channel can provide three generations of Marshall sounds, while the lead channel balances gain with factors such as headroom to produce high *perceived* gain, without sacrificing tone or dynamics. The automatic control over damping factor ensures that the clean sounds are well defined, with the sound loosened up for "crunch" and lead selections. An indicator warns of power valve failure, but the amplifier can still be used with reduced power. Other features include half/full power operation, effects loop, low volume compensation, frequency adjusted recording output, and a MIDI channel control facility. Celestion speakers have been central to the "British sound"; the G12 series has been fitted to most Marshall cabinets for the last thirty years.

Comparing heads
The 1960s' JTM45 (top) and the modern Jubilee head (above) can be compared. The first has simple speaker outputs and a bakelite socket with a fuse. The modern Marshall head has a switching unit and an effects loop.

RACK-MOUNTED SYSTEMS

THE ULTIMATE SET-UP FOR THE MODERN GUITARIST

MIDI

"Musical Instrument Digital Interface" is a standardized system that allows communication between the microprocessors built into many types of modern effects units, switching systems, pre-amps and, occasionally, amplifiers. This allows a guitarist to control programmed and pre-set changes from a switching system or other source such as a sequencer. It is also commonly used for linking synthesizers, drum machines, and sequencers.

In recent years, portable rack-mounted amplification and sound processing equipment has become increasingly popular. These systems enable guitarists to obtain a sound with the sort of quality and control normally exclusive to the recording studio. Portable rack-mounted equipment can be assembled with flexibility. Each item is fitted with bolts to the front of a standard 19-inch rack frame. Items such as power supplies and patch bays can be mounted at the back.

Mono or stereo?

To recreate studio sounds and effects in a live performance many guitarists are now using some form of stereo amplification. These can range from a basic 2x12 stereo combo with a stereo chorus effect to large rack systems incorporating studio-quality signal processors.

STAGE AND STUDIO RACK SYSTEM

The system shown over the next four pages was designed and put together by the guitarist Jim Barber for playing both on stage and in the recording studio. It consists of an extensive range of high-quality amplifiers, equalizers, and speaker simulators that have been assembled in such a way that a particular type of guitar can be matched with the right amplifier and routed through specified rack-mounted effects to create a mono or stereo image for stage or recording use.

THE SYSTEM IN ACTION

When playing a solo with the Gibson Les Paul, the guitar is routed through the Marshall 4500 amplifier to give an overdriven sound, a Palmer PDI-03 speaker simulator, and one of the PAST equalizers through to a combination of effects. These may include a stereo delay with panning, and additional reverb. The programmable VCA (*Voltage Controlled Amplifier*) and H*ush* noise reduction, can also be used to increase the level of the chosen pre-set, and eliminate any unwanted noise. Alternatively, if the Fender XII twelve-string guitar is used, a clear sound for chordal picking is likely to be required. In this case, the guitar can be routed through the clean channel of the CAE pre-amplifier, and channel one of a Palmer PDI-05 speaker simulator through to the Eventide harmonizer with added reverb and the TC1210 chorus unit, which will create a wide stereo effect.

Fender XII

This Fender XII twelve-string Stratocaster was made in Japan. It is refinished in a fluorescent yellow colour and features a simulated mother-of-pearl pickguard.

Jackson Soloist

This early Soloist was built by Grover Jackson for Jeff Beck. It has an unusual pickguard that shows the influence of a Fender Precision bass. It has an orange finish, an ebony fingerboard with dot inlays, three single-coil pickups, and a Floyd Rose tremolo unit.

Gibson Les Paul Custom

This black Les Paul Custom has a Seymour Duncan bridge pickup and a prototype ESP neck pickup. Unusually, a Floyd Rose unit with a locking nut has been specially fitted, making it a powerful and versatile instrument, combining traditional design with modern hardware.

LIVE MONITORING

To give a clear and precise reproduction of the amplification and effects, the rack system shown below uses four Marshall 4x12, 400-watt speaker cabinets fitted with Celestion G12 speakers. An HH V800 transistor power amplifier is used to produce distortion-free power at any level of volume. This enables the player to achieve a specific sound and alter the volume without having to change the characteristics. This approach is especially useful for monitoring a guitar sound in a live situation. Many players have a preference for the warmth of valve-power amplification, but there are inherent problems that result from the alteration of the volume level. Using Celestion G12M 25-watt speakers can also help to produce a vintage sound with more character. They have less definition, though, as well as a tendency to distort. The four cabinets may be positioned and separated as two pairs, to create a wider stereo image, or placed close together.

Marshall 4500 amplifier This standard unmodified 50-watt dual reverb amplifier is one of the Marshall JCM 900 series.

Rear of the rack Housed at the back of the rack is a Sonus MT 70 MIDI router and TC Electronic 1210 stereo chorus/flanger.

Marshall 2100 amplifier Also from the JCM 900 series, this model is a standard 100-watt master volume amplifier.

Furman PL8+ power conditioner/light unit

Blank panel

TC Electronic 1128 programmable graphic equalizer (MIDI)

TC Electronic M5000 digital audio mainframe (MIDI) with two reverb modules

TC Electronic 2290 dynamic digital delay (MIDI)

Eventide H3000 SE harmonizer (MIDI)

Spectra Sonics 610 compressor

Korg DT1 digital tuner

Furman PL8+ power conditioner/light unit

Panel with markings for mixer (below)

Rocktron G612 stereo line mixer

Rocktron/Bradshaw RSB-18-R switching system (MIDI)

Valley Arts MIDI patcher for 4500, 2100, and Mesa/Boogie amplifiers

Furman PL8+ power conditioner/light unit

Blank panel

Custom Audio Electronics 3+ pre-amplifier

Marshall JMP-1 MIDI pre-amplifier

Palmer PDI-05 speaker simulator

PAST equalizers for 4500 and 2100 amplifiers

Palmer PDI-03 mono speaker simulators for 4500, 2100, and Mesa/Boogie amplifiers

Palmer PDI-05 two-channel speaker simulator for main outputs

Mesa/Boogie Mk11 100-watt amplifier

HH V800 400-watt stereo power amplifier

Pedal board

The guitar is plugged into a Roland FV2 volume pedal. The signal is then fed into the RSB-18-R in the rack. All switching functions of amplifiers and effects, including MIDI, are controlled by the Rocktron/Bradshaw RSB-18-F footswitch unit, mounted on the pedal board. If a radio system is used the receiver is plugged into the volume pedal, then into the RSB-18-F input.

RACK SYSTEM DIAGRAM

There is considerable variance in the way rack-mounted systems are put together and used. The different approaches are largely due to individual tastes and styles of music. The system on the previous page is shown here as a chart, with a detailed description of the components (below). The audio links between each unit are shown with arrows depicting the direction of flow. The MIDI links are indicated by a series of dotted lines. This system was designed by Jim Barber to emulate the sounds effected in a recording studio, in a live situation. A major benefit of using this type of system, with its extensive use of new technology, is that it enables the musician to record an album and then faithfully reproduce on stage the sounds and textures associated with particular tracks.

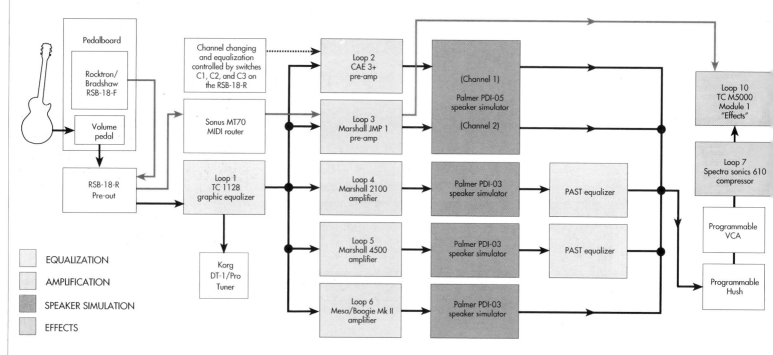

EQUALIZATION

AMPLIFICATION

SPEAKER SIMULATION

EFFECTS

SWITCHING SYSTEM

The heart of this system is built around the Rocktron/Bradshaw switching system, which controls the signal routing through the different stages of amplification and effect processing. The system consists of ten mono loops (marked as L1–L10) and one stereo loop (L11). A *loop* is simply a circuit comprising a *send* signal fed to the input of an effect (or chain of effects) and a *return* signal from the output of the same effect. There are also twenty-five banks of five presets. These can be used to program twenty-five songs with five variations in each. Using MIDI, this allows different combinations of amplifier and effects in different parts of a song. For example: preset 1 – introduction; 2 – verse; 3 – chorus; 4 – middle-eight; 5 – soloing. The switching system controls all MIDI-compatible units, although there are also four control switches which allow for the bypassing of non-MIDI effects. The guitar is plugged into a volume pedal mounted on the pedalboard; the output from this feeds to the RSB-18-R, which is mounted in the rack. The floor unit – RSB-18-F – also connects to the RSB-18-R.

LEVEL MATCHING AND TUNING

The first item in the chain is the TC 1128 programmable graphic equalizer, which is patched into loop 1. The equalizer is on all the time, and is used to balance the input levels of any guitars used in the system. In this case, it would be used to match up the levels from the Jackson to the Les Paul, which have considerably different output levels. A signal is also fed to the Korg DT-1 guitar tuner, which is permanently monitoring the guitar signal.

Control cable This links the footswitch to the RSB-18-R rack unit.

Loop selector switch There are ten mono loops; Loop 3 controls the Marshall JMP 1 pre-amp.

Hush noise reduction switch

Control switch There are four control switches; C4 is set up as a bypass switch to the chorus unit.

Output

Input

Bank selection

Bank presets

Stereo loop Loop 11 controls the stereo reverb.

Volume pedal

Pedalboard

The custom-built floor unit consists of an electronic switching system made by Rocktron/Bradshaw with a volume pedal. The switching system uses MIDI to control amplification and effect processing. It features twenty-five groups of "song" presets. Each bank contains five individual presets.

MIDI

MIDI plays an important role in this system. The control computer built into the Rocktron/Bradshaw footswitch controls all MIDI functions through the Sonus MT70 MIDI router. This enables a constant flow of MIDI data preventing MIDI messages from occurring.

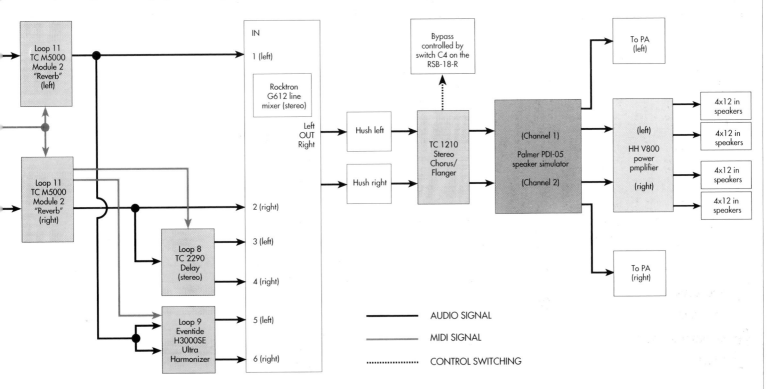

AUDIO SIGNAL

MIDI SIGNAL

CONTROL SWITCHING

AMPLIFICATION, EQUALIZATION, AND SPEAKER SIMULATION

The signal runs to loops 2, 3, 4, 5, or 6, depending on which is selected. **Loop 2** is a CAE 3+ pre-amplifier, which goes into channel 1 of a Palmer PDI-05 speaker simulator. The channels of the pre-amp are switched by control switches **C1** ("crunch"), **C2** ("lead"), and **C3** ("EQ"). **Loop 3** activates the Marshall JMP 1 pre-amp, which goes into channel 2 of a Palmer PDI-05 speaker simulator. **Loop 4** controls the 100-watt Marshall 2100 amplifier, the output of which goes into a Palmer PDI-03 speaker simulator and then the PAST equalizer. **Loop 5** runs the Marshall 4500 amplifier, which goes into a Palmer PDI-03 speaker simulator and then the PAST equalizer. **Loop 6** controls the Mesa/Boogie Mk II amplifier, which goes into a Palmer PDI-03 speaker simulator.

All these loops pass through a programmable Hush and VCA for noise reduction and level control, which is programmed into their presets. For example, when soloing and driving an amplifier at high volumes, the VCA would be adjusted for greater level, and the Hush

would have a more extreme setting to compensate for added noise resulting from changes in volume.

THE SOUND-PROCESSING STAGE

Loop 7 is a Spectra Sonics 610 (mono) compressor. This feeds **loop 10** containing a TC M5000 digital audio mainframe. This is mainly used for room simulation effects. This loop splits into **loop 11**, which is also a TC M5000 and provides stereo reverb. The left output channel of the reverb feeds channel 1 of the Rocktron G612 mixer (panned left), and **loop 9**, which is the Eventide H3000SE Ultra Harmonizer. The stereo outputs of this are fed into channels 5 and 6 of the mixer (panned extreme left and right). The right output channel of the reverb feeds channel 2 on the mixer (panned right) and **loop 8**, a TC 2290 stereo digital delay, whose stereo outputs go into channel 3 (panned left) and channel 4 (panned right) of the mixer.

OUTPUTS

The stereo output from the mixer passes through a secondary Hush in the RSB-18-R rack unit. This signal then passes into the TC 1210 chorus unit. The on/off bypass of

the chorus unit can be switched via control switch **C4** on the pedalboard. Finally, the stereo signal from the chorus unit goes to the left and right channels of the Palmer PDI-05 speaker simulator.

LIVE USE

In a live situation, the balanced outputs of the PDI-05 speaker simulators are fed directly into the PA system's monitor console and then to the front-of-house console. This eliminates the need for miking up the speaker cabinets. The *thru* signal from the PDI-05 is fed into the HH V800 power amplifier, which is linked up to the Marshall 4x12 speaker cabinets. When used in this way, the amplifier and speakers become the monitor system for the guitar, but have no effect on the level or the balanced signal sent to the PA.

STUDIO USE

In a recording studio, the balanced outputs are taken directly to the mixing console, again eliminating the need for miking. If necessary, the *thru* signal from the PDI-05 can be used to feed a valve power amplifier and vintage 4x12 in speakers. This sound can then be mixed with speaker simulators.

RECORDING

RECORDING THE GUITAR IN A STUDIO AND AT HOME

The modern studio
Studios comprise rooms for recording performances, and a separate control room housing the mixing desk and computers. The mixing desk has a number of separate channels, each with various sound-processing functions so that a combination of tracks, such as rhythm and solo, can be controlled, edited, and assembled in stages.

Before the invention of the tape recorder in the 1930s, sound was recorded by etching a pattern mechanically onto disc: once a recording was made it could not be altered. The advantage of using a magnetic tape recorder was that tape could be wiped clean and the same section used to record again. The principles of sound-on-sound – recording layers of sound on top of one another – and multi-tracking, where the sounds are recorded as tracks on separate tape channels, were developed in the 1940s. This allowed two or more pieces of music to be recorded onto tape and played back at the same time. So, a guitar rhythm track could be recorded and have a melody laid over it. The two tracks could be played back and heard together. These basic principles have been used ever since.

Recording the guitar
The guitar is often recorded at the same time as other instruments. Isolating each sound can be achieved using separating screens or different rooms: players can listen to each other on headphones. A song is often recorded starting with a guide track, which may include a rhythm guitar part. Additional guitar parts are played over this rhythm track, at which point the guide track is sometimes re-recorded or removed.

THE COMPUTER

Today computers have virtually replaced tape recorders in studios. Normal "analogue" sound is converted to a digital code, routed through converters and computers and stored on hard disks. Computers sit at the heart of the control process and can replace almost any piece of musical equipment, although "outboard" equipment is still used. There are almost unlimited numbers of channels, and computers can give tremendous control when it comes to altering and editing music. Mistakes or unwanted ideas can be cut and stored, and single notes or entire sections can be dropped in or pasted anywhere, using on-screen controls that show the music as graphic wave forms and as scores. It is possible to record and entirely change the character of the sound through on-screen software manipulation.

Mixing desk Modern mixing desks, such as this SSL, have computer-controlled consoles.

The Beatles (*above*)
The Beatles perform their single All You Need Is Love *for a worldwide audience broadcast by the BBC from Abbey Road's Studio 1 in June 1967. With producer George Martin and the studio engineers, the Beatles used innovative recording studio techniques and approaches to, for instance, sound processing, to advantage.*

Real World (*right*)
Real World studios, situated in the rural setting of Box in Wiltshire, were opened in 1987. There are four separate studios, fitted out with Otari, Studer, and Mitsubishi tape recorders and three SSL mixing consoles. Part-owner Peter Gabriel, the Happy Mondays, and New Order have all recorded here.

THE MIXING DESK

The signals that make up a piece of music are routed into the separate channels of a mixing desk (or mixing console) to create mono and stereo "images". An example of this process is to make a recording using two microphones positioned (panned) left and right in the stereo "field". In addition to controlling the balance of the recording as a whole, each individual channel of the mixing desk can be used to modify the sound either in volume or equalization or by adding various types of effect.

CHANNELS

A group of individual channels can be run into a single channel that can then be used to control the group as a whole. For example, a drum kit consisting of twelve individual channels can be sub-mixed into a pair of channels panned left and right. This provides the master volume for an overall stereo drum sound. Grouping can also be used where a guitar sound comes from a number of different sources, e.g., a speaker with three different microphone signals, and one from a speaker simulator. Mixing desks are frequently described by the number of input channels, grouped channels, and output channels on board. For example, a console described as "twenty-four into eight into two" (24-8-2) has twenty-four input channels, eight sub-group channels, and two output channels.

SOUND PROCESSING

The effects units commonly used in the recording studio are similar in principle to dedicated guitar pedals, but are built to a much higher specification. They can be used to process sound in a wide variety of ways, including delay (phasing, chorus, flanging, and echo), adding a digitally generated harmony (harmonizing), and compressing the signal. Sound processing is often connected to the mixing desk using a send and return loop: auxiliary volume controls on each channel of the desk are normally used to control how much of the effect is added to the signal. It is possible to add effects during the recording stage. However, most studio engineers prefer to record a dry signal, adding effects during the final mix-down. Effects are often built-in to some of the more sophisticated mixing desks.

The Power Station

Started in the late 1970s, the Power Station studio in New York can cater for anything up to ninety-six-track recording facilities. It features four separate studios fitted with Studer analogue and Sony digital tape recorders and SSL and Neve mixing consoles. A number of the best-known names in rock music have recorded here.

Abbey Road control room

Now one of the world's legendary studios, Abbey Road was officially opened as EMI Recording Studios by Sir Edward Elgar in 1931. This is one of the control rooms where engineers, producers, and musicians listen back to the music through various types of monitoring speakers using an SSL desk and computers. There are four studios and extensive facilities. Abbey Road has been used for recording a vast amount of music in all kinds of fields from film music scores through to pop albums. Today, studios such as Abbey Road continually evolve with modern technology, which is incredibly sophisticated and wide ranging in its creative possibilities. Any music can be imported as digital material and used seamlessly with real sounds.

RECORDING TECHNIQUES

Before starting a recording, it is a good idea to make a plan of which instruments are to be played on every track. A *track sheet* is often used to plan the overall structure of the music and the role of guitar parts in relation to the music as a whole. The desired sound will be set up with an electric or acoustic guitar, and the source of the sound – an amplifier or an acoustic instrument – will be recorded. At the start of a track, a count-in containing one or two bars of beats should be recorded. This gives the musician advance warning of when he or she should start to play.

OVERDUBBING TRACKS

The technique in which a number of tracks are played back, allowing the musician to listen to them and play and record additional material, is known as *overdubbing*. In this instance, the computer or tape machine plays back material from certain tracks and simultaneously records material on new tracks. This is usually achieved by running the guitar into a new input channel on the mixing desk, and assigning the signal to a new track.

MONITORING

Foldback monitoring for recording is usually heard through headphones. This enables players to hear the sound of their own instruments and other instruments via the mixing desk, while adding a melody or rhythm part. These instruments may be playing live at the same time, or they may be on tracks that have been previously recorded. Monitoring controls are placed in line with the input controls for each channel or in a separate bank on the desk.

RECORDING WITH MICROPHONES

After experimenting with sound settings in the studio, the guitar amplifier will be recorded using microphones placed in a number of positions. They can be situated near the combo or cabinet speakers (*close miking*), or at a distance, picking up room sound (*ambient miking*). Microphones have widely differing characteristics, and the position in which they are placed in relation to the sound source is important. The distance of the microphone, the angle in relation to the speaker, its relationship to the acoustics of the room, and its

---

INPUT CHANNEL COMPOSITION

Each input channel on the mixing desk has an identical set of functions.

Gain control and pad switch
Different types of microphone and line input rarely have the same output levels. The **gain** is effectively a volume control used to adjust an incoming signal to a level compatible with the mixing desk. The **pad** switch has a similar function, except that it is not variable – it reduces the sensitivity of a microphone input by a specific value, usually one that is outside the range of the gain.

Phantom powering
Some types of microphone require DC power to operate. The **phantom** switch, providing between twelve and forty-eight volts, provides this power from the desk.

Equalization
Equalization (or tone) controls come in a number of forms. The most common types allow low, middle, and high frequencies to be adjusted. They can be used to change the brightness of the treble and the presence in the middle and bass range, which can make a piece of music sound fuller or less defined. High- and low-pass filters can be used to cut out any unwanted frequencies above or below specified levels.

Sound processing/auxiliary send
Where sound processing is required, the **auxiliary send** controls the amount of the original signal being sent into an external unit. Effects inputs can be set either before or after the equalization stage. It is also possible to create a loop (see p. 172) using the channel's **insert point**.

Channel grouping
Group sends route the signal from specific channels into one or more other channels. An example of their use is in drum-sound production, where the individual sounds are grouped into two channels, producing a stereo sub-mix. These channels are then used to control the volume of the drums relative to the rest of the mix.

Mute and solo switches
The **mute** switch simply prevents the entire signal from the channel being heard. The **solo** switch is used to isolate individual tracks within a mix.

Panning
The **pan** control is used to feed the signal through to the left and right master output channels, controlling the position of the sound in the stereo "field".

Channel fader
The sliding faders usually found at the bottom of the desk control the volume for each channel.

Patch bay | Channels 1–8 (from left to right) | Channels 9–16 (from left to right) | Channels 17–24 (from left to right) | Channels 25–3 (from left to righ

Engineer's table

Solid State Logic console
The *Solid State Logic SL4064 G is a 48-32-48 mixing console. The desk has forty-eight channel modules: both the input and output controls – as well as separate compressor, limiter, expander, and noise gate modules – are contained within each channel module. A computer keyboard, with a VDU, housed* in the centre of the console, is used to control any of the individual settings for each channel. This "Total Recall" system can memorize and store specific mixes, moving the faders automatically during playback. The main record and transport controls for the tape machines can also be operated from the console. If necessary, the system is expandable to sixty-four tracks.

irectional capacities determine the
quality and colour of the recorded sound.
f the signal from the guitar is split, and
played through more than one amplifier
t the same time, it is possible for each
ound to be recorded onto a separate
hannel, and then mixed down and edited
t a later stage.

DIRECT INPUT AND SIMULATORS

Direct input evolved partly through the need
o separate out instruments so that their
ound did not spill during live playing.
Where several microphones are used to
ecord instruments playing together
t the same time, separating screens or
ooths are used. However, rather than
peing played through an amplifier, the
guitar can be plugged into either a DI *box*
or the mixing console, where pre-amp gain

takes the signal to tape. In recent years,
DI boxes have been replaced by *speaker
simulators* (see p. 171), which run the signal
from a guitar amplifier output straight into
the desk. The speaker simulator takes the
line output from the amplifier; imparts a
filtered sound, giving the characteristics of
a speaker cabinet; and reduces the signal
down to line level, where it is then fed
into the desk. Some producers prefer to
use a mixture of both systems, recording
speaker simulator on one channel and a
miked-up speaker cabinet on another.

ACOUSTIC RECORDING

An acoustic guitar usually has one or
more microphones positioned to pick
up the direction of the sound. Minor
movements with a microphone can lead
to tonal imbalance or left-hand playing

noise. Acoustic instruments often benefit
from a room with reflective surfaces to give
a live sound. Classical recordings are often
made with a pair of microphones running
to a portable DAT machine: churches
or other buildings that enhance the
acoustics are often used for this purpose.

DROPPING-IN

It is not necessary to record a piece of
music from start to finish: a section on
one track can be *dropped in* (or *punched in*)
by listening to the track, switching the
computer or tape machine *in* to record
mode, playing over the section, and then
switching *out* of record mode. With skill
and care, it is possible to replace single
notes and chords. This technique is widely
used for correcting mistakes without
having to repeat an entire section.

Visual display unit
The settings for each
channel can be displayed
on this small screen.

Channels 33–40
(from left to right)

Channels 41–48
(from left to right)

Multi-track routing
The patching system
provides the link between
the mixing console and
the recording machines.

Back panel The rear of the mixing
console houses a series of sockets.
These include separate line and
microphone inputs, outputs, and insert
points for connecting to peripheral effects.

VU meters Channel volume and tape input
levels are indicated by a series of VU meters.

Dynamics controls Each channel has compressor,
limiter, expander, and noise gate functions.

Equalization section Each channel of
the console features four-band parametric
equalization and "hi/lo" filters.

Auxiliary send bank The console features
four mono sends and one stereo auxiliary
send. These controls "send" a signal from
the channel into a sound-processing unit.

Blank panels Additional groups of channels
can be added as they are required.

**QWERTY
keyboard**

**Computer-
controlled
automation
system**

**Master
output
fader**

Channel fader
The volume for an
individual channel is
controlled by this fader.

Pan control This
controls the position
of the channel in
the stereo spectrum.

Solo button This switch
allows an individual channel
to be heard by cutting
out the other channels.

RECORDING THE GUITAR

The first step in recording any guitar is to ensure the strings are new enough to produce good tone and intonation. Consider, too, the room acoustics – these largely define the sound and cannot be removed. So it is safer to record "dry", often as simple as placing acoustically absorbent material near the instrument.

The type of microphone is crucial. A small diaphragm condenser (pencil microphone) is ideal for acoustic guitar, because it is sensitive yet not prone to boom. A dynamic microphone can reproduce a tougher quality of tone and reject unwanted sound. For electric guitars a combination of dynamic and condenser microphones is typical. With acoustic guitar, place the microphone in front of the 12th fret and 20–30cm (8–12in) away. Make a test recording and listen back, comparing it to the actual sound of the guitar. If it lacks bass bring the microphone closer to the soundhole. If it lacks definition, move it futher away. With electric guitar, a dynamic microphone such as a Shure SM 57 is often placed close to the amplifier, offcentre from the speaker cone. Movements of just a few centimetres affect the sound, which brightens towards the centre and is intensely bright in the middle. Experiment with test recordings, moving the mic until the sound is right, and consider the amplifier settings. If the recording is to be a solo guitar, ambient microphones create a bigger sound. Each microphone has a separate track and can be blended and panned with the close microphone to broaden and liven the image.

Transport buttons The panel controls the basic functions of the sequencer such as play, record, and locate. The numerical readout displays time in bars and beats as well as hours, minutes, and seconds.

Yellow bar This indicates a highlighted area ready to be edited, cut, trimmed or otherwise processed.

Computer power The computer, here an Apple Macintosh running Digital Performer, is an indispensable tool for detailed editing and manipulation of audio, such as repairing mistakes in a performance with cutting, pasting, dropping in, or even retuning.

Waveform This represents 100th of a second of the sound captured by a condenser microphone 30cm (12in) from the 12th fret of an acoustic guitar.

Stereo waveform This shows the sound captured by two equidistant ambient microphones a stride away pointing to the bridge of the guitar.

The computer
Computers have closed the gap between home recording and the professional studio, making commercial-quality recordings possible in a home environment. A software program such as Digital Performer, Logic Audio, or ProTools has the capability of replicating an entire recording studio in virtual form, including the mixer and multitrack recorder, as well as outboard effects such as reverb delay and chorus.

Connecting up
The microphone is routed to the computer via a preamp, which boosts the output level, and an audio interface, which converts the signal into digital form for storage and manipulation. Both of these stages have a substantial effect on the recorded quality.

GLOSSARY OF EFFECTS

AUTOMATIC DOUBLE-TRACKING A delay-based effect usually referred to as "ADT". The effect is created on digital or analogue units capable of producing a fast single repeat of a signal. It is also sometimes referred to as "doubling".

BYPASS Most effect units can be bypassed by switching the signal to a route where the sound is not processed.

CHORUS This is a delay-based effect (between 5 and 35 milliseconds) designed to simulate what happens when two instruments play the same part. With real-life double-tracking there are always slight differences in timing and pitch between the parts – chorus recreates this effect electronically. For example, a 6-string guitar can be chorused to sound more like a 12-string guitar. Most units offer "Modulation" (rate) and "Depth" controls. A number of combos exist with built-in chorus, often in stereo, with an amplifier and a speaker for each channel.

COMPRESSOR Using compression, quiet notes are boosted in level, while louder signals – such as a heavily struck chord – are reduced in level. The unit averages out the natural differences in level as you play, making finger-picked passages sound smoother, and giving a feeling of "flow" to clean lead passages. The controls – usually Threshold and Compression – allow for a wide array of effects. With heavy compression, the percussive front end of a heavily picked note is taken away to give a softer start; as the note fades, the unit increases volume, keeping the level virtually constant.

DELAY When sound is reflected from a distant surface, a delayed version of the original is heard later. Echo-units copy this natural effect, by either analogue or digital means. Solid-state units store the signal electronically; analogue devices pass the signal down a long chain repeatedly until it is needed, while digital units encode the signal in digital form, store it in memory until it is required, then decode it. Digital units can offer stereo operation, allowing multi-tapped signals to be placed left, right, and centre-stage or even appear to bounce from one side to the other.

DIGITAL EFFECTS Almost every effect can now be produced digitally. When using digital effects, a signal is converted to binary code – a series of ones and zeros – so that it can be processed in a variety of ways and converted back to an analogue signal.

DISTORTION When extra gain and distortion cannot be achieved by an amplifier, traditionally a distortion pedal (or fuzz-box/overdriver) is used. A clean signal is plugged in, and a distorted, sustaining sound is produced. Many early fuzz-boxes were simply crude trigger-mechanisms, so that no matter how you played, the same "buzzy", square-wave sound would result. Modern pedals allow the amount of distortion to be more easily controlled. Some units include pre-amp valves to give good tone and dynamics coupled with genuine valve overdrive. Digitally produced distortion, while increasingly common, is generally thought to be too harsh for the tastes of most guitarists.

ENHANCERS This device processes an audio signal to improve the sound and definition. The early enhancers, called "aural exciters", boosted a harmonic element in the music to produce a brighter effect. Other systems use phase correction to place signals precisely in phase so that frequencies are not lost as a result of phase cancellation.

EXPANDER The opposite effect of compression is called expansion. These units are used to increase the dynamic range of a signal.

FLANGER A delay-based effect that originated with tape recorders. The tape was slowed down by pressing the fingers against the reel, and the sound produced was mixed with a normal signal from a second tape recorder. The flanging sound is created electronically by playing back a delayed signal of up to 20 milliseconds, with controlled pitch modulation, against the original signal. The "feedback" or "regeneration" control found on some flanging units creates an unusual pitch-modulated sound. The effect can be produced on most modern digital delay lines.

GRAPHIC EQUALIZER A graphic equalizer is a tone control that divides the sound spectrum into frequency-bands, allowing the level of each band to be boosted or cut separately. The word "graphic" refers to the fact that it is possible to see at a glance what particular "shape" is being used. For example, a V-shape boosts the top- and bottom-end, while the opposite response adds mid-range warmth. Although the tonal emphasis can be changed, it is not possible to improve the basic quality of tone.

HARMONIZER Also known as a "pitch-shifter", the effect has two main uses. It can enrich the sound of a guitar, using a harmonizer to add overtones which are in harmony with the original signal and sound similar to **chorus**. The harmonizer can also generate a harmony note. Until recently, only fixed-interval harmonies were possible; however, new "intelligent" units allow the player to select specific types of scale, which result in automatically adjusted harmonies.

LESLIE CABINET The Leslie is a rotary speaker cabinet designed for use with an organ. In the 1960s, players such as Jimi Hendrix found that by feeding the guitar signal through a Leslie cabinet they could produce a delicate, ethereal sound. Nowadays the effect is simulated electronically.

MIDI Musical Instrument Digital Interface (MIDI) was developed in 1981 by the Sequential Circuits company as a universal interfacing system for synthesizers and sequencers. MIDI is widely used within effects units as a way of controlling parameters or stored settings from either footswitches or sequencers.

MULTI-EFFECTS UNITS There is an increasing trend towards single units that are capable of producing reverb, phasing, flanging, chorus, delay, harmonizing, and many other effects. These units are generally digital, MIDI-controllable, and capable of chaining effects together and storing settings.

OCTAVE DIVIDER This analogue effect (an early forerunner of the harmonizer) added a single note either an interval of an octave above, or an octave below, the original signal.

PANNING The location of a signal within a stereo "field". It can also refer to the dynamic behaviour of the signal – for example, where echo repeats are "panned" from left to right.

PHASING If two identical versions of a signal are "out-of-phase", so that the peaks in one precisely coincide with the troughs in the other, the two signals will cancel each other out, leading – in theory – to silence. If the signals are partially out-of-phase, a characteristic colouration to the sound will result. Phasing can be achieved electronically, the results varying from a mild "whooshing" to sounds reminiscent of a jet plane.

PRE-AMPLIFIER To help overload the input-stages of the amplifier, a "pre-amp" can be used to generate extra gain. The pre-amp often acts as a tone control when used in conjunction with a main amplifier. It can also be used to boost the signal when used with amplified acoustic instruments.

REVERBERATION A "reverb" unit mimics the natural effect of overlapping sound reflections caused by sound bouncing around an interior space such as a room. Spring reverb is the traditional effect built into many guitar amplifiers, but digital reverb (offering fine control of the many parameters involved, and a crisp, bright sound) is now more common.

STEREO CHORUS This term can refer to a **chorus** effect that is panned over stereo outputs to give the impression of spatial movement. It can also describe the sound created by playing a dry signal through one channel and a chorused signal through the other.

TAPE-ECHO The traditional method of producing delay. The original signal is recorded on tape and played back slightly later by one or more replay heads, giving either a single repeat or "multi-tap" effects. Feeding the delayed signal back to the recording head gives a heavily textured sound.

TONE PEDAL See **WAH-WAH PEDAL**.

TREBLE BOOSTER In the early 1960s, many of the cheaper amplifiers and guitars lacked the top-end produced by high-quality equipment. To overcome this, small battery-powered treble boosters were used.

TREMOLO This rhythmic pulsing effect is obtained by modulating the volume of the signal. It was built into many early combos, being relatively easy to engineer with valve circuitry, and could give anything from a fast rippling sound to a deep throbbing effect. Note that Fender always called their tremolo effect "vibrato" – this is technically incorrect (see below).

VIBRATO This effect is obtained by modulating the pitch of the signal. The sound produced can vary from a subtle enhancement to an extreme variation. Early valve combos such as the Vox AC30 offered vibrato as well as tremolo; however, the feature is more often seen on chorus pedals or digital multi-effects units.

VOLUME PEDAL This passive device allows players to vary the volume at will while continuing to play. Its main use (apart from altering overall volume level) is as a "swell" pedal; a particularly attractive effect may be achieved by eliminating the percussive attack at the beginning of notes and chords letting them "float in". This also works well with string-bends and harmonics.

WAH-WAH PEDAL This foot-operated tone control came into vogue in the late 1960s. When the pedal is flat, a high-treble sound is produced; raising the pedal gradually increases the bass sound. It can be used in several ways: rocking it gently backwards and forwards while playing produces a "talking guitar" effect or a soft "wah" sound, while a fast "chopping" effect is used by many funk players. It can also be set to an in-between position, to select a certain tone. MIDI-controlled, rack-mounted auto-wah devices have recently been developed.

CARE AND MAINTENANCE

KEEPING YOUR INSTRUMENT IN THE BEST POSSIBLE CONDITION

Considering climate
The need for periodic maintenance, apart from the general wear and tear of a working instrument, is largely due to wood being used as the main material for construction. Being hygroscopic, wood is subject to movement through changes in temperature and humidity. Usually, small adjustments will compensate for any changes in the instrument, but failure to protect a guitar from extreme climates can result in serious damage.

In terms of its sound, playability, and appearance, a properly set-up, well-maintained guitar can be an inspiration to the player. To keep a guitar in good order, one must first acquire some knowledge of the workings of the instrument; one must also be aware of the various problems that might occur, so that damage can be prevented wherever possible. Most repair and maintenance work requires a high degree of skill and experience, and specialist tools and equipment. Therefore it is advisable to consult a reputable repairer to undertake any work that you do not feel is within your capabilities. Vintage, expensive, or rare instruments are especially likely to need specialist attention. However, there is a great deal that the ordinary player can do to ensure that the guitar stays in top condition.

Evaluating repair work
Whilst there is much common ground in the maintenance of different types of guitar, each will have its own special requirements. Setting-up can also be tailored to suit a player's own style and technique, but it is important that the guitar is free of major defects before routine adjustments are made. With care and attention, surprising good results can be obtained even from inexpensive guitars but if extensive repair work is needed, the costs should be considered in the context of the value of the instrument.

STRING CARE

For the best possible results, guitar strings must be correctly fitted, in good condition, and appropriate for the guitar and the player. Many problems, such as poor intonation, tuning difficulties, rattles and buzzes, and loss of volume and elasticity, can be attributed to playing with strings that are old or worn. Strings should be renewed in proportion to the amount and the conditions of use. Perspiration and dirt will rapidly shorten string life: cleaning strings with a dry, lint-free cloth immediately after use will not only help to counteract this, but will also help prolong the life of the frets and fingerboard.

RE-STRINGING

The following tools are recommended for string installation and removal: a small pair of pointed-nose pliers incorporating a wire-cutter; a string winder; a tuning pitch reference such as an electronic tuner, a

String-winder The slot is placed over the end of the machine head. This allows the string to be wound on evenly with greater speed.

tuning fork, or pitch pipes (see p. 42). There are a number of acceptable ways to install strings, although the methods used vary according to the type of guitar. Players should adopt the method that suits them best in terms of speed and efficiency. For example, some people prefer to change the strings one at a time, keeping the others tuned to pitch, whereas others prefer to remove all the strings, giving access for cleaning the fingerboard. New strings always take a little time to settle; gently pulling the tuned string away from the fingerboard – or *stretching-in* as it is sometimes called – will help tuning stability. On the next page are some tips to help the beginner (and sometimes the experienced player) avoid some common mistakes.

RE-STRINGING SOLID-BODY GUITARS

The method of attaching the ball-end of the string will differ according to the make of guitar, but will in all cases be self-evident. One way of attaching the string to the machine head capstan is shown below. This is a quick and simple method, and the string will not slip. There are many other

String ends The winding around the capstan traps the end of the string in place.

acceptable ways to do this; to some extent it is a matter of personal choice. The *wound* strings, for example, can simply be threaded through and wound downward on the capstan. This may be preferable when using heavy-gauge strings. One type of capstan (common to many Fender guitars) has a hole in the top. This variation on the usual design is shown right. Recently developed *locking* machine heads enable the strings to be locked to the capstan, usually by means of a thumbscrew. The string is drawn through the capstan, leaving virtually no slack. It is then locked and can be tuned to pitch with less than one full turn of the capstan. You should always remember to de-tune the strings fully before unlocking this type of mechanism.

Vertical capstan hole
Cut the string to the required length and insert the end into the capstan hole. Bend to one side and wind on. With this method, the string ends are kept neatly out of the way. The slot in the capstan also allows the string to be fitted as shown on the right.

Tremolo arm Some tremolo systems can be held in place with shims when the strings have been removed.

Shim When the guitar is tuned, the shims become free.

RE-STRINGING SOLID-BODY GUITARS WITH TREMOLO

With most guitars that have tremolo systems, re-stringing methods are similar to those used on non-tremolo guitars. If all the strings are removed they should be de-tuned in turn, in gradual steps to prevent spring tension and thereby string breakage. Remember that altering the tuning of one string will affect the others, so fine-tuning takes longer. Locking tremolo systems are different: they often require the strings to be clamped at the nut and the bridge, so the ball-end of the string must be cut off before the string is clamped to the bridge saddle. When doing this, all the over-wrap should also be cut off. Place the string in the bridge and tighten the clamp securely. Before clamping the nut, set the fine-tuners on the tremolo to a mid-way position, stretch-in the strings, and tune to pitch.

STRING INSTALLATION TIPS

- Never put steel or steel-core strings on a guitar designed for nylon or gut strings. If in doubt, seek advice.
- Always remove old strings with great care, as the sharp ends can damage the finish of the instrument.
- Do not wind too much string onto the capstan. Allow just enough slack to achieve approximately two to four turns when the string is tuned.
- Wind the string turns on the capstan downwards towards the headstock. Keep the turns neat, and avoid overlapping.
- On guitars with slotted headstocks, wind the turns around the capstan in the direction that results in the smallest angle through the nut.
- Hold the string taut while winding to the capstan, and avoid making any sharp bends or kinks in the string.
- Wind on all of the slack, ideally with a string winder. Do not wrap the string around the capstan by hand – this can distort the string wrap.
- It is not necessary to thread the string through the capstan hole more than once: this only makes future string-changing difficult.
- Where the string needs to be cut to length before fitting, make a 90-degree bend and cut the excess string off approximately 1.2 cm (½ in) from the bend. This prevents string wrap slippage.
- Changing string gauges may necessitate adjustments of the truss rod, string slots at the nut, and tremolo tension to compensate.
- Avoid stretching-in new strings too much as this can also distort the string wrap.
- A string that breaks suddenly can be dangerous. When bringing strings to pitch, keep your eyes well clear.
- As a safety precaution, snip off the excess string close to the capstan. This will avoid sharp string-ends protruding from the headstock.

STRING TYPES

Choosing strings can be confusing for the beginner. Experience will ultimately be the best guide in selecting the most suitable types. The main differences in strings and their applications are: the materials used for manufacture, design, gauge (diameter), and tension. String types fall into two distinct categories: nylon and steel. The main differences between the steel string designs used for different guitars concern the type of string-wrap. Roundwound strings are used on acoustic and electric guitars. Flatwound strings are designed to eliminate finger noise, and are mostly used on archtop instruments. Groundwound strings are a compromise between the two. When choosing strings, attention should be given to their gauge. Factors to consider are volume (heavier gauges produce more volume), tone, and ease of playing. With most strings, a heavier gauge will result in heavier string tension.

Nylon strings This high-quality set of Augustine "Gold" nylon strings are used for classical guitars.

Bronze-wound strings The string gauges are .052, .042, .032, .025, .016, and .012. This set was produced by Martin.

Nickel-wound electric guitar strings These Ernie Ball strings have the following gauges: .038, .030, .022, .014, .011, and .008.

Nylon strings

Nylon strings are used exclusively on classical and flamenco guitars. The three treble strings are made from a monofilament nylon. The lower strings are made from a multi-filament nylon core and are invariably roundwound, with a silver-plated copper, bronze, or other alloy wrap; some manufacturers produce strings with polished or compressed wrapping to reduce finger noise. Nylon strings are available in low, medium, high, and extra-high tensions.

Steel strings

Steel strings used for acoustic and electric guitars are all made with steel cores. For electric guitars the wrap is made from a nickel/iron alloy, nickel-plated steel, stainless or other metal, or alloy. The various materials used for the wrap will give different tonal responses and slightly different levels of output when amplified. On steel strings for acoustic guitars, the wrap is usually made from bronze, brass, or similar alloys. "Phosphor bronze" strings produce a rich tone with strong bass response. "Bronze" or brass strings are brighter and more "bell-like" in tone. Sometimes these strings are labelled with the "copper/zinc or tin" alloy ratio. As a rough guide, the closer the ratio, the "brighter" the tone will be. Roundwound strings are used for both acoustic and electric guitars. They are characterized by their wide tonal response, richness in harmonies, sustain, and brightness. Flatwound strings are designed to eliminate finger noise, and have a perfectly smooth feel, but are duller in sound, with a pronounced mid-range response and less sustain.

NYLON-STRING GUITARS

The suggested methods for the string-ties on the bridge and capstan of a nylon-string guitar are illustrated below. It is useful to make a small knot at the very end of the treble strings, after the tie at the bridge. This stops the string slipping through the bridge if the string-tie fails: the "whipping" effect of a tensioned string slipping can cause considerable damage to the body. Some wound strings have a few centimetres of loose winding at one end: this section should not be used at any of the string-ties. It takes a few days for new strings to settle fully. The plain treble strings improve with age, becoming brighter and louder as the nylon hardens under tension. These can last a long time before being replaced. The wound strings, however, will deteriorate and lose tone more rapidly; for this reason many players change the bass strings more frequently.

String-ties at the bridge (above)
Pass approximately 7 cm (2.7 in) of the string through the front of the tie-block situated at the back-end of the bridge unit. Pull the end of the string back over the tie-block, passing it under the string's original point of entry. Wrap the end around itself to hold the string in place. This should be done twice for wound strings, and four times for treble strings. Finally, secure the tie by stretching the string towards the headstock. It is important to ensure that the final wrap is positioned at the back of the tie-block.

Stringing the capstan (right)
Turn the machine head until the capstan hole is at ninety degrees to the headstock face, and thread the string down through the capstan hole. Bring the string-end around the back of the capstan, and thread the string beneath itself, forming a knot.

Nylon-string headstock (left)
To achieve the optimum angle between the capstan and the nut, the 1st and 6th strings on a nylon-string acoustic guitar should be wound towards the outer side of the headstock: the opposite direction to the other four strings.

FLAMENCO GUITARS

Flamenco guitars are usually fitted with friction pegs rather than geared machine heads. If the pegs do not fit tightly enough, accurate tuning will become difficult – *peg paste* used by violinists can be applied to improve grip. Stringing at the headstock is the same as for a nylon-string guitar.

FLAT-TOP ACOUSTICS

On a flat-top acoustic guitar, the string tension is taken by the hardwood bridge plate glued to the underside of the top immediately below the bridge. There are two types of bridge pin commonly used. One type has a recess running down one side to accommodate the string. The second type has no recess: instead there is a slot cut at the leading side of the pin hole in the bridge where the string sits. Always fully de-tune a string before removing the bridge pin. Use the facility provided on the string-winder to lever the pin gently from the bridge. Pins should fit snugly in their holes: modification may be necessary if they are either over-tight or too loose. Bend the ball end of the new string slightly to one side to fit under the bridge plate, as illustrated. Refit the bridge pin and ensure that it remains properly seated when tuning to pitch. Some makers use an alternative to the pin bridge, similar in principle to the bridge on a nylon-string guitar. Here the ball-ends are retained at the back edge of the bridge, When restringing it is advisable to protect the top of the guitar immediately behind the bridge to avoid dents and scratches as the string is pulled through.

Bridge pin cross-section
*This cross-section shows the type of bridge used on a flat-top acoustic guitar. Note that the purpose of the bridge pin is to hold the ball end in position under the bridge plate, **not** to take the string tension.*

ARCHTOP GUITARS

Traditionally, a tailpiece retains the strings on this type of guitar. Some tailpieces are hinged and will fall onto the guitar top if all the strings are removed, so again protection between the tailpiece and top is recommended. The bridge is not usually attached to the top but held in position by the string tension. As the position and seating of the bridge is critical, it is essential that it is relocated correctly when restringing. Changing the strings individually is advisable as this avoids bridge movement. When tuning to pitch, check that there is no forward tilting on the bridge, and that it remains in perfect contact with the top of the guitar. When stringing at the headstock of an archtop guitar follow exactly the same procedure as for the electric guitar.

CLEANING THE BODY

It is important that any agents used for cleaning should be compatible with the type of body finish. Preventing dirt accumulating by wiping after use is the best way to keep a guitar clean. For all wiping and polishing, use a clean, 100%-cotton cloth. Extensive cleaning may be carried out with a clean cloth moistened with warm water. The finish should then be buffed with a dry cloth. Cellulose and synthetic finishes can be cleaned with purpose-made guitar polish.

Body cleaner   String cleaner

Cleaning cloth   Buffing cloth

Cleaning fluids
A wide variety of specialized cleaning and polishing fluids are available for the body and strings.

CLEANING STRINGS

Strings must be clean in order to produce a good tone and accurate tuning. Dirt and grease rapidly build up while playing, and the salt from perspiration causes corrosion if left on the strings, even for short periods. Clean the strings after use with a dry, lint-free cloth. This can be wrapped under the strings and drawn along their entire length a few times. Some players prefer to clean each string individually, lifting the string from the nut slot, and continuing past the nut. String lubricants can prevent corrosion and keep the strings in good condition. If used, be sure to remove any surplus. Note: string lubricants should never be used on nylon strings.

Do not use cleaning agents that contain silicone – this can permeate the finish, making future refinishing work extremely difficult. Wax polish may also have an adverse effect – it can become sticky in warm temperatures, attracting more dirt. Waxes used in guitar polish are emulsified and blended with cleaning agents, thus avoiding these problems. French polish finishes, commonly found on high-quality classical guitars, are very delicate and should be cleaned by wiping lightly with a barely damp cloth or chamois, followed by buffing with a dry cloth. Never use abrasive cleaners or regular guitar polishes on this type of finish. Exceptionally soiled synthetic finishes can be "revived" with a liquid burnishing cream containing a mild abrasive additive. This should be used rarely, as the abrasives not only cut through the dirt but also remove some of the lacquer. Cotton wool is good for applying this type of cream, working in small areas at a time, and rubbing in a circular motion, finishing in the direction of the wood grain. A liquid glaze cream can then be applied to remove rubbing marks, before buffing with a clean, dry cloth. Dust

THE FINGERBOARD

Keeping the strings clean also prevents dirt and grease building up on the fingerboard. Each time the strings are changed, wipe the fingerboard with a dry, clean cloth. On ebony or rosewood fingerboards, a little lemon oil can be applied to help loosen grease and dirt. This also "feeds" the wood, preventing it becoming too dry. The oil should be left on for a few minutes, then cleaned off with a dry cloth. A heavily soiled fingerboard will be far more difficult to clean. In this case, leave the lemon oil on a little longer, then wipe off and clean the fretboard and frets with very fine steel wool, working with a small circular motion, and finishing with the grain. Remove residual dirt from the fret sides by wrapping a cloth moistened with lemon oil around a plectrum (or thumbnail) and running it along each side where the fret meets the fingerboard. Finally, vigorously polish the whole of the fingerboard with a clean, dry cloth. Lacquered maple fingerboards can be cleaned in a similar way, although steel wool should not be used unless a matted finish is desired. Note: when using steel wool on electric guitars, mask the pick-ups to prevent steel particles being attracted to the magnets.

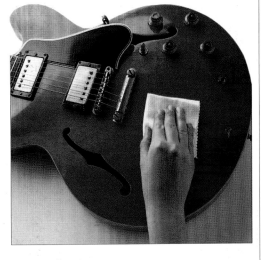

Routine cleaning
It is a good idea getting into the habit of cleaning a guitar regularly after use.

can accumulate inside the body of acoustic guitars which can attract and trap moisture, and affect the sound. This can be removed by periodically vacuuming or blowing through the sound hole.

HARDWARE

Plated metal parts should also regularly be cleaned. Chrome cleaners or burnishing cream can be used for cleaning chrome- and nickel-plated parts. Gold-plated parts should be wiped clean with a soft cloth. Corrosion can usually be remedied by removing and soaking the affected parts in penetrating oil. Be sure to wipe off the excess oil before refitting. Finally, a small artists' brush is useful for keeping tremolo units, bridges, and other small parts free from dust. Regular cleaning will not only prolong the life of your guitar, but will keep it sounding, feeling, and looking at its best.

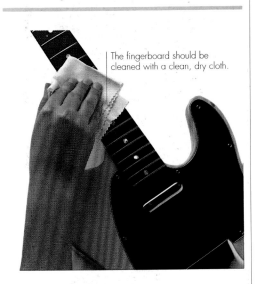

The fingerboard should be cleaned with a clean, dry cloth.

SETTING UP

The term *setting up* describes adjustments made to achieve the best possible sound and playing action. There is no definitive set-up; ultimately the aim should be to accommodate the individual player's style and technique within the adjustment limitations of the instrument. For the purposes of describing the elements of the set-up, it is assumed that the instrument is in a reasonably good condition throughout and free from structural defects. The actual feel and sound of the guitar are the best guides to help you to assess the existing set-up condition, so you will gradually become more discriminating as you gain playing experience. The guidelines shown over the next two pages are intended to help you to assess the kind of setting-up work that may be required. It is recommended that most of the work involved in setting-up be carried out by a specialist, although many players may wish to make simple adjustments themselves. Measurements can be made using a fine-graded steel rule and a set of feeler gauges. To begin with, strings of the desired gauge must be installed and tuned to the correct pitch.

ACTION

The term *action* refers to the playability of the guitar. Many factors contribute to the action, but essentially it is determined by the height of the strings above the frets. This is usually measured between the top of the 12th fret and the bottom of the string: for electric guitars the average figure ranges from 0.13 to 0.2 cm (0.05 to 0.08 in), and for acoustics, 0.2 to 0.28 cm (0.08 to 0.11 in). On electric guitars, the bridge saddles and/or bridge are adjustable and can simply be raised or lowered to adjust the action. On flat-top acoustic guitars the saddle is usually pre-formed from bone or synthetic material, and the action can be lowered by accurately filing the bottom of the saddle.

Saddle screws are used to adjust the bridge

Measuring the action
Place a ruler on top of the 12th fret and measure the distance to the bottom of the string. Ensure that the ruler is of the type where the scale starts at the tip.

Adjusting the action
Action is changed by altering the height of the saddles on the bridge. Turning the saddle screws clockwise usually raises the height of the saddle, and so increases the space between the string and the fret.

NUT

The nut governs the height of the open strings above the 1st fret. Measurements are taken from the top of the 1st fret to the bottom of the string: for electric guitars these range on average from 0.025 to 0.05 cm (0.01 to 0.02 in), and for acoustics, 0.035 to 0.065 cm (0.015 to 0.03 in). Adjustments are made by either refiling the nut slots or replacing the nut. It is essential that the string slots in the nut are filed at a precise angle, to provide the string with a clean "take-off" point, and that each slot is proportional to the string diameter. The material used for the nut affects the sound quality of the open strings. Bone or hard synthetic materials are commonly used. Teflon or graphite-based materials are recommended when using a non-locking tremolo system.

CAMBER

The setting of the individual string heights at the bridge and nut must conform with the *camber*, or the radius of the fingerboard. This is checked by measuring the height of each string at the 12th fret and the 1st fret. You will notice that the action is set highest on the bass side. This is because the heavier strings need greater clearance to vibrate freely. The camber of the bridge and nut should be set so that the action of each string gradually increases from the 1st to the 6th strings. On electric guitars with individually adjustable saddles this can easily be set. On flat-top acoustic guitars the saddle crown can be carefully reworked or, if necessary, a new saddle can be made for the guitar. Classical and Flamenco guitars normally have no bridge and fingerboard camber.

MEASURING NECK RELIEF

Neck relief is the curve along the length of the neck. Looking along the length of the fingerboard from the nut or bridge will give an indication of the curve. Relief is measured by holding the string down at the first and last frets and measuring the gap between the bottom of the string and the top of the fret. At the deepest point of the curve, usually around the 7th or 8th fret, this averages from 0.015 to 0.05 cm (0.005 to 0.020 in).

Feeler gauge
The measurement should be made at the deepest point of the curve.

Last fret The string should also be held down at the last fret while the measurement is being made.

Capo When making the relief measurements, a capo can be used to hold down the strings at the 1st fret.

INTONATION

For the intonation to be as accurate as possible, the vibrating length of the string must be set proportionally to scale length, action, and string gauge. Without correctly set intonation, accurate tuning over the entire fingerboard cannot be achieved. It is important to install new strings prior to adjusting the intonation, as well as checking that nut height, relief, and action are correctly adjusted and that the frets are in a reasonable condition. On most electric guitars, adjustable saddles allow each string to be intonated individually. Tune to pitch and compare the note produced by the open string with that produced at the 12th fret. If the 12th-fret note is flat, the string length must be shortened by moving the saddle closer to the nut. If the 12th-fret note is sharp, the opposite adjustment must be made. The adjustments are continued until the two

notes are in tune. An electronic tuner is useful for setting the intonation, but, if it is done by ear, it may be preferable to use for comparison the harmonic produced above the 12th fret instead of the open string. Most acoustic guitars have a fixed saddle, in which case intonation adjustments are best left to a specialist.

FRET CONDITION

Frets should be ideally of uniform height and properly fitted; however, as frets are being constantly worn, maintenance will be necessary. Frets can be *reprofiled* several times, but will eventually need replacing by a specialist. Fret height can be checked by holding a string down on two adjacent frets and using a *feeler gauge* to measure the gap between the fingerboard and the bottom of the string. Measurements should be taken where fret wear is most apparent on the fingerboard. Refretting may be needed if this reading is less than 0.025 in (0.6 mm).

Fret wear Excessively worn frets will almost certainly need replacing.

TRUSS ROD

The truss rod reinforces the neck against string tension. Most rods are adjusted by means of a hex, or slotted nut, situated at the heel or headstock end of the neck. Slackening the rod by turning the nut anticlockwise increases relief; tightening it decreases relief. Although this is simple in principle, in practice the results can be very complex and specialist attention is recommended. The many different types of truss rod, together with the quality and types of timber used for the neck and fingerboard,

Adjusting relief Some truss rods are adjusted at the "body end" of the neck.

will produce varying results from adjustment. Even the necks of two apparently identical instruments may behave in different ways when similar adjustments are made. With this in mind, you may wish to attempt some minor adjustments to improve the action or test different string gauges. If so, first check the relief (see p. 184). If there is no relief, the neck may be convex – the rod should be slackened until relief is obtained. Adjustments should be made in increments of a half-turn of the hex/slotted nut, and the relief rechecked. Adjustments greater than a full turn in either direction are not recommended. Finally, remember that the action at the nut and bridge will be affected by truss-rod adjustment.

Headstock end Truss rods with adjustment at the headstock end are often made with allen keys.

STORAGE AND TRANSPORTATION CHECKLIST

• Keep the guitar in its case when it is not being used. A good-quality hardshell case is best.
• Avoid exposing the guitar to extremes of temperature. If travelling in exceptionally hot conditions, de-tune the strings.
• If moving the guitar from cold to warm surroundings or vice versa, leave it in the case and allow it to acclimatize for as long as possible.
• Periodically check the instrument thoroughly for signs of climatic effects, such as a noticeable change of the action, splits and cracks, protruding fret ends, lacquer cracking, movement in glue joints, and distortion of the woods. Any problems of this kind should be dealt with by a specialist as soon as possible.
• If travelling by air, where possible arrange with the airline in advance to take the instrument on board as hand luggage. If this is not possible and the guitar travels in the cargo hold, a good-quality flight case should be used. The string tension should always be slackened for air transport.
• Insure the instrument against loss or damage.
• If storing the guitar for long periods, first clean it thoroughly and slacken the strings, leaving a minimum amount of tension.
• Store in a safe place of reasonably constant temperature and humidity, in its case. Do not store in attics, lofts, or basements.

GLOSSARY

ACCENT An emphasised note or chord.

ACCIDENTAL A symbol used to raise or lower the pitch of a note.

ACOUSTIC GUITAR A classical or steel-string instrument with a sound chamber.

ACTION The height of the strings in relation to the frets and the fingerboard.

AEOLIAN MODE The mode starting on the sixth degree of the major scale.

AMPLIFIER Electronic device for boosting the signal from a pickup or microphone.

ARCHTOP An instrument with a curved top and back carved or made from laminated wood.

ARPEGGIO A succession of chord tones.

AUGMENTED An augmented chord is a major triad with a raised fifth. Certain intervals raised by a semitone are termed augmented.

AVANT GARDE Modern experimental music often featuring modified instruments, unusual techniques, and improvisation with atonality.

BAR A bar or measure is a section of music for grouping note values over a given length of time.

BARRE Method of placing the first or other fingers across the strings to hold down adjacent chord notes.

BASS NOTE The lowest pitched note in a chord or harmonic movement.

BELLY Term applied to an archtop soundboard.

BIGSBY A type of tremolo or vibrato unit.

BINDING A continuous strip of wood around the edge of a guitar body.

BLUES A term applied to an expressive form of North American folk music.

BOTTLENECK A technique for sliding a metal bar or tube along the strings to play notes and chords.

BOUT A term applied to the upper and lower section of the guitar body.

BRACING Strips of wood underneath an acoustic soundboard for support and tonal distribution.

BRIDGE Section for fixing and supporting the strings on an acoustic guitar. The method of supporting the strings on an electric or acoustic guitar.

CAMBER Curvature of the fingerboard, often referred to as the radius.

CAPO A device clamped to the strings with a screw or a strong elastic strip. It holds the strings across any of the lower fret positions enabling open strings on higher fret positions to be played. It also lowers the action.

CHORD Two or more notes sounded together.

CHROMATIC Full scale including all twelve notes a semitone apart within an octave.

CLASSICAL Standard compositional repertoire played on a classical instrument.

CLEF Symbol for fixing the stave at a given pitch.

COMPOUND INTERVAL Interval larger than one octave.

CONTROLS Normally rotary pots or switches used to control electrical signals.

COUNTERPOINT Two or more lines of melody played at the same time.

COURSE Normally a pair of strings placed together to be played with normal fingering.

CUTAWAY A section of the body cut away to give access to the upper part or register of the fingerboard.

CYCLE Series of related musical structures, e.g., the cycle of keys.

DIATONIC The seven note major and minor scale system.

DIMINISHED Term applied to a minor chord with a lowered 5th and a chord comprising of minor 3rd intervals. Scale composed of successive tones and semitones.

DOBRO A type of resonator guitar.

DOMINANT The note or chord on the fifth degree of a diatonic scale. This is often marked with the Roman numeral **V**.

DORIAN MODE The mode starting on the second degree of the major scale.

DREADNOUGHT A large acoustic steel-string guitar.

EFFECT The result of some form of processing to modify sound.

EQUALIZER A control for filtering frequencies to modify tone.

EXTEMPORISATION *see improvisation*

FEEDBACK A sound produced by a string or microphone picking up and amplifying its own signal from a loudspeaker.

"F"-HOLE Ornamental sound holes on archtop and thinline electric guitars.

FINGERBOARD Wooden section with mounted frets for stopping the strings with the left hand. Also called a fretboard.

FIXED MELODIC MINOR This is an Aeolian mode with a raised sixth and seventh in both the ascending and descending form.

FLAMENCO The indigenous music and dance of Andalusia in Southern Spain.

FLAT Symbol (♭) used for lowering a note by a semitone. A double-flat (♭♭) moves the note down by two semitones (one tone).

FLAT TOP A steel-string guitar with a flat soundboard

FREQUENCY The number of cycles per second, which determines pitch.

FRET Metal strips placed across the fingerboard to determine semitonal spacing.

FRICTION PEG A round wooden peg to hold each string on a solid headstock.

GOLPEADOR A type of pickguard for tapping rhythms on flamenco guitars.

HAMMER A technique for sounding notes with the left-hand fingers.

HARMONIC These are upper parts of a note, related to the fundamental which are played by touching a string at certain points.

HARMONIC MINOR An Aeolian mode with a raised seventh.

HARMONY The simultaneous relationship and order of musical notes.

HEADSTOCK Section for mounting the machineheads or pegs.

HEAVY METAL Intense guitar-based rock music played at high volume and speed, often featuring sustain, overdrive, virtuoso playing.

HEEL A reinforced section supporting the neck where it joins the body.

IMPROVISATION Creative process of composing music or soloing ad lib.

INTABULATION Music in tablature form.

INTERVAL The distance between two notes.

INVERSION The order of notes in a chord from the bass note.

IONIAN MODE Another term for the major scale.

JAZZ American vocal and instrumental music which has evolved over the past hundred years with a wide diversity of forms and styles.

KEY The reference pitch for a diatonic system.

LEAD A cable for carrying electrical signals. Also a term for single note playing and soloing.

LEADING NOTE The note or chord on the seventh degree of the major scale. Often marked with the Roman numeral **VII**.

LEDGER LINE Small line for placing notes above and below the stave.

LEGATO A smooth, even approach to playing consecutive notes.

LIGADO Term for hammering and pulling-off notes.

LINE A succession of single notes.

LOCRIAN MODE The mode starting on the seventh degree of the major scale.

LUTHIER A guitar maker. Usually associated with the construction of classical instruments.

LYDIAN MODE The mode starting on the fourth degree of the major scale.

MACHINE HEAD Mechanical device for adjusting pitch.

MAJOR Chord with a major third between the root and the third. Scale with major and perfect intervals.

MEDIANT The note or chord on the third degree of the major scale. Often marked marked with the Roman numeral **III**.

MELODIC MINOR This is an Aeolian mode with a raised sixth and seventh in an ascending form, and a normal Aeolian mode in its descending form.

MELODY Single notes in a recognisable pattern.

MINOR Chord with a minor third between the root and the third. Scale with minor and perfect intervals.

MIXING Method for controlling and blending recorded sounds.

MIXOLYDIAN MODE The mode starting on the fifth degree of the major scale.

MODE A scale.

MODULATION Movement from a section of music in one key to another key.

MULTITRACKING Storing separate tracks on a reel of tape.

NATURAL Symbol (♮) for cancelling the effect of a sharp or flat.

NUT Point at which the strings are supported as they run from the fingerboard to the headstock.

OCTAVE An interval of twelve semitones. The same note vibrating mathematically related frequencies.

PENTATONIC A five-note scale.

PHRASE A musical sentence.

PHRYGIAN MODE The mode starting on the third degree of the major scale.

PICKGUARD A plate for protecting the guitar body.

PICKUP A coil wound with fine wire which converts the sound into electrical signals.

PIMA Letter names for the right-hand fingers, derived from the Spanish language.

PITCH The frequency of a note.

PLANTILLA The outline shape of a classical guitar.

PLECTRUM Object for sriking the strings held by the right hand. Also known as a pick or flatpick.

POLEPIECE Individual metal poles under each string on a pickup.

POT Potentiometer for controlling a signal.

PREAMP A signal-boosting device.

PSYCHEDELIA Drug-based popular music featuring various types of sound treatment, multi-textured sound layers, and unusual forms. Pioneered by British and American groups during the late 1960s.

PULL OFF Left-hand technique for sounding a note.

PURFLING Decorative inlays next to the binding.

RASGUEDO Method of strumming used by flamenco guitarists.

RELATIVE MINOR The minor system starting on the sixth degree of the major scale

REST A period of silence.

RHYTHM A pattern of notes and accents.

RIBS The sides of the guitar.

ROCK Music derived from blues and country music in the 1950s.

ROOT The letter-name reference note for a chord.

ROSETTE The circular decoration round the soundhole.

SADDLE(S) The point on the bridge for supporting the strings.

SCALE The string length between the nut and the saddle.

SEQUENCE Often a term for a song or a chordal pattern.

SHAPE The outline form of a chord on the fingerboard.

SHARP Symbol (♯) for raising a note by a semitone. A double-sharp (𝄪) is used to raise a note by two semitones (one tone).

SLIDE Method for sliding in pitch between notes.

SOL-FA A system of one-syllable abbreviations for scale notes. The notes are Do-Re-Me-Far-Sol-La-Ti-Do.

SOLO An improvised passage over music.

SOLID-STATE The use of modern transistors.

SOUNDBOARD The top or table of the guitar.

SOUNDHOLE Normally a circular section cut out of the top to allow sound and energy to project from the soundchamber.

SPACE The gap between the lines on a stave.

SPEAKER Circular cone for projecting amplified sound.

STAVE A grid for placing music.

STRUM Method for striking chords with the right hand.

STUDIO A room for recording or practising.

SUBDOMINANT The note or chord on the fourth degree of the major scale. This is often marked with the Roman numeral **IV**.

SUBMEDIANT The note or chord on the sixth degree of the major scale. Often marked with the Roman numeral **VI**.

SUPERTONIC The note or chord on the second degree of the major scale. Often marked with the Roman numeral **II**.

SYNCOPATION A rhythm emphasising offbeats.

SYNTHETIC SCALE A non-diatonic succession of notes.

TABLATURE A method for writing music down showing the position of notes on the frets and strings.

TAILPIECE Metal frame or stud for holding the strings on the body of the guitar.

TEMPO The speed of the music in relation to the beats or pulse.

TIME SIGNATURE Two-tier symbol showing the number of notes and their value in a bar.

TONALITY Relationship to a keynote or pivotal tone for a harmonic system.

TONE 1 A major second. **2** The colour or quality of the sound. **3** A note.

TONIC The note or chord on the first degree of a diatonic scale. Often marked marked with the Roman numeral **I**.

TRANSDUCER A device for transferring energy from one form to another. Used to describe a form of pickup used for amplifying acoustic instruments.

TRANSPOSITION Moving a section or a piece of music to a key with a new pitch.

TREMOLO 1 Used for a mechanical (vibrato) arm for controlling pitch. **2** A sound-processing effect **3** The fast repetition of a single note. **4** A term for Vibrato.

TRIAD A three-note chord with intervals of thirds in root inversion.

TRITONE This is an interval using three whole-tones (tri-tone). It is normally an augmented fourth, or a diminished fifth.

TRUSS ROD Reinforcing metal rod for stabilising and adjusting the neck.

TUNERS Machine heads.

VALVE Glass tube which amplifies sound using a cathode and anode.

VIBRATO 1 Used for a mechanical arm for controlling pitch. **2** A sound processing effect. **3** A technique whereby a fretted note is moved rapidly (a minor fluctuation in pitch) to create an effect or enhance tone.

WHOLE TONE An interval of a major second. A six-note scale using whole tones over an octave.

WOLF NOTE A note which is irregular or weak due to the properties of acoustic resonance.

INDEX

Music titles are in *italics*

ACKNOWLEDGMENTS

THE AUTHOR Richard Chapman would firstly like to thank his agent Julian Alexander, and Christopher Davis and Stephanie Jackson at Dorling Kindersley for their help in bringing about an improved, updated, and expanded version of *The Complete Guitarist*.

I would particularly like to thank the contributors: Bill Puplett for the care and maintenance section, John Seabury, Jim Barber, and Terry Burrows for the majority of the sound and amplification section, and Hugh Manson for material on his electric guitar.

I want to give a special thank you to Veryan Weston for contributing his fascinating system on pentatonic scales and modulation on page 164.

Both the consultants have been tremendously helpful: guitarist Rafael at www.flamencoguitarist.com for flamenco and engineer and producer Joe Leach at The Cowshed Recording Studio www.cowshedstudio.com for recording techniques.

I wholeheartedly thank the people who have worked on this new edition. They have been great! Adèle Hayward and Karen Self for excellent management, Anna Fischel for constructive support and thoughtful editorial work, Ted Kinsey for thoroughly professional design, Neil Lockley and Kevin Ryan for editorial, design, and general help.
Also Trevor Bounford and his company for his important contribution with music setting and graphic elements.

I would also like to take this opportunity to thank Robert Cornford (1940-83) for his inspiration and encouragement.

Thanks to: The Acoustic Centre; Arbiter; Fiona Austin; Tony Bacon; Stephen Barber; Martin Booth; Sheila Bounford; Trevor Bounford; Nigel Bradley; Dave Brewis; Karen Brock; Alan Buckingham; Dave Burrluck; Rod Butcher ; Steve Byrd; Capitol Records; Carter; Doug Chandler; Paula Chandler at Chandler Guitars ; Carol Chapman; Matthew Chattle; David Clifton; James Coppock at FCN; The Cocteau Twins; Brian Cohen; Pete Cornish; Fin Costello;

Jamie Crompton at Fender Artist Relations; Christopher Dean; Denise ; Paul Fischer; Scott Fischer; Russell Fong; Gerald Garcia; Michael Gee; Dave Gladden; Tracey Hambleton-Miles; Phil Harris; Steve Hart; Vincent Hastwell; Mark Hayward; Steve Hazell; Lol Henderson; Andy Holdsworth; Nick Hooper; Steve Hoyland; Grover Jackson; Katie Johns; Rose Jones; Max Kay; Jane Laing; Joe Leach; Alex Lee; Richard Leyens; Heather McCarry; Pete McPhail; Andy Manson; Neville Martin ; Tom Mates; Roger Mayer; Charles Measures; John Monteleone; Paul Morgan; Nigel Moyse; Tom Nolan; Sean Moore; Alan Murphy; Nigel Osborne ; Nick Peraticos; Les Paul; Colin Pringle at SSL; Mervyn Rhys-Jones; Gurinder Purewall; Rafael; Rose Morris; Nick Rowlands; Iain Scott; Damon Smith; Sally Stockwell; Mike Tamborino; Dawn Terrey; Daniel Thomas; Pat Thomas; Ced Thorose; Dave Townsend; Paul Trynka; Helen Turner at JHS ; Ray Ursell; Jerry Uwins; Mike Vanden; Tina Vaughan; Carey Wallace at Christie's; Simon Wallace; Kevin Walsh; Adam Watson; James Westbrook; David Weston; Larry Wexer; Martin Wheatley; Marty Williamson; Andreas Young.

DORLING KINDERSLEY would like to thank Matthew Ward for new photography; Francessca Agati, Rochele Whyte, Daniel Thomas, and David Weston for modelling on pages 34–35 and 40–41; Margaret McCormack for indexing; Diana Morris for picture research; Mike Tamborino for the John Monteleone guitar on page 22 and Dave Brewis for the Flying V on the Contents page.

Bibliography:
R. Aspen Pittman *The Tube Amp Book* (1982); Tony Bacon *The Ultimate Guitar Book* (Dorling Kindersley, 1991); Ralph Denyer *The Guitar Handbook* (Dorling Kindersley, 1982); Mike Doyle *The History of Marshall Valve Guitar Amplifiers* (New Musical Services, 1982); Tom and Mary Ann Evans *Guitars from the Renaissance to Rock* (Oxford University Press, 1977); George Gruhn and Walter Carter *Gruhn's Guide to Vintage Guitars* (GPI, 1991); Brent Hurtig *Multi-track Recording* (GPI, 1988); Juan Martín *El Arte Flamenco de la Guitarra* (United Music, 1978); Norman Mongan *History of the guitar in jazz* (Oak, 1983); Frederick Noad *Solo Guitar Playing Books 1 and 2* (Macmillan, 1968); Vincent Persichetti *Twentieth Century Harmony* (W W Norton, 1961); Professor Walter Piston *Harmony* (Victor Gollancz, 1941); Nicolas Slonimsky *Thesaurus of Scales and Melodic Patterns* (Scrivener's, 1947) Don Randel *The New Harvard Dictionary of Music* (Harvard University Press, 1986); José Romanillos *Antonio de Torres* (Element, 1987); Harry Shapiro and Caesar Glebbeek *Jimi Hendrix: Electric Gypsy* (Mandarin, 1990); Michael Stimpson *The Guitar* (Oxford University Press, 1988); James Tyler *The Early Guitar* (Oxford University Press, 1980); Tom Wheeler *American Guitars* (Harper and Rowe, 1982).

Photography:
Matthew Ward; Visual 7 Photography; Steve Gorton; Andy Crawford; Tim Ridley.

Computer artwork:
Bounford.com

Picture credits:
p.5 Michael Tamborino: r.
p.6 Rose Jones: tl.
p.7 David Redfern/Redferns: b.
p.14 Finn Costello/Redferns.
p.15 Ashmolean Museum; Matthew Chattel; Edinburgh University Collection.
p.19 Country Music Hall of Fame.
p.22 Michael Tamborino: br.
p.25 Robert Knight/Redferns: bl.
p.27 David Redfern/Redferns: cr.
p.169 Sothebys.
p.190 David Magnus/Rex Features: cl.
p.191 Abbey Road Studios www.abbeyroad.com: br.
p.194 Joe Leach: b.

Music credit:
All The Things You Are
Words by Oscar Hammerstein II Music by Jerome Kern
© Copyright 1939 T.B. Harms & Company Incorporated, USA.
Universal Music Publishing Limited, Used By Permission Of Music Sales Limited.
All Rights Reserved. International Copyright Secured.

My eyes are nearly as big as my head. Can you guess what I am?

I am a Fly!

A fly's eye is made up of thousands of tiny parts. They are very good at seeing movement, which is why they are so hard to catch.

My wings are as colourful as the flowers I fly through. Can you guess what I am?

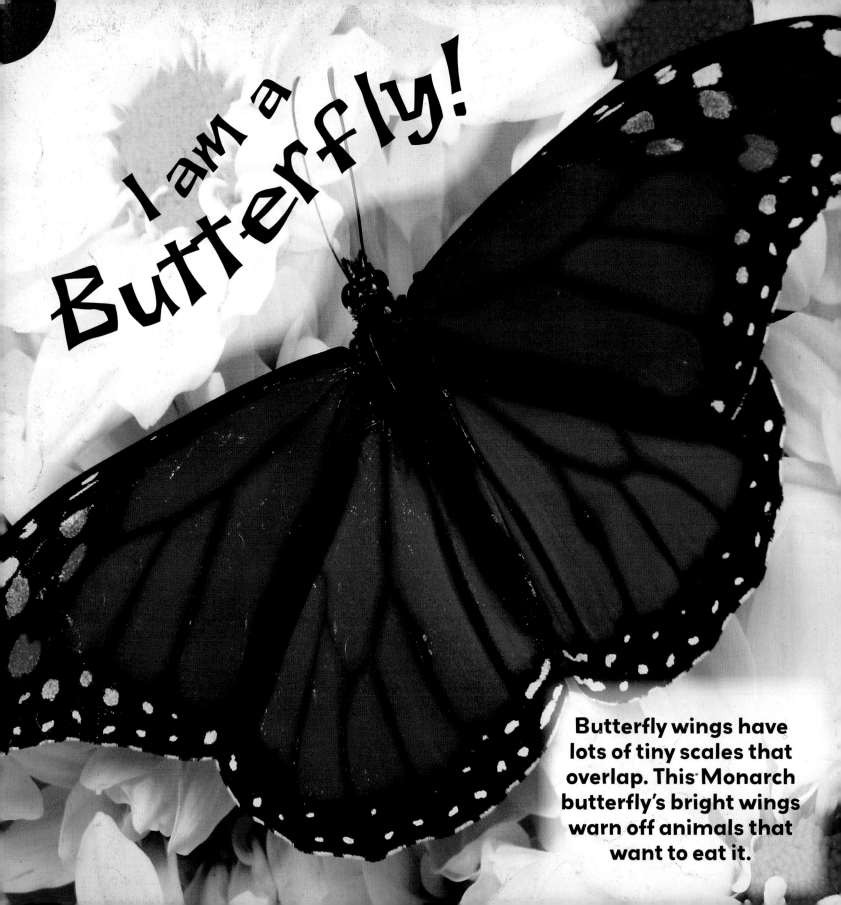

I am a Butterfly!

Butterfly wings have lots of tiny scales that overlap. This Monarch butterfly's bright wings warn off animals that want to eat it.

My big, round eyes are on top of my head. Can you guess what I am?

I am a Frog!

Frogs can pull their eyes into their head! This helps them to swallow their dinner. It pushes their food into their stomach.

My whiskers may twitch when you stroke me. Can you guess what I am?

I am a Cat!

Cats' whiskers help them hunt in the dark. They use their whiskers to pick up smells in the air and sense the shape and size of things around them.

My colourful feathers make sure everyone notices me. Can you guess what I am?

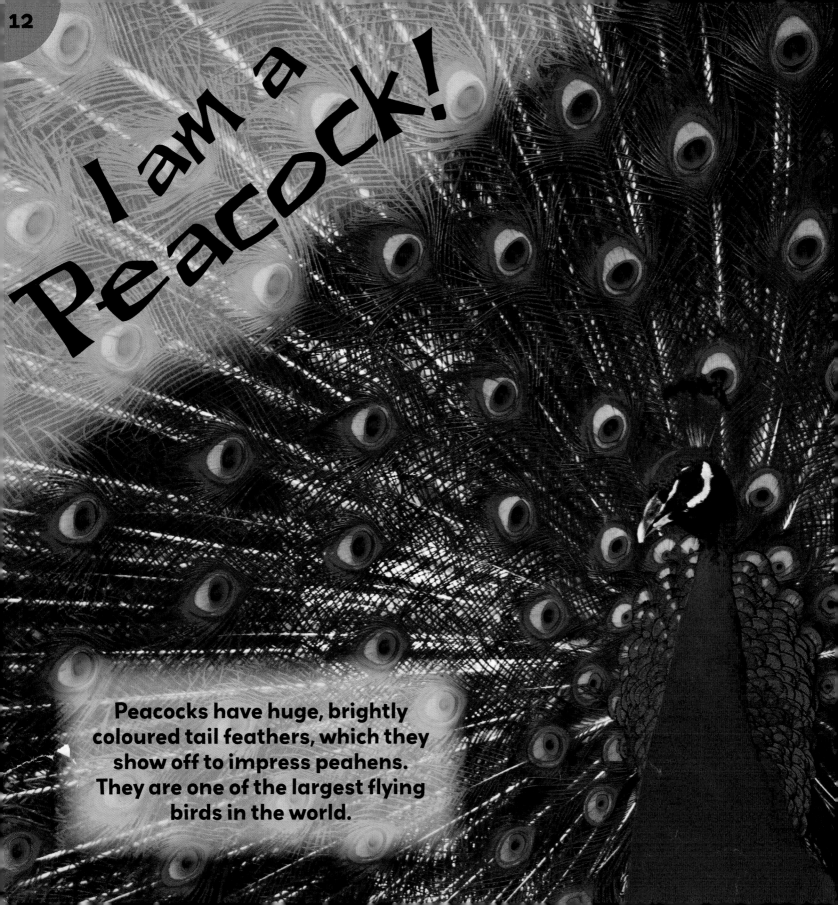

I am a Peacock!

Peacocks have huge, brightly coloured tail feathers, which they show off to impress peahens. They are one of the largest flying birds in the world.

I am a Snake!

Snake skin is usually smooth and dry. It is covered in scales, which allow it to grip surfaces. A snake will shed its whole skin many times during its life.

My stripes help me hide in the grasslands of Africa. Can you guess what I am?

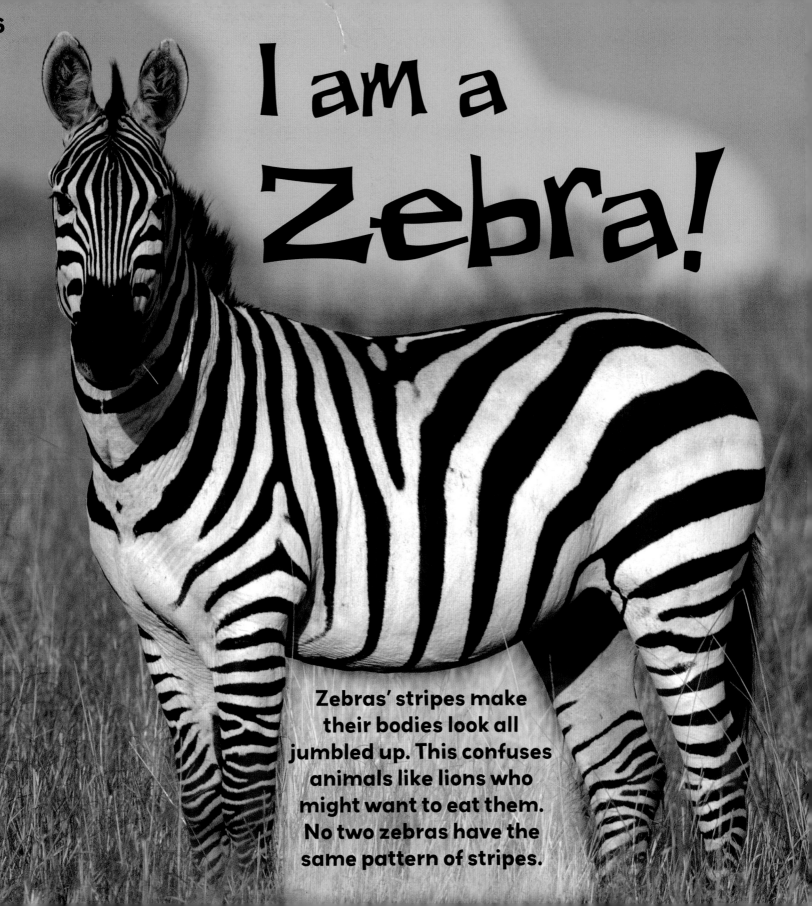

I am a Zebra!

Zebras' stripes make their bodies look all jumbled up. This confuses animals like lions who might want to eat them. No two zebras have the same pattern of stripes.

I'm big, furry and I live in the ice and snow. Can you guess what I am?

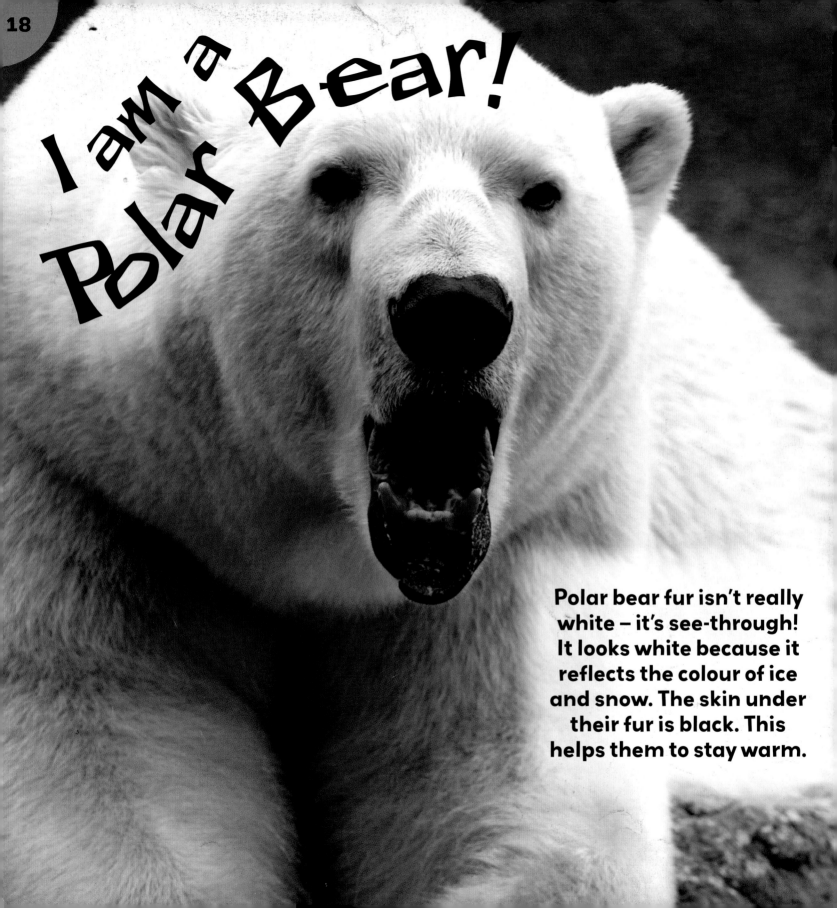

I am a Polar Bear!

Polar bear fur isn't really white – it's see-through! It looks white because it reflects the colour of ice and snow. The skin under their fur is black. This helps them to stay warm.

My ears are huge and my skin is very wrinkly. Can you guess what I am?

I am an Elephant!

African elephants live in hot countries. Their skin is thick but very sensitive. They roll in mud to protect it from the Sun. They also flap their huge ears to help them keep cool.

Now try this...

Make it!

Take a really close look at an animal or a picture of an animal – and choose a small part to focus on. Then make a picture of that part for people to guess what the animal is. You could look at patterns, or perhaps use scraps of paper or material to make a collage.

Mix it!

Take a large picture of an animal and cut it into smaller pieces to make a jigsaw puzzle. Remember – the more pieces you have, the harder your jigsaw will be!

Write it!

Think of your favourite animal. It could be a pet or a wild animal. Think about what makes your animal special – a lion has sharp claws and a dog has a waggy tail. Write a short poem about your chosen animal.